PROMISED

LAND

How the Rise of the
Middle Class Transformed America,
1929–1968

DAVID STEBENNE

SCRIBNER

New York   London   Toronto   Sydney   New Delhi

Scribner
An Imprint of Simon & Schuster, Inc.
1230 Avenue of the Americas
New York, NY 10020

First Scribner hardcover edition July 2020

SCRIBNER and design are registered trademarks of The Gale Group, Inc.,
used under license by Simon & Schuster, Inc., the publisher of this work.

For information about special discounts for bulk purchases,
please contact Simon & Schuster Special Sales at 1-866-506-1949
or business@simonandschuster.com.

The Simon & Schuster Speakers Bureau can bring authors to your live event.
For more information or to book an event, contact the Simon & Schuster Speakers Bureau
at 1-866-248-3049 or visit our website at www.simonspeakers.com.

Manufactured in the United States of America

1 3 5 7 9 10 8 6 4 2

Library of Congress Cataloging-in-Publication Data has been applied for.

ISBN 978-1-9821-0270-8
ISBN 978-1-9821-0272-2 (ebook)

To Karen and Ben

Contents

Introduction

One of the most unexpected developments of the twentieth century was the rise of the middle class as a defining feature of American society from the 1930s through the 1960s. So transformative was that overall experience that even some prominent historians working during that period came to believe that the USA had *always* been dominated by its middle class. Dominant groups tend to see their current situation as somehow natural and timeless. Only when a group holding sway is displaced by another do they see how misleading those assumptions had been. When the middle class began to fracture and stop growing in the later 1960s, those changes helped bring into clearer focus just what was most distinctive about the previous era.[1]

Let's start with a definition of that often-elusive term *middle class*. Most Americans then and now would probably agree that it applies to people who cannot fairly be described as either rich or poor. In mid-twentieth-century America, the middle three-fifths of the income distribution, roughly speaking, fit that description. Inside that elastic category were prosperous families of blue-collar workers who toiled in such places as auto plants, coal mines, and steel mills, as well as families of lower-level white-collar workers such as accountants, civil servants, and reporters. Most—but not all—were white, native-born, with no more than a grade-school education or a college degree paid for by the government in return for military service. They were people of modest means, but supported by steady jobs that enabled them to build and protect their economic security if they lived cautiously, which they typically did.[2]

Their place in the middle class, we should bear in mind, had not simply been handed to them. That middle-class majority hadn't existed in the early decades of the twentieth century; it took an enormous effort to transform the country into a predominantly middle-class nation, at least for a while. *Promised Land* tells the story of how and why that transformation came about, what life was like during the heyday of the middle class, and why, beginning in the later 1960s, that process slowed down and eventually stopped.

Social conditions can be measured and characterized in many ways, and one of the trickiest is with averages. For example, a polarized society (in terms of income) has mostly really expensive homes and really cheap ones with relatively few homes in between. Calculating the average price of a home in that society wouldn't tell us much about what most of the housing actually costs. One of the most striking things about the rise of the American middle class was that averages became steadily more meaningful numbers because increasing numbers of people were grouped into that big bell-curve bulge in the middle, and outliers became steadily less numerous. In a country as big and varied as the USA, referring to "average Americans" can still be somewhat misleading, even during the height of the middle class, because even then there were a lot of exceptions. *Belonging to the majority group* or *sharing in the majority experience* are phrases that capture better what is meant by *average* in that time and are preferred in this book.

The rise of the middle class also meant more than having a certain level of income or amount of accumulated wealth. Being middle class described a state of mind and a way of life, and so the story told here explores not just the economic aspects of that change, but also the interrelated political, social, and cultural factors.

Thus, almost all of those in the middle-class majority were mainline Protestant, Catholic, or Jewish people—morally traditional, though usually not extremely so. Politically, they tended to be either Democrats or Republicans and typically leaned more toward the center of their party than toward its wings. Patriotic and populist, they tended to embrace middlebrow messages in books, movies, radio, and TV. Though worldly in some ways, not many people in that middle three-fifths saw the inside of an opera house, or a juke joint in the Deep South. In short, the middle class, in its heyday, tended to stick to the middle of the road, economically, politically, socially, and culturally. Its members prized a sense of belonging, taking pride in their families, neighborhoods, communities, and country. One of the great questions about this phenomenon is to what degree the middle class of the mid-twentieth century, and especially its preference for the group ethos over individualism, was shaped by government policy and corporate strategy, and to what degree the middle class and that preference were rooted in the people's wish to find more common ground, growing out of such seismic historical upheavals as the Great Depression, World War II, and the Cold War. Certainly, all of these factors were relevant, and part of the shared experience of most Americans, but their relative influence can be debated.

As much as we think about the mid-twentieth-century middle class as conformist, it was neither monolithic nor completely homogeneous. It's easy to think of the history of the middle class as the history of the white middle class, and while that perception isn't entirely wrong, the reality was more complex. Without doubt, the various mechanisms that fueled the rise of the middle class in the middle of the last century were all geared toward improving the lives of the majority group, which generally meant white people of European ancestry. Even as the middle class expanded and carried other kinds of people into it, such as some African Americans, Asian Americans, and Latinos, these more marginalized populations were never central to policymakers' or corporations' calculations and tended to participate in the rise of the middle class much less equally. During the heyday of the middle class, Americans did come to have more in common, but they still tended to live apart, segregated into groups based on such things as race, ethnicity, and religion. The majority experience, even within the middle class, was never the same for everyone.

The same reality held when it came to gender because men and women usually experienced the rise of the middle class very differently. Middle-class dominance in the mid-twentieth century meant male dominance, in the workplace and the public sphere, to an extent that seems positively shocking to subsequent generations. Some women *did* play leading roles in this era, but not many, and even the most influential operated within sharply defined constraints. The reemphasis on domestic roles for women raises, too, the question of to what extent that was imposed on them, and to what extent it reflected their own preferences shaped by the Depression and war, which together disrupted family life for many people and increased the appeal of domesticity for some women.

These more troubling aspects of the rise of the middle class grew out of deeply rooted historical experience as well as conscious later choices. Societies are not completely malleable, even when they are as new and dynamic by world historical standards as the United States. Building a predominantly middle-class nation began at a specific moment in American history—the end of the 1920s—when the country had assumed a form that greatly affected the workings of that social process.

By that point, the American people, while in theory a unified group, had, broadly speaking, become separated into three distinct components. The most numerous and influential was made up of whites of primarily northern and western European ancestry, mostly Protestant, and many descended from colonial-era settlers. This group made up more than half of the overall population of slightly more than 123 million in 1930 and dominated what we today call the establishment. They occupied virtually all the highest positions in business, the professions, government, education, and the arts. These "real Americans," as they tended to see themselves, had been around for a long time and saw their anglophone-influenced customs and folkways as the only truly American ones. They naturally assumed that, over time, everyone else would adopt those ways and assimilate into their culture.[3]

The next group in size and influence comprised more recent immigrants—those who had arrived within the previous fifty years. The 1930 census reported that 36 percent of Americans (44.3 million) were of foreign background, meaning that either they or at least one parent had been born abroad. That was the largest such percentage in modern American history. America had been a land of immigrants since before its founding in 1776, but what set these new immigrants apart were their countries of origin. Virtually no immigrants had come from Italy before 1890, or from Russia before 1900, to give just two examples. Not only did most of this wave of immigrants come from southern or eastern Europe, but they tended to be Catholic or Jewish, and to settle in the larger towns and cities, where there was work. Their America was urban and industrial, putting them at a considerable distance—economically, politically, socially, and culturally—from the majority of Americans still living in small towns and rural areas. New York City, by itself, had become home to 2 million Jewish people, and a million of Italian Catholic ancestry. Many of these relative newcomers were viewed as not quite white by more established Americans of northern and western European ancestry. The newer immigrants were changing the nature of the country in fundamental ways. Even though America's leaders—past and present—considered it a Protestant country, nearly one in six inhabitants identified as Catholic. Despite their different faith traditions, these newer Americans, especially the younger ones, assimilated rapidly due to the influence of schools, employers, and newly burgeoning mass media—movies, then radio—which did not require literacy to understand.[4]

Changes in immigration patterns and policies over the previous fifteen years had actually hastened the assimilation of many such Americans. The outbreak of World War I in the summer of 1914 had stemmed the flow of migration from Europe; however, when the war ended more than four years later, established Americans suddenly had visions of masses of poor and politically radical migrants pouring out of a ravaged and destitute Europe and crowding into the country, and not being as easily assimilated. Such bigoted fears triggered the nation's leaders to move quickly and decisively to restrict immigration, first by temporary measures, then, in 1924, by a major new federal law establishing strictly limited national quotas, and in 1929, "final" national quota legislation, all of which drastically reduced the influx of newcomers. So, over a fifty-year period starting right after World War I, the foreign-born population in the United States crested, then steadily fell. As a consequence, the average age of those born abroad began to climb, while their children and grandchildren became a larger percentage of the newer American population. Still, even if those younger generations felt more at home in America, few could be found in important positions in heavy industry or in the professions, and hardly any in genteel country clubs.[5]

The third major population group—the one with the smallest numbers and least influence—were African Americans. The 1930 census reported that almost 80 percent of the nation's 11.9 million black people still lived in the South, with most of the rest clustered in big northern cities such as Chicago, Cleveland, Detroit, New York, and

Philadelphia. African Americans in the South, like their white neighbors, mostly still lived in rural areas and small towns. In their part of America, poverty was the norm, and connections to the wider society of the other two major population groups was limited, often due to a factor as simple, yet profound, as a lack of electricity, which meant no radio. For black people the South was still basically a closed society as institutional racism did not allow them to vote, to hold public office, or to play other kinds of civic roles in society. Determined to preserve that social arrangement, white southerners tried hard to keep black people from being exposed to the somewhat different—though still segregated—life of the urban North. The roughly 20 percent of the black population living outside the South was concentrated in the poorest urban neighborhoods, where they lived almost exclusively among other African Americans. They were better off in some ways than black people in the South because they could vote and hold public office (Chicago, for example, had a black congressman by then), but even in the urban North, African Americans still lived near the bottom of the social totem pole.

Black people were not invisible to the majority white population, but were usually depicted in the mass media in ways that strengthened prejudice rather than undermined it. The *Amos 'n' Andy* radio program, which premiered on NBC (the National Broadcasting Company network) in August 1929, was a leading case in point. The show, intended as a comedy, revolved around the lives of two black men living in the South, but the characters were played by white actors using caricatured voices and performing scripts that routinely trafficked in stereotypes. *Amos 'n' Andy* was distorted and demeaning, yet it quickly became the most popular show on radio by affirming racist conceptions of black people. By the late 1920s, African Americans had achieved positive visibility in other realms of endeavor, such as jazz music, but most white Americans, both the established and the new, simply weren't paying attention.[6]

Thus "three Americas" coexisted in uneasy parallel, their members perhaps passing each other on the street or in some commercial areas, but always finding their way back to segregated and sealed neighborhoods and social worlds. Sometimes, the tensions between them would flare out into the open, such as during the presidential campaign in 1928. Commerce Secretary Herbert Hoover ran against Governor Al Smith, Democrat of New York, an Irish Catholic born and raised in New York City. Hoover had trounced Smith, except in the biggest cities, which had split almost evenly between the two candidates, and in some heavily Democratic states in the South that still saw Hoover's GOP as "the party of Lincoln." Catholics especially had taken Smith's defeat hard, feeling that it underscored their outsider status in the eyes of the power structure. Newer Americans, who were often either Catholic or Jewish, faced a glass ceiling on their social achievement and acceptance, and Smith's career exemplified it.[7]

Black Americans, though usually deeply rooted in the country, found their ceiling much lower. Unlike newer white Americans, many black people found their fundamental citizenship rights denied daily. Even the African Americans in the northern cities who had greater access to the polling booth were so vastly outnumbered by whites that voting provided them little voice in the nation's governance. The typical African American of the period was politically powerless, which gave rise to simmering tensions that were difficult to express openly for fear of death or other serious reprisal.[8]

In 1929, the iconic trumpeter, singer, and entertainer Louis Armstrong probably came closer than anyone else to the role of leader of the black community on a national scale in the eyes of the white majority. Much better known to them than such leading figures within the black community as historian W. E. B. Du Bois or black nationalist Marcus Garvey, Armstrong was the greatest star of the 1920s Jazz Age. A gifted soloist in an art form that had, up until then, celebrated creative collaboration, he had emerged as a kind of American Bach whose innovations had transformed jazz. But Armstrong could never make a real impression on America's conservatories, the gatekeepers of the music establishment, which never allowed themselves to consider jazz as culturally significant as classical music.

Born in New Orleans in 1901, Armstrong had migrated north, first to Chicago, before coming to New York to take a spot in the pit orchestra of a popular, all-black revue called *Hot Chocolates*. During the show each night, he was given a short cameo to perform "Ain't Misbehavin'," his bestselling record to date, and would routinely steal the show. Louis Armstrong's rise to fame reflected the outer limits of what was possible then in social achievement and acceptance for African Americans.[9]

The circumstances of a person's life were decisively shaped by which group the person belonged to, but *where* in America one lived mattered as well. The country broke down into three distinct geographic regions, the most populous of which became known as the manufacturing belt, which stretched from New England south through New York, New Jersey, Pennsylvania, and Maryland and west to Wisconsin, Illinois, and Missouri. A large majority of Americans lived there because the region's many factories and offices had created so much wealth and employment. Its percentage of the overall population continued to rise as more and more people migrated up from the heavily rural and impoverished Southeast.

That second major part of the country—the Southeast—had been depressed since the Civil War, which had destroyed so much of its cotton-based wealth. The expansion of cotton production in other parts of the world had driven up supply so much as to depress prices substantially, which made the effort to revive the antebellum wealth of the "Cotton Kingdom" impossible. Heavily indebted to northern bankers for the capital needed to rebuild southern infrastructure and to start industrialization, the Southeast's leaders pursued a low-wage strategy that helped make poverty there commonplace.

The Far West was locked into a similarly colonial relationship with the manufacturing belt and, with the notable exceptions of California and Texas, was thinly populated. Much of its wealth came from extractive industries such as oil and gas; ranching, with vast herds of cattle and sheep; and large agribusinesses of the sort for which California became famous. All of these sectors tended to produce fabulous profits for owners and typically meager wages for workers.[10]

These three regions, though still distinct, had become somewhat better linked in the 1920s, with the spread of electrification, improved trains and telephone communication, and more roads, which made travel by cars and trucks between these regions more common. Air travel also expanded, which did much to speed up mail delivery.

Of all of those changes, the one that came fastest in the twenties was driving. The United States became the first nation ever to experience mass automobility, and the proliferation of cars and trucks did a great deal not only to expand people's horizons, but also to connect Americans to one another, although at first more within each region than between regions. The change was apparent in large metropolitan areas as well as in rural America, where farmers had discovered how Henry Ford's cheap Model Ts made trips to town and to market so much easier. Iowa became the state with the most cars per capita. The proliferation of cars and trucks held the long-term promise of tying the country's major regions much more closely together, as roads improved and highways were built.[11]

Something similar was happening by the end of the 1920s with the advent of radio. By that time, America's cities and towns had been wired for electricity. Even though much of the impetus for that change had stemmed from consumer demand for more and better appliances such as washers, refrigerators, mixers, and fans, it nonetheless made possible a revolutionary new means of communication. NBC, the leading radio network, and second-place CBS (Columbia Broadcasting System), had spread from coast to coast, tying together the disparate locales and population groups of metropolitan America. More than 45 percent of households had radios, almost all of them in the cities and larger towns, and most owners kept their radios switched on for hours every day. Radio was cheap to listen to because the cost of electricity was low and programming was paid for by advertising dollars. Funding radio programming that way meant that station and network owners went where the money was—the middle class and especially the more affluent. Thus, the dominant programs and commercials featured characters that fit the expectations of more prosperous white Americans, no matter how stereotyped those expectations might have been. Shows and commercials were also set disproportionately in upper-class America, reinforcing the notion that most of the country looked and felt like that, and that most Americans lived some version of that life.[12]

The image projected by radio programs and their advertisers did not reflect the reality of America in 1929, when 71 percent of households had incomes below $2,500, which was considered to be the minimum needed for a decent life with housing, food, clothing, and other basic necessities. Even allowing for a lower cost of living in rural areas and small towns, around half of the nation's population likely lived near the poverty level, or below it. While poverty was disproportionately concentrated in the heavily rural Southeast and the Far West, and in the working-class neighborhoods of cities and factory towns in the manufacturing belt, farming areas and smaller towns everywhere knew poverty. European agriculture had revived after World War I, reducing demand for American farm exports, and the farm sector never fully recovered. As a result, the 1920s saw the steady movement of people from rural areas not just in the Southeast but also those within the manufacturing belt to its cities and towns in search of better jobs.[13]

The decline in farmwork had begun seventy-five years earlier with the industrial revolution. By 1929, this trend was transforming not just the economy, but also Americans' sense of who and what they were, how they worked, and where they lived. As fewer people worked in agriculture, the family-farm employment model—in which parents and children worked together to produce the household income— declined. With more Americans working in the manufacturing and service sectors, a new model was taking form, in which men worked in paying jobs (if they could find them) and women mostly stayed home, managing the household and raising children, who spent most of their time in school. This was still not a solid majority of Americans, given that close to half of them still lived in rural areas and mostly farmed, with its older, less gender-divided employment model, and because poor women in urban areas often had no choice but to take some kind of paid work, often part-time. But as the shift toward living in major metropolitan areas steadily gained ground, reaching about a third of all Americans by 1929, the male-breadwinner model did, too. Most of the nation's population growth by then was in such metropolitan areas, which fueled a growing division in social roles between men who worked for pay or for profit, and women who did not.[14]

However, even within prosperous households in major metropolitan areas, these gender roles were not always so clearly delineated. Many young women held paying jobs before getting married and starting families, and a good number of older women did volunteer work for a variety of worthwhile social causes such as aiding the poor, helping run churches and synagogues, and caring for elderly relatives.

INTRODUCTION

Women's ability to engage in civic life had grown since they were granted the vote in 1920. A new era was dawning, largely for a small group of more affluent white women, who were launching careers in fields as varied as law and business. The average white, middle-class woman from a working family had much less chance of availing herself of such opportunities, and black women in the South—still denied the franchise—none at all, but for women of privilege and education, some long-closed doors began to open in the twenties. But even those professional women operated within much greater constraints in the workplace and the public sphere than most men.[15]

Such was the nature of American life on the eve of the rise of the middle class. Given how unequally different kinds of Americans lived, it should come as no surprise that the shift thereafter toward a more middle-class country and culture produced nothing like a uniform result. To the beginning of that story we now turn.

PROMISED
LAND

CHAPTER 1

A Dream Deferred

In March 1929, fifty-four-year-old Herbert Hoover became president, having campaigned on the promise of a future in which most Americans would be truly middle class. Despite increasing economic inequality, some indications of economic progress gave Hoover confidence. "We in America today," he told his supporters on August 11, 1928, "are nearer to the final triumph over poverty than ever before in the history of the land." In his stump speeches, Hoover had spelled out his expectations. He talked about home ownership for city and town dwellers, and farm ownership for the almost half of the population still living in rural areas. He envisioned a kind of middle-class standard, with two cars per household, and even more schooling as the norm. Hoover's vision—breathtaking for a country in which so many people were poor or almost so—also encompassed a more stable kind of life for an expanded middle-class majority, in which employment was steady and savings assured, and ever more people were protected by privately provided insurance against death, accidents, and other major income disruptions and able to sustain themselves in old age. Twenty years later, as he looked back on his most important goals for Americans in 1929, Hoover wrote simply, "We want[ed] them all secure."[1]

Hoover promised—and tried to deliver—that dream, but things went terribly wrong for his presidency, the United States, and for the world after 1929 when the stock market crashed. While much of that dream would eventually come true, it wouldn't be for another quarter of a century, during which time the country would endure an economic depression and a major military conflict. The great big middle class was forged largely in the crucible of those two calamities.

Many and probably most people believe the cataclysmic stock market crash of October 29, 1929, was the primary cause of the Great Depression, but large-scale economic disasters rarely stem from one single factor. The crash revealed multiple weak points in the economy. The first was the fragility of the international economic system of which America had become such an important player. After World War I, Germany assumed heavy debt to the European victors. Responding to the anger of their citizen populations, who had suffered terrible losses in life, property, and money as a result of German aggression, the leaders of England, France, and Italy insisted that Germany make what came to be known as reparations. The American government insisted that their wartime allies, such as the British, French, and Italians, repay the money borrowed to make war. The German government had signed a treaty obliging it to financially compensate damage done to civilians, as well as to pay the full cost of the pensions of the Allied soldiers. The British, French, and Italian governments intended to use some of that income to repay the money they had borrowed from the United States to finance their war efforts.[2]

The plan made sense politically, but less so economically. John Maynard Keynes, the renowned academic economist and British civil servant, argued that the plan would ultimately be self-defeating, but the optimists believed that in time, the anger in England, France, and Italy that led their governments to insist on an unworkable reparations approach would fade, and that Americans would come to see the wisdom of moving away from their insistence on repayment. The softening of attitudes would enable a comprehensive renegotiation of war debts such that the taxpayers of all the nations involved would share the conflict's heavy costs more equally. In this vision, Germany, the main loser, would be required to pay less, and the USA, the big financial winner, would pay more by forgiving debts owed to it by Britain, France, and Italy. That step would facilitate the restoration of long-term international economic stability and head off the kind of economic disaster that began in 1929.[3] British politicians and treasury officials, with visions of returning their country to its prewar position of dominance in the global economy, favored war debts forgiveness, but they aimed too high, and not just with respect to their hopes for how quickly public resistance to forgiveness might fade. Seeking in vain to make the British pound the world's benchmark currency once again, the British government had gone back to the gold standard in 1925. But with its wealth depleted after the war, England was unable to fully back the pound with gold, so the move backfired. With an overvalued currency that interfered with world trade, the country was unable to contribute much to an international economic solution.[4]

Other miscalculations also helped doom hopes for long-term international economic restabilization. Public demands in France, England, and Italy to "make Germany pay" did not fade quickly in the 1920s, nor did the American insistence on repayment from wartime allies. The eventual economic disaster was papered over for a while, thanks to the willingness of the United States, the only major country actually enriched by the war, to lend money to Germany for its reparations payments to the victorious European nations, which they used to make payments on what they owed to the Americans. The basic problem with that approach was that if America's lending to Germany stopped before war debt forgiveness became politically possible, the global economy would collapse. By the fall of 1929, with so much invested in European economic recovery, America was as much at risk as Europe. When the New York Stock Exchange crashed in October, many banks, facing declining assets, stopped lending to Germany. Its government could no longer make payments to Britain, France, and Italy, which meant they could no longer pay back America.[5]

The weakened demand in Europe for US exports also contributed to the slump. Before World War I, a generally prosperous Europe had enriched America by buying significant quantities of what we had to sell. Even with American loans, Europe had much less money to spend on those products after the war and was able to purchase even less as the US loan money began to dry up. Making things even worse, the United States continued to stick to an outmoded protectionist trade policy, even after the transformation in our economic relationship with Europe brought on by the war.[6]

The changes in the US-Europe economic relationship, in which the United States went from being a debtor nation to being a creditor nation, came on rather suddenly, in just a few years. America's leaders were not prepared for such a dramatic transformation, and the ensuing confusion led to misguided decision-making, such as the stand on war debt repayment and the failure to modernize trade policy to fit the new world order. The ruinous war in Europe had pushed the United States into an international leadership position for which it was not prepared, and which it played badly.[7]

Several aspects of the American economy having nothing to do with the upheaval of the war in Europe also helped produce the Great Depression. The boom of the 1920s relied too heavily on too few industries, most notably cars and construction. The economy simply lacked sufficient diversification to compensate when those industries declined near the end of the decade.[8]

At the same time, income and wealth inequality was growing, which was creating a practical problem. The ideas of Henry Ford had propelled American prosperity during this decade. He envisioned expanding the market for one's product by making it more cheaply, and by paying workers so well that more of them could afford to buy it, thereby expanding the market further. He only needed to make a modest profit on each car sold because he could sell them in such great numbers that his overall profit would be huge. However, an economy based on mass production and mass consumption—what Europeans called Fordism—was a new concept, and few people understood the long-term ramifications for overall income and wealth distribution. Excessive inequality would eventually mean that ordinary people would no longer be able to buy what American farms, factories, and offices were churning out in ever-greater amounts. That's exactly what had begun to happen, especially with respect to cars, consumer appliances, and houses. For a while, the reality of the situation was disguised by the practice of making these goods available on credit, via new "installment plans," and the availability of ambitious, balloon-type mortgages to buy homes. That lasted only as long as employment and incomes remained steady, but both fell due to the 1929 crash and the other underlying weaknesses in the American economy.[9] An even more serious consequence, in some ways, of growing income and wealth inequality was that the upper class—so prominent in the media and the advertising of the day—acquired an outsize influence on the buying habits of the rest of the population. The ones with the most money to spend and invest acquired a lot of consumer goods and bid up the prices of stocks and real estate far beyond what they were worth. Less affluent Americans, taking their cues about what was normal in consumption from magazines, movies, and radio shows aimed at the upscale market, took on more and more debt in the effort to keep up. Perhaps if interest rates had been higher, more money would have found its way into savings accounts rather than needless consumption and unwise investments, but rates had been kept low to encourage that kind of borrowing and spending, and to make repayment of debts easier. Those low interest rates encouraged Americans, whether of the investor class or of more modest means, to buy more and make riskier investments. By the time the Federal Reserve took action to correct that problem, by raising interest rates charged to member banks, the investment bubble had become too big to puncture gently. When it burst instead, it helped bring on the stock market crash.[10]

As the 1920s drew to a close, the previously booming American economy had clearly started to slow down. With corporate profits on the decline, executives began to reduce their investments in new plants and equipment, which further weakened the dragging economy. They also started laying off workers, which made sense from the perspective of individual firms, but which made the economy that much more fragile. With less investment by major corporations and less consumption by an increasing number of idled workers, all that remained to power the economy in any meaningful way was government, but it, too, was doing less and less to promote prosperity.[11]

One of the most striking things about the years immediately preceding the crash of 1929 was how little the federal government was doing to keep the economy moving forward. Treasury Secretary Andrew Mellon had committed himself to reducing substantially the large federal debt amassed to fight World War I, and to bringing down the high wartime-era taxes on America's investor class. Mellon needed to free up money for private investment in new industries, and to breathe new life into older ones. For a while, these policies brought about the desired result, as the federal government ran surpluses while paying down the national debt. This was accomplished with lower taxes that were producing more total revenue than before as the overall economy expanded. Mellon's tax cuts helped stimulate the economy, but his quest to run budget surpluses led him to de-emphasize direct economic stimulus by government spending on goods and services for public purposes. In 1929, almost the entire federal budget went toward national security in some form, and even that wasn't much; total federal spending amounted to just 3 percent of the gross national product. (For comparison, federal spending hovered around 20 percent of GNP in the early 2000s.) At the state and local levels, governments were spending more than ever on roads and schools and other public necessities, using taxes collected from the general working population. Should the income of that population decline, so, too, would the spending by these other, smaller governmental bodies, which is exactly what happened after the crash.[12]

All these problems combined to put intense pressure on the American banking system by the end of 1930. Increasingly, Europeans couldn't afford to repay what they owed each other or the United States. Strapped American farmers and urban consumers struggled to pay their debts, or even the interest on them. Over the next three years, more than five thousand banks, whose deposits were uninsured, succumbed to the pressures exerted by stock-market losses, foreign-government loan defaults, capital flight from America, insolvent farmers, and savings-account withdrawals by urban workers. When the Federal Reserve once again raised the interest rate it charged member banks, this time to stem the flow of capital out of the country, the banks were again forced to raise the rates charged to borrowers and paid to depositors.

Those moves depressed the economy even further, in a variety of ways. Higher interest rates made money more expensive to borrow, which discouraged consumption and investment. Higher rates also forced banks to sell more of their assets at depressed prices to raise cash to pay interest on remaining deposits, making the banks even more insolvent. The tighter monetary policy of the early 1930s turned up the heat on a banking system already in hot water.

One by one, America's banks closed their doors, some of them at least hoping to reopen in the future. Not just the number of bank closings scared people, but also the size of the banks. As ever-bigger banking dominoes fell, the economic catastrophe gained momentum. The Great Depression, a disaster of much greater magnitude than seen before in American or world history, had arrived.[13]

The unprecedented nature of the unfolding human tragedy was revealed by official unemployment figures. The ranks of the jobless expanded from 5 million at the end of 1930 to 9 million just one year later, and 13 million a year after that. Even those grim numbers understated the problem, since only people actively seeking jobs were officially categorized as unemployed. When the United States enjoyed high employment, as it usually had up until then, this measure was fairly accurate, but it became increasingly misleading as the economic crisis deepened and frustrated job seekers gave up looking for work. Thus, as the Depression grew worse, the official government statistics that documented it grew more inaccurate. The official unemployment rate peaked at around 25 percent in 1932, but the real number was probably closer to a third of Americans wanting and needing jobs.[14]

This kind of disconnect was not uncommon in the America of the early 1930s. For most ordinary citizens things were getting harder, but they lacked a coherent and realistic overall picture of the extent of the nation's woes. The public normally looked to the popular press for that wider perspective, but in the hard times of the 1930s, newspaper editors and publishers avoided printing stories that weakened the public confidence on which a market system partly depended. Important reporting of the reality of the economic decline was thus inhibited.

Making matters worse were the Republican leanings of most major newspaper owners, who did not want to make the Hoover administration or congressional Republicans look any worse than they already did. The leadership class—the power elite of the day—likely remained disconnected from everyday reality, insulated as they were by wealth or privilege, and basing their understanding on misleading government statistics and inaccurate reporting in the press. Despite memorable public displays of hardship—the apple sellers on downtown city streets and the long lines at soup kitchens—the majority of jobless Americans, embarrassed by their plight, were still more likely to hide out in their homes. People of the upper-middle class spent less of their money on nonessential shopping and entertainment and so spent less of their time in downtown business districts, where they would have been exposed to the consequences of mass unemployment.[15]

The increasing concentration of the population in cities as America industrialized also helped magnify the harshness of the Depression. For most of the nation's history, most Americans lived in rural areas, where they established and sustained their households by accessing the bounty of the natural world around them. The ability to hunt, fish, grow produce, raise animals for dairy and meat, or find wood for fuel and shelter enabled them to fend for themselves, especially during hard times. Such had been the case during the country's last prolonged economic downturn forty years earlier, when a much greater percentage of people lived on farms. The much higher fraction of Americans living in cities by the 1930s contributed to the unprecedented misery of the Great Depression. At first, a number of city dwellers with family ties to farming areas did return, but simultaneously, the growing number of farm foreclosures drove dispossessed rural migrants toward the urban areas, where they hoped at least to find soup kitchens, breadlines, and other forms of public assistance, however inadequate. As the urban population grew, the opportunities to turn to traditional methods of sustaining oneself off the land declined, an aspect of the overall picture that people still living in rural areas couldn't quite grasp. They had become the exception, and no longer the rule.[16]

The lack of reliable information also played into the fear of dependency that already existed among more affluent Americans. The well-off tended to underestimate the magnitude of the social problems created by mass unemployment. They focused instead on the potential harm to the legendary American work ethic done by a more generous welfare system—"relief," as it was called then. Inaccurate reporting and misleading federal statistics reinforced their reluctance to support such governmental action.

But among the constantly expanding ranks of the unemployed, the social problems kept mounting. More people were experiencing hunger, and mental and physical health declined as a result. Rates of violent crime and suicide rose to all-time highs by 1932. It was not a great time for family stability. Although the divorce rate actually declined, that was perhaps only because a divorce cost money in legal fees and so became harder for many to even consider. Informal and unregistered marital breakups increased, but didn't turn up in any official statistics. At the same time, as more and more Americans found themselves without work, people crowded into the homes of their relatives, driving up the tension and conflict.

As these harmful effects worsened, the funds in state, local, and private relief coffers dwindled. But with a national leadership drawn largely from more affluent Americans and the pain of the Depression felt most strongly by working people and those already vulnerable, no federal relief program surfaced during the four years of Herbert Hoover's presidency.[17]

What emerged instead was a grimly Darwinian struggle for survival, often expressed in conflicts over who should get those few jobs still available. The prevailing sentiment was that no family could be allowed to hold more than one well-paying job, so a kind of job-rationing system evolved. That hardening of social attitude was a double-edged sword for some people. For instance, married women who held fairly secure public-sector jobs such as librarian or schoolteacher faced resentment if their husbands also had work. But if a husband had been laid off and hadn't found other work, his wife's efforts to make ends meet for the family would be accepted and even applauded.

At the lower end of the economic scale, the struggle for jobs had racial and ethnic implications. African Americans in more menial jobs, such as street sweepers and garbage haulers, almost all of them male, found themselves displaced by white men, especially in border states and in the South. In the Southwest in the early 1930s, Latino field workers saw their jobs getting handed over to dispossessed rural white people. These trends accelerated as the Depression worsened.[18]

The Depression reached deep into people's personal lives, coming to bear on decisions such as whether and when to marry, or even to have intimate relations, whether to have children, or how best to raise them. Marriage and birth rates fell to historic lows, in an era when birth-control devices were not always available or morally acceptable, suggesting that sexual activity underwent some kind of significant change.[19] Families that chose to have children saw those children spending more years in school than previous generations had.

In the 1930s, the propensity to stay in school tended to rise, especially outside the mostly rural and impoverished southern states. In the more heavily populated North—its cities and towns especially—the majority of kids began staying through high school because there were few jobs for adults, never mind adolescents, as an alternative. Many Americans still believed that holding a job in the real world was a critical part of a young person's education, but that approach was hardly viable during the early years of the Depression.

In the ensuing boom in public education, a growing fraction of society came to depend on it because it was free (unlike private schools) and because it gave the young something constructive to do. As demand for public education increased, the public budgets that supported it grew tighter, as the Depression hollowed out state and local tax bases. Still, even many hard-pressed upper-middle-class families gravitated away from private institutions and toward public schools, intensifying the elite's support for better public education. This began a major shift with major social consequences.[20]

With incomes declining, and home and farm foreclosures mounting, government at all levels needed to find new sources of tax revenue, which led to another major change in the social landscape of the early 1930s: the end of Prohibition. As the decade began, the public still seemed to mostly favor Prohibition, but the liquor lobby convincingly made the case that ending it could help solve the problem of vanishing revenue from income and property taxes. Legalized drinking could also provide an escape from the trials of unemployment, especially among men. As an added benefit, ending the "noble experiment," as Hoover called it, could deal a major blow to organized crime, which had jumped on the opportunity to rake in massive profits off illegal booze. Strong arguments could also be made for keeping Prohibition in place. Alcohol became a terrible addiction for some or triggered mayhem and had a depressant effect, the last thing people needed when so many already suffered from depression. In addition, the ready availability of liquor could drain already tight family incomes. Worse yet, drinking now posed a whole new threat in a society recently transformed by mass automobility. Recognizing the sensitivity of the issue, Congress opted to require the states to establish ratifying conventions to approve what became the Twenty-First Amendment to the Constitution, rather than go the usual route through the state legislatures, where rural areas, generally hostile to repeal, were overrepresented.[21]

The repeal campaign had far-reaching implications for partisan politics on a national level. In the preceding decade, Prohibition, more than any other issue, had divided the Democratic Party, between its big-city "wets" and its southern "dries." When the tide of public opinion turned against Prohibition after 1930, that "wedge issue" faded in importance. Albert Ritchie, the governor of Maryland and chief elected Democratic cheerleader for repeal, neatly epitomized that shift. Maryland was a unique border state, with a major city—Baltimore—that felt somewhat northern, but also smaller towns and rural areas with a distinctly southern character. Ritchie sought the Democratic presidential nomination in 1932—and while he didn't win, his advocacy of repeal brought him positive national attention. He was at home with big-city politicians, as well as with the Dixiecrats, as the southern Democrats were known, which made him a unifying force in the party. Ritchie argued persuasively that by enacting repeal, the Democrats could put the divisive issue behind them and thus become more competitive as a party on the national level.[22]

The desire for escape that helped drive the repeal movement also sustained the extraordinary spread of radio that had begun in the 1920s. With more expensive forms of entertainment, such as restaurants, movies, and theater, out of reach for so many, people could always turn to radio to get them through the idle hours. By 1934, almost exactly two-thirds of American households had a radio, with ownership practically universal in cities and larger towns. Only rural areas, many of which still lacked electricity, lagged behind. As with the expansion of public education, the ubiquity of radio contributed to the commonality of social and cultural experience. With the great majority of Americans listening to the same kinds of programs each day and each night, a more uniform national culture began to emerge.[23]

The prevailing social conditions of the day reshaped the content that filled the radio airwaves. Programmers served the need for escape among adult listeners, while making sure to provide important social messages for younger audience members. On the radio, romantic love flourished, families found happiness together, and crime never paid. Happy endings were the order of the day, along with bright, cheerful music and upbeat advertising. The consumer companies that sponsored the programs worked hand in hand with producers to shape shows and ads that together met the needs of the public. Even Herbert Hoover, so isolated in important ways from the experience of ordinary Americans, knew the value of more optimism on the radio.

He told Rudy Vallee, the enormously popular singer whose voice reached millions over the radio, "If you can write a song that makes people forget about their troubles, I'll give you a medal."[24]

Depression-era radio inaugurated a profound shift toward the middlebrow in American popular culture, and away from the upper-class orientation of twenties programming. Radio's new middlebrow messages resonated with people who had some social standing, but were not so well-off as to find the themes and morally traditional messages trivial or Pollyannaish, nor so poor as to find them false or unrealistic.

The motion-picture industry had to find ways to keep up with the runaway popularity of radio, lest it—and the decline in incomes brought by the Depression—shrink movie attendance. More optimistic movies were one obvious answer, but Hollywood could also offer an alternative, a more disturbing entertainment that the more tightly regulated radio programmers could not. Filmmakers began adding more sex and violence to their movies in the early 1930s, which did not sit well with urban American parents, whose children had more ready access to movie theaters after school and on weekends, out of sight of the adults, who could at least control the radio at home.

The film industry had earlier recognized the need to regulate itself, but as hard times continued across the country, filmmakers slipped back into making films that featured violent gangsters and salacious love scenes. The demand arose among urban Americans for federal censorship that would minimize the exposure of their precious youngsters, especially boys, to the base values and dysfunctional behavior playing out on the silver screen. The Hoover administration's resistance to federal intervention, in this area as in others, angered much of the public, especially within the heavily Catholic neighborhoods of America's big cities.[25]

Herbert Hoover saw his star fade in the early 1930s. His governing philosophy was totally out of step with the needs of the day, his conception of the federal government's role inadequate to meet the crises facing America both at home and abroad. On the domestic side, Hoover envisioned a system in which the levers of government were operated primarily at the state and local level, mostly in service to private organized groups such as the Chamber of Commerce and the American Red Cross. The role of government was to provide useful information and suggestions to nongovernmental groups, which could take the lead in solving social problems.

In foreign policy, Hoover favored diplomacy over force and believed in the need for international cooperation, the stabilizing effects of international trade, and the effectiveness of economic sanctions against aggressor nations. These ideas did the country little good in the face of the Great Depression, but Hoover could not break free of them. He allowed the federal government to take some small steps to alleviate the economic crisis, but when he saw that they would lead to a permanently big and interventionist national government, he quickly pulled back. For instance, he supported the creation of a kind of federal lender to big business, the Reconstruction Finance Corporation (RFC), but couldn't bring himself to let it operate at a level that would have made a difference. He stubbornly blocked such popular proposals as a temporary federal relief program and a system of federal insurance for bank deposits.[26]

Hoover had been pushed to the GOP nomination in 1928 by the party's business wing. Republican Party chieftains had never been enthusiastic about a Hoover presidency and soured on him even further once the Depression began. Essentially shy and thin-skinned, and prone to making long speeches on dull subjects, Hoover proved a thoroughly uninspiring leader during a national catastrophe. More an administrator by temperament than a skilled political operator, he disliked professional politicians regardless of party affiliation and, once in office, compounded his troubles through his inept dealings with Congress.[27]

That dysfunctional relationship led to a public-policy fiasco in 1930 when Hoover was unable to engage forcefully enough with members of Congress to block passage of a bill raising taxes on imports. The measure, touted as a way of protecting American industry from cheap foreign competition, was blasted by most academic economists as utterly self-defeating. They correctly predicted that other nations would respond in kind, further reducing the already depressed volume of international trade.

When Congress passed the bill anyway, Hoover meekly signed it into law. Raising American trade barriers that were already high undermined the country's influence abroad and fueled nationalism and militarism in such nations as Germany, Italy, and Japan. Hoover made that problem worse by supporting a reduction in US military spending as a way to eliminate waste and help bring the faltering federal budget into balance. That decision undermined the credibility of the military force that backstopped US diplomacy. Why would aggressor nations around the world take American diplomatic initiatives seriously if they could see the American army getting smaller and weaker?[28]

As the presidential election of 1932 loomed on the horizon, Hoover presented the sorry spectacle of a highly intelligent and previously successful man unable to adapt to the demands of a changing world. He became as unpopular a president as anyone could remember, drawing unprecedented jeers along the campaign trail. The Secret Service was concerned enough about his safety that he discontinued the presidential custom of greeting tourists visiting the White House. Knowing that he had no chance of winning reelection, Hoover focused his campaign on defending himself and his ideas, rather than trying to convince voters to stick with him.

Perhaps most sadly, America had not moved any closer to the middle-class millennium he had promised in 1928. If anything, the country had moved in the opposite direction. Ironically, the massive loss of wealth among the investor class had indeed narrowed the gap between them and the rest of the population, but the record-breaking joblessness and shattering poverty of the early Depression years made a mockery of Hoover's optimistic predictions of a bright future. Instead, as Democratic National Committee publicist Charles Michelson kept pointing out, America had become a nation of "Hoover blankets" (yesterday's newspaper), "Hoovervilles" (shantytowns), and "Hoover flags" (empty pockets turned inside out).[29] Herbert Hoover's inability to adapt to change reflected a wider social phenomenon across the United States. Most Americans met the arrival of the Depression, and the continued worsening of conditions, with striking passivity. Instinctively reluctant to surrender their optimism about the future, and having no way of knowing that the situation would drag on for years, they mostly clung to traditional values and beliefs and behaviors that were ill-suited to their new circumstances. If they suffered financial reverses, they tended to blame themselves rather than the American economic system or misguided public policies. If they needed help of any kind, they turned to family, friends, and neighbors, and not to the government. If they couldn't find work, they simply knuckled down and tried harder, at least for a while. Even the rise in crime grimly reflected Americans' preference for personal initiative.[30]

The upheavals of the early 1930s played out in microcosm in the lives of countless individuals, ordinary Americans whose stories illustrated the unfolding history of the day. One of those citizens, Beatrice Bauch of Maquoketa, Iowa, had been studying at Columbia University's Teachers College in New York before the crash. Her parents were hit so hard financially by the Great Depression that Beatrice soon found herself back in Maquoketa, taking in other people's laundry to help make ends meet for her family.

Or, there was George Perkins, married and the father of two children. In 1929, George was comfortably employed managing a service station in the tony suburb of West Hartford, Connecticut (where a young Katharine Hepburn once brought her car in for repair), but he lost that job in 1932. Perkins retreated with his family to his mother's house in Providence, Rhode Island, while looking for steady work. The traumas of these experiences colored the rest of Beatrice's and George's lives, much the same as with countless other Americans.[31]

Despite the passive acceptance and slow response of most Americans to the onset of the Depression, suspicion did start to simmer below the surface that someone somewhere was to blame, at least partly, for what had gone wrong. That discontentment burst into the open during the presidential election of 1932, which even Herbert Hoover knew would usher in a new leader. Franklin Roosevelt's candidacy appealed most to people such as Beatrice and George, who had fallen so suddenly from the middle of the social scale.[32]

FDR's single most important role model was his distant cousin Teddy Roosevelt, who rose to prominence near the end of America's Gilded Age. In that era, the very public opulence of the nation's rich masked the widespread hardship of a working class transitioning from an agrarian to an industrial economy. Teddy had charted a course that Franklin would almost slavishly follow. Although the two men aligned themselves with different parties, Teddy left a large footprint that marked the way for Franklin. It even influenced FDR's choice of a bride; Teddy had acted as a surrogate father figure for his orphaned niece Eleanor, which made him Franklin's de facto father-in-law when Franklin married Eleanor. Teddy had just begun his second term in the White House when he gave Eleanor away at the wedding, effectively cementing young Franklin's family connection to a sitting and popular president.[33]

Five years later, in 1910, FDR began climbing virtually the same career ladder in politics that Teddy had, beginning with his election to the New York State legislature. From there, he went on to serve as assistant secretary of the navy, as his party's candidate for vice president, and as governor of New York, as Teddy had done earlier. FDR's association with a beloved Progressive Republican widened his bipartisan appeal. Once FDR was elected governor of New York in 1928, his views on the business-government relationship followed the lead of his cousin Teddy, even though by then they seemed utterly out of step with the prevailing mood of the country. Thus, in FDR's first year as governor, he pushed to expand the production of electricity by building water-powered generating stations along the St. Lawrence River in northern New York State. Roosevelt had noted the low utility rates charged by public power plants built by the Canadian government on its side of the river and believed that public plants built on the American side could serve rural areas not yet electrified. His proposal didn't sit well with private utility companies, which naturally opposed what they derided as "public power." When Wall Street financier J. P. Morgan Jr. indicated his support for a private monopoly to build and operate such plants, which was favored by Republicans in the state legislature and their allies in the press, FDR took to the radio airwaves to argue that this approach would cost consumers more.

He continued to press his case in a speech at Tammany Hall, the Democrats' New York City headquarters, on July 4, 1929. There, he sounded the alarm about "a new feudal control" by big business, which put the fight against Morgan and the private utility companies in a larger context of a crusade against excessive corporate power. That attitude endeared him to the fifteen hundred Democratic partisans cheering him on that day in New York and drew national attention.

Soon his ideas were gaining traction outside his home state, especially once the economy began its spectacular collapse that fall.[34]

The Democratic presidential hopeful knew that Teddy Roosevelt's popularity had been rooted in the belief that he favored the interests of regular Americans over those of the corporate titans. FDR highlighted that same perspective in a widely heard radio speech in the spring of 1932: "These unhappy times call for the building of plans that . . . build from the bottom up and not the top down, that put their faith once more in the forgotten man at the bottom of the economic pyramid."[35] He made another bold public statement reminiscent of TR when he flew from New York to the Democratic convention in Chicago to accept the party's presidential nomination in person, something no major-party candidate had done before.[36]

Voters felt the desperation of the era and longed for decisive and reassuring leadership after the frustrating passivity of Herbert Hoover. In accepting the Democratic nomination, FDR clearly articulated his priorities: "The people of America want, more than anything else, two things: work, with all the moral and spiritual values that go with it, and with work, a reasonable measure of security—security for themselves and for their wives and children."[37] Implicit in FDR's words was the assumption that the only breadwinners in American life were men. To be sure, the proportion of women in the paid labor force was vastly smaller than it is now, and the job rationing that had taken hold after the 1929 crash ensured that virtually all decent jobs went to the husbands and fathers who needed them. The male-breadwinner model that FDR took for granted tended to fit the majority of Americans who occupied the middle of the economic spectrum. It meant less to those at the high end, where women tended to be more educated and had help with their domestic responsibilities. At the bottom end of the spectrum, the model was essentially irrelevant, since the men, even if employed, earned too little money to support their families, which meant that many women worked out of necessity. For these reasons, Franklin Roosevelt especially captured the attention and affection of that vast economic middle.[38]

With his sincerity and eloquence and popular ideas reaching into homes via the radio, FDR had helped turn the nation's bitter disappointment in Herbert Hoover into a landslide victory for the Democrats. Hoover, unable to overcome his disastrous resistance to federal relief and aid to failing banks, won only six of the forty-eight states. What the broad middle of the electorate wanted was more action from Washington. That's exactly what FDR would give them.[39]

CHAPTER 2

Roosevelt to the Rescue

FDR was a man of instinct, not doctrine. He described himself as "a Christian and a Democrat—that's all," although he was an unapologetic reformer. That Progressive instinct, however, along with the policies that underpinned his New Deal, evolved over time, constantly adapting to suit changing circumstances. Roosevelt's administration juggled a great many initiatives without always giving a lot of forethought to how they would relate to one another. These initiatives, rolled out in the unique cultural context of Depression-era America, brought to the fore the interests of the great majority of citizens in the middle ground between rich and poor.[1]

Although we tend to think of the New Deal as a well-orchestrated set of coordinated programs, this transformative social movement actually unfolded in three distinct phases. The first phase, essentially emergency measures intended to rescue Americans devastated by the Depression, commenced on the day of FDR's inauguration in March of 1933 and lasted for two years. The administration had no time to waste and raced ahead on many fronts in the effort to quickly stabilize the economy. They sought to regulate banks, the stock market, and the value of the dollar; to raise household incomes; and to refinance mortgages on homes and farms. The pressure to move quickly ensured that White House staffers and cabinet departments took the crafting of specific proposals out of the hands of Congress. Refreshingly, FDR brought all kinds of talented people to Washington with him, regardless of their social pedigree. Reflecting the changing demographics of the country, citizens from families of recent immigrants filled many key positions in the federal government. Among the most influential of these were the strategists Ben Cohen, a soft-spoken man from a Jewish family in Muncie, Indiana, and Tommy Corcoran, a gregarious Irish American Catholic from a Rhode Island mill town. Both were protégés of Harvard law professor Felix Frankfurter, whom FDR eventually appointed to the Supreme Court. Cohen and Corcoran were able to quickly and brilliantly draft laws that sailed through a cooperative Congress with Democratic majorities in both the House and the Senate, in some cases with only the most cursory of inspections. While some members of Congress grumbled about the dangers of making new laws on the fly, the overall result was positive: by the summer of 1933 the nation's downward economic spiral had been halted.[2]

Americans were not accustomed to the president and the federal government taking such a strong hand in responding to economic crises. That had long been the job of state and local governments, but officials at those levels found themselves unable to cope with the sweeping social problems caused by the Depression, or to fashion practical solutions. Herbert Hoover's White House had done nothing to alter that expectation, but under FDR, the federal government stepped up to tackle the job. The public, relieved that someone had taken charge, grew to accept the new order. Just as it had brought Americans closer together culturally, the rise of radio as a mass medium helped enable this shift by making the federal government—those faceless politicians in faraway Washington—seem less remote in the great expanse of America.

The Emergency Banking Act of 1933 was a complicated measure that provided government aid to banks, helped the ones that still had liquid assets to reopen, and established a procedure to reorganize those that didn't, while also giving the president control over gold and permitting more issuing of Federal Reserve currency. It could not have succeeded unless ordinary people understood it well enough to believe it would protect the money they kept in banks. Once the bill passed Congress on March 9—only the fifth day of FDR's administration—he decided to give the first of what would become known as his fireside chats over the radio. Three days later, at 10:00 p.m., the new president spoke directly, via the national radio networks CBS and NBC, reaching an estimated 60 million people—nearly half the nation's population at the time. With characteristic warmth, Roosevelt reassured the country that the federal government was extending aid to the banks so they could resume operations, bringing renewed stability and security to the banking industry.

The tactic worked. When the banks reopened the following day, more money was deposited than withdrawn in every city in the country. A second banking measure, the Glass-Steagall Act, separated deposit banking from the riskier investment kind and mandated federal insurance of bank deposits, which reassured nervous depositors even more. The restored public confidence in the banks that was so essential to their recovery was enhanced even more by the president's new approach to communicating with the people. FDR's radio broadcasts established a direct connection between them and the federal government and conveyed the clear message that not only did Washington bear the responsibility for addressing this national emergency, but that it was on the case. That reassurance may be the most important part of what was new about the New Deal.[3]

The administration took other regulatory steps to strengthen the foundations of the economy. Congressional investigations had revealed unethical practices on Wall Street that contributed to the speculative boom in stocks that precipitated the market's collapse. Assisted by its brilliant counsel, Ferdinand Pecora, the son of Sicilian immigrants, the Senate Banking Committee brought to light that financial executives had paid themselves astronomical bonuses while rigging investment pools and pegging bond prices artificially high. The public was eager to see the mess on Wall Street cleaned up, and FDR quickly stepped in. On March 18, 1933, he proposed legislation that gave the Federal Trade Commission power to police the issuing of new securities. Each new stock issue would now have to include detailed financial information, and company directors would be held legally liable for any misrepresentations in that material. By emphasizing full disclosure by the financial institutions, rather than more intrusive government intervention in the markets, Roosevelt ensured bipartisan support for the measure. Even Herbert Hoover strongly supported it. The biggest beneficiaries would be middle-class investors. Wealthy speculators already had access to this kind of information, and the poor simply did not buy stocks. But even those people at the extreme ends of the economic scale stood to gain as the nation turned a corner, with these reforms helping to bring an end to the sickening plunge in stock prices and in the broader economy.[4]

A more traumatic leveling of the playing field, at least for the investor class, was Roosevelt's proposal to create a federal Securities and Exchange Commission (SEC) to act as a watchdog over the daily workings of the stock market. He sent the bill to Congress in February 1934, and it was signed into law in June. The act demanded that stockbrokers and all other traders fully disclose all relevant information when they offered any stock for sale. While enforcing the disclosure requirements of the earlier law, the SEC would also ensure that reputable outside auditors confirmed all relevant public information about stocks. The act further protected the market from runaway speculation by regulating the extent to which investors could use credit to purchase securities (called buying on margin).

FDR shrewdly appointed veteran Wall Street speculator Joseph P. Kennedy Sr. as head of the SEC. FDR figured that if anybody knew the darkest secrets of the stock market, it would be Joe Kennedy. Here was an unusual product of the newer immigrant America, someone so talented, ambitious, and successful as to have crossed over, partway at least, into the overwhelmingly more established American world of high finance. Kennedy was so well informed about the market's looming problems in the twenties that he quietly unloaded his common stocks before the crash, then astutely reinvested afterward, making his influential family richer than ever. The Securities Exchange Act of 1934 successfully ended the casino-like shenanigans of the 1920s, turning many prominent business leaders—much of the upper class in America—against the Roosevelt administration. But again, the middle class, which blamed the big-pocket speculators for the crash and the Depression, was cheering.[5]

In April 1933, Roosevelt made the controversial decision to take the country off the gold standard, meaning that no longer would the amount of paper money printed be limited by the amount of gold in the government's possession. The United States was not alone in taking this step (Britain had done the same thing two years earlier), but conservative business leaders and high-stakes investors saw it as sacrilege. From now on, monetary experts in the government would determine the appropriate amount of paper money to have in circulation, based on existing economic conditions. Traditionally, economists feared that printing too much paper money could trigger excessive inflation. But the administration didn't think that was likely in the early 1930s, when interest rates were high and the economy was so weak that prices for most goods and services were plummeting. In those conditions, the problem was more likely to be deflation, which meant that money itself became more valuable. That was good news for savers, but because of bank failures and mass layoffs, most Americans of the day had no savings to speak of. For debtors, deflation was a disaster because the real value of what was owed grew as money became scarcer and more valuable.[6]

After taking the country off the gold standard, Roosevelt's economic team tried to reverse the deflationary trend by manipulating the price of gold. That decision, unlike the much more sensible one to abandon the gold standard, was ill-considered from the start. Even though the value of the dollar was no longer directly tied to that of gold, people still took the precious metal seriously and believed that it influenced prices. For three months, from October 1933 to January 1934, the government followed a program of officially raising the price of gold every morning. Over breakfast, FDR, Henry Morgenthau Jr., and two other aides would decide what the raise for that day would be. The Treasury would then purchase gold on the open market at the new price, effectively raising the market to that level. Sometimes, the president would pretend to settle randomly on a particular figure, just to see the horrified look on Morgenthau's face. The exact amount didn't matter to FDR, as long as gold's price steadily increased in an unpredictable manner that would discourage speculators. Some economists believed that such maneuvering would drive up commodities prices, thus stopping deflation in its tracks.

This turned out to be among the New Deal's flakiest experiments. Plenty of good reasons existed for going off the gold standard, but boosting commodities prices by buying up gold didn't work out, and Roosevelt would stop the practice. The best reason to abandon the gold standard was that it wouldn't allow the government to run bigger budget deficits, even during a deep depression. FDR needed to free up the government to pursue the expansionist economic policies that defined the New Deal, such as spending on public works and relief.

Here was the problem: If the nation's currency was redeemable in gold and the government created a large budget deficit, the big savers and investors, fearing inflation, would hasten to exchange their dollars for gold. That would shrink the nation's gold supply and force the government to take some paper money out of circulation to compensate for the reduced gold in its coffers. As long as the gold standard continued, less gold in the government's vaults would necessitate a smaller money supply, creating *more de*flationary pressure. The administration had again made policy decisions that best served the interests of people of relatively modest means.

The rich, no longer able to redeem their dollars for gold, were predictably outraged. The effort to reverse the downward spiral in prices also made the poorest Americans nervous, with its prospect of having to pay more for consumer goods when their incomes were low. The thinner slices of population at the top and the bottom of society again opposed FDR's machinations, but the great numbers in the economic middle saw the promise of stability.[7]

The greater flexibility in economic policy made possible by these financial moves enabled the federal government to act in even more direct and unprecedented ways to rescue the dispossessed and to raise incomes. The administration could now expand relief programs and public works projects even though that meant running a budget deficit. In addition, FDR moved to prop up farm prices and to establish a system of wage and price floors in other sectors of the economy. By March 1933, state and local governments were tapped out, with no more relief funds available to provide the unemployed and their families enough to subsist on. Even some *Republican* leaders at those levels turned to Washington for support and direction. Before FDR took office, Pennsylvania governor Gifford Pinchot, who had served under Teddy Roosevelt as head of the US Forest Service, had pleaded with Herbert Hoover to provide emergency federal aid to state relief agencies. Hoover had turned a deaf ear, but now that FDR was in the White House, he stepped up. After all, he himself had seen the desperate need for such assistance when he was governor of New York.

As his federal relief czar, Roosevelt installed Harry Hopkins, a small-town Iowan with a background in urban social work. Hopkins had seen the grim face of poverty up close, which most of the upper-crust politicians had not, and understood well the urgency of the problem. In his first two hours on the job, working from a temporary desk in a hallway, Hopkins wrote checks totaling over $5 million to state relief agencies. FDR shared Hoover's fear that a permanent federal dole could foster dependency, but the new president didn't let that stop him. His thought was to minimize that danger by making the main relief measure temporary. Roosevelt built that disclaimer right into the title of the agency that Hopkins headed, the Federal Emergency Relief Administration (FERA). Right at the outset, the administration signaled that the $500 million in federal grant money infused into state and local relief agencies to replenish their coffers was intended to alleviate a specific crisis, not meant to make Washington responsible for assistance over the long run.[8]

The surest way to raise income is to create jobs, and the Roosevelt team began that effort by setting up the Civilian Conservation Corps (CCC). The US Army provided most of the key personnel who ran the CCC, including Colonel George Catlett Marshall, who would lend his name to the European Recovery Program after World War II—the Marshall Plan. Marshall oversaw seventeen CCC camps in the Southeast. In its first year, the CCC hired a quarter of a million unemployed young men, and that number would rise to 3 million by the time the program ended in 1942. The men were put to work in the national forests and parks, building firebreaks and lookouts, bridges, campgrounds, trails, and museums. In return, they got room and board in work camps run by the military, plus $30 a month (about $580 in 2019 dollars), $25 of which had to be sent home to their families. That requirement, of an all-male workforce, to send money back home, can today be seen as a piece of social engineering that reinforced the pervasiveness of the male-breadwinner model. New Dealers invariably thought in terms of households, rather than individuals, and simply assumed that those households would be headed by men. Most Americans must have shared that perspective; the CCC was one of the most popular programs, not to mention one of the most enduring symbols of the New Deal.[9]

Roosevelt then launched the Civil Works Administration (CWA), a federal public works effort aimed at helping the overall population get through the winter of 1933–34, and that was less rigid about gender.

Under the astute direction of Harry Hopkins, who wore many administrative hats during the 1930s, the CWA spent nearly $200 million a month from November 1933 to March 1934, and put 4.2 million needy men and women to work on light construction and housing projects: upgrading roads and bridges, laying sewer pipe, fixing up schools and hospitals, and building 150,000 outhouses for farm families. One reason for the program's popularity was that, like the CCC, it paid people for work, affording some dignity and sidestepping the stigma of relief. In its brief five months of operation, the CWA drew most of its administrative staff from other, more lasting government agencies. That the program was temporary again illustrated Roosevelt's concern that this type of assistance might prove so popular with those who benefited from it that it would take on a life of its own. The CWA was shuttered on schedule as the winter of 1933–34 ended, even though millions of workers still lacked paying jobs.[10]

The most iconic and longest-lasting New Deal public works project also primarily benefited male breadwinners. On April 10, 1933, Roosevelt urged Congress to get behind a massive public power project in the Tennessee River Valley. Some version of this idea had been kicking around since World War I, when the US government had erected the Wilson Dam along the river in northern Alabama to generate hydroelectric power for a munitions plant. Even the concept's most fervent champion, Progressive Republican senator George Norris of Nebraska, never imagined it on as grand a scale as FDR did. In the president's conception, the federal government would employ thousands of workers to construct a series of large dams to produce electricity cheaply throughout the region. Not only would the project electrify an isolated, largely rural area stretching from southwestern Virginia through Tennessee to northwestern Mississippi, and extending into portions of North Carolina, Georgia, Alabama, and Kentucky, it would also attract industry and create jobs. With strong support from Dixiecrats who applauded the direct benefits to the South, Congress quickly passed the measure. But when Roosevelt signed the Tennessee Valley Authority (TVA) into law, only five short weeks after introducing it, a howl went up from certain corners of the nation.[11]

For starters, the project largely ignored black Americans, employing whites almost exclusively, a reflection of the strictly segregated

South where it was built. It also drew hostility from the other end of the socioeconomic spectrum, the wealthy, conservative, and powerful business leaders, of whom utility executive Wendell Willkie of Commonwealth and Southern Corporation became the most famous. It wasn't just that the TVA was unmanageably large, according to these critics, but it would be built and run entirely by the government, without even a partnership role for private industry. The new power plants it built would compete with private-sector plants already in operation. In describing what he saw as the real problem with the TVA, Willkie coined a term that would become a permanent part of the American political vocabulary: *big government*.[12]

Roosevelt could have taken steps to calm the fears of these free-market conservatives. He could have made them a part of the process from the start or arranged to sell off the completed power plants after the TVA dams were finished. But FDR lacked faith in the private sector to get the job done properly and insisted on an entirely government-owned and government-operated venture. The right-wing rich could only suspect creeping socialism when they heard TVA head David Lilienthal describe the enterprise as "democracy on the march." To them, the engineers and administrators assembled in the Knoxville headquarters might as well have been Soviet commissars supervising some piece of the latest five-year plan. As much as the TVA came to symbolize the achievements of the New Deal for white, middle-class men and their families, it revealed how polarizing it was, representing discrimination to America's black citizens and governmental overreach to many of its business leaders.[13]

Also in 1933, the Roosevelt administration instituted a system of price supports for farmers, to raise their incomes through federal subsidies rather than through relief programs or public works. Farm incomes had been depressed during the 1920s, then had fallen faster and further than urban workers' incomes after the crash. Despite the ongoing migration of Americans to the urban manufacturing centers, roughly 30 percent of the population still lived off farms in some way, and huge numbers of them now stood to lose everything to foreclosure. America had a soft spot for farmers, a sympathy also felt in state legislatures, which typically overrepresented rural areas. (Since 1900, many states had resisted reapportioning their legislatures after each census because that would have transferred more clout from the countryside to the fast-growing cities.) Powerful farm lobby groups, notably the American Farm Bureau Federation, exploited the increasing sympathy for farmers during the Great Depression.[14]

Support remained strong for what became a lasting federal policy of paying farmers to limit how much they grew, as a way of driving up prices for those agricultural products. This was true despite an early public relations fiasco that took years to live down. By the time the farm subsidies went into effect in May of 1933, farmers had already planted their spring crops. Since the idea was to increase prices by reducing the supply, it became necessary to plow under huge fields of growing corn and wheat. Critics of the New Deal on both the right and the left seized upon the spectacle of farmers destroying food crops while many Americans were going hungry. Likewise, the slaughtering of more than 6 million piglets and more than two hundred thousand sows because of a ruinous glut in the hog market horrified both America's hungry and its animal lovers. Equally shocking was the plowing up of over 10 million acres of cotton when so many people couldn't afford to put clothes on their backs. That this was a necessary, one-time adjustment in agricultural production didn't matter; the jarring, incongruous images stuck in the minds of many people, some of whom came to believe for years afterward that this kind of destruction was an annual ritual.

Despite the nearly disastrous rollout, the new system of farm price supports soon achieved what its advocates had promised. The timing of the implementation was fortuitous, as the drought and dust storms of the 1930s—the Dust Bowl years—ravaged the Midwest and depressed farm production even further. Farm income rose 50 percent during Roosevelt's first term in the White House, almost entirely making up the losses since 1929. Still, the farm sector continued to shrink, since most of the subsidies went to the biggest, most successful farm operations, but the devastating pace of family-farm failures was greatly slowed.[15]

The unique circumstances of each of the three distinct regional components of 1930s America could be seen in the different ways the New Deal's farm policies played out around the country. In the parts of the Northeast and Midwest that hadn't yet been urbanized, and where the highest concentration of family farms still existed, the policies functioned more or less as planned. Not coincidentally, Roosevelt's secretary of agriculture, Henry Wallace, was born and bred in Iowa. Wallace had made a fortune developing high-yield hybrid corn, and he firmly believed that family farming, backstopped by mechanization, could remain vibrant in America. He drew on his vast personal experience to get the price-support system up and running quickly, which helped to calm rising turbulence in the Midwest, where mass foreclosures had given rise to some instances of violent vigilantism. Across the heartland, public, court-ordered sales of family farms were increasingly met with calls for armed resistance on the part of the farmers.

The reception in the South, a part of the country wholly unfamiliar to the likes of Henry Wallace, was different. In this region, dominated by large landowners who relied more on low-wage laborers than machinery, as opposed to the smaller but more mechanized family farm operations up North, the same policies produced much harsher results. Owners of the big southern farms would withdraw land from production, keeping the federal subsidy checks for themselves instead of sharing the money with their sharecroppers, and laying off the workers who had previously tilled that land. Then the plantation owners turned the steady stream of government money into new tractors, harvesters, and threshers, jumping on the bandwagon of mechanization pioneered by better-off farmers in the North and out West. As the demand for agricultural labor fell drastically in the South, a growing multitude of poor, landless farmhands, both black and white, saw no option but to leave for the nation's larger towns and cities outside the region. The exodus out of the South that had begun during World War I accelerated during the thirties and forties, making the farm sector there much more like the big mechanized agricultural operations of California. The transformation felt much less like real reform than it did in the more heavily populated Northeast and Midwest, proving the difficulty of creating a national farm policy that treated the varied regions of the country fairly.[16]

In the South, the benefits accrued primarily to the well-off minority that held political power. The Democrats basically enjoyed one-party rule in the South, and over time, the Dixiecrats' stature in Washington had risen. Southerners in the House and Senate had piled up many years in office, and the seniority system on Capitol Hill ensured that they now occupied top-ranking positions on almost every committee. Once the Democrats won big majorities in the election that swept FDR into office, Republican dominance on Capitol Hill, which had been the norm since the Civil War, vanished almost overnight. That revolution gave the Dixiecrats lasting leverage in shaping national policy. They were New Dealers, too, but of a different sort from Roosevelt and his mostly northern advisers. Here was the native-born establishment sector of the New Deal coalition, but an unusual slice of that socially dominant group. Dixiecrats tended to be as rural and agrarian in economic background as northern New Dealers were urban and industrial. Neither group made any specific effort to include black Americans in 1933, but the Dixiecrats were more rigidly committed to segregation than northern New Dealers were. The South's poverty helped bridge the gap with northern liberals, who represented urban workers in economic distress, but many points of tension existed between the two factions.

Nothing exemplified that pattern of crossover and conflict better than religion. Southern Baptists and northern Catholics often overlapped on morality but conflicted on theology. The Democratic Party that FDR now led had been badly divided by region and religion during the 1920s, and he knew he had to keep the powerful Dixiecrats happy if he wanted to get his programs through Congress. That meant, at a minimum, refraining from serious challenges to Jim Crow in the South, and greater federal efforts to help the region prosper.[17]

Beset by economic crisis, Roosevelt looked for allies wherever he could. With the private sector still stronger than the public one, he supported the creation of a Business Advisory Council (BAC) within the US Department of Commerce to advise the administration regarding economic policy. While the BAC might have looked to some like a publicity stunt, a bone the president could throw to the business community, it actually gave its members a formal role in shaping new and sorely needed policy initiatives. In a break with precedent, Commerce Secretary Daniel Roper urged the group to take the broad view and consider all aspects of the US economy, rather than focus narrowly on what might be good for their own firms or business sectors. With the economy reeling, these business leaders were open to setting their individual interests to the side and working toward a larger goal.[18]

Franklin Roosevelt was fortunate to have the consistent support of his friend and neighbor Thomas J. Watson Sr., the head of IBM, who served on the BAC from the beginning and played an influential role behind the scenes. Watson would enjoy national celebrity beginning in the Depression years, respected across the country as much for being on the cutting edge of technology as he was for standing by his company and his workers even during the worst years of the Depression. More important, he was a true believer in the New Deal and worked hard to convert his skeptical fellow business leaders. He knew that the Roosevelt revolution would benefit business, too, if only they would give it the chance. Watson could point to his own company as his most persuasive argument: a relatively small enterprise in 1932 it had, by the end of FDR's presidency, become a moneymaking colossus, largely by doing business with the greatly expanded federal government.[19]

FDR remained focused on winning over the business community and knew that bringing its leaders into the administration's decision-making processes would help make them part of the solution. That determination shaped passage of the National Industrial Recovery Act, with the intent of raising incomes for corporations and for their employees. The act called for business executives to play an active role in policing American economic life, by taking the lead in drafting and enforcing codes of fair competition. This included setting wage and price floors in a variety of industries, so as to stop the downward spiral on both fronts. The biggest businesses dominated that process, not only because they were able to throw their weight around through high-priced lawyers, but also because their pockets were deep enough that they could play the corporate statesman role without losing so much in profits as to endanger their firms' survival. Smaller businesses typically operated on profit margins so slim that they generally needed a shove from some higher authority to show generosity to their employees. The codes, it was believed, would prevent "unfair" competition over prices, wages, and working conditions and so help break the cycle of economic decline. Launched in the summer of 1933 with great fanfare and headed by Hugh Johnson, a colorful ex-general turned businessman with public relations savvy, the National Recovery Administration (NRA) succeeded in making its purpose known to the public and exerted some influence on economic life for about a year and a half.[20]

The program ran into trouble after that, however. Predictably, many small businesses resented an approach to national economics that represented more of a burden on them than on the bigger firms. (The lawsuit that ultimately sank the NRA had been brought by the four Schechter brothers from Brooklyn, whose small business butchered and sold chickens without strictly following all the new poultry codes.) Big businesses, as well, helped fuel dissatisfaction with the codes by laying off their lowest-paid workers—such as children and African American adults—rather than raise wages for them up to the level of the floors set by the new codes. These layoffs hit the poorest working families the hardest, as they depended on the money these low-wage workers had earned. Many black people grew equally hostile toward the NRA, claiming the acronym stood for Negroes Ruined Again. And, as always, the insistent drumbeat of complaint about intrusive government regulation came from some conservative businessmen still not convinced about the New Deal. Herbert Hoover, still a spokesman for Republican orthodoxy, objected to the NRA, insisting that the federal government should not *require* business to do anything, but rather should help spur private-sector efforts to fight the Depression by organizing conferences and providing information.[21]

In a pattern that would come to typify the New Deal, the NRA's policy of promoting fewer but better-paying jobs favored the vast socioeconomic middle, but drew fire from Americans at both the top and the bottom of the scale. Soon even the bigger businesses got fed up with the NRA, growing resentful about losing the freedom to control their own wages and prices, even though they had been primarily responsible for writing the codes. As objections multiplied, and more and more businesses balked at compliance, the NRA quickly faded. When the US Supreme Court ruled unanimously in May 1935 that the act unconstitutionally delegated legislative power to business, the NRA experiment came to an end. Ironically, even the Schechter brothers of Brooklyn, who had filed the suit, felt conflicting emotions about the result. Jewish immigrants from Hungary, they feared the fascism growing in Europe and supported Roosevelt's New Deal as a viable and constructive alternative. They couldn't help but feel a tinge of regret that their objection to a single NRA code had put such a dent in the spirit of national unity that FDR's early efforts had tried to foster.[22]

The Roosevelt administration moved on another critical front to rescue the newly poor by stemming the flood tide of house and farm foreclosures. In the spring of 1933, half of all home mortgages in the United States were in default, with home mortgage foreclosures averaging over a thousand each day. The entire home-financing system was close to collapse, a crisis that overwhelmingly affected the great majority of Americans in the middle of the income spectrum. (The wealthy didn't, for the most part, need the aid, and the very poor, not to mention most black Americans, could generally not afford to buy homes or farms.) Any action taken to address the crisis would thus benefit that middle-income group. This time, the steps taken by FDR and his people were both successful and durable.[23]

At the president's urging, and with bipartisan support, Congress enacted the Home Owners' Loan Act in June of 1933. The new law allowed lending institutions—banks and savings-and-loan societies—to exchange defaulted loans for guaranteed government bonds and refinance the terms of the loans. Troubled borrowers benefited in three critical ways: they could stretch out the repayment schedule much longer than had previously been allowed; they could lower the interest rates paid; and they could make uniform monthly payments over the term of the mortgage. The emergence of the Home Owners' Loan Corporation (HOLC) as a major lender led to the debut of the thirty-year fixed mortgage in America, not to mention the demise of the killer balloon payment at the end of the loan's term. The HOLC would enable the refinancing of one-fifth of all urban mortgages in the country, although in the long run the act would prove controversial as the government necessarily became influential in deciding which mortgages were good risks and which were not.

The thirty-year fixed mortgage, while helping many by making monthly mortgage payments lower and more uniform, hurt some others because those whose incomes seemed insecure could not be considered good prospects for mortgage repayment over such a long term. That tended to disqualify the almost poor, which affected a greater proportion of the black population. The law also reinforced segregation in housing by both income and race, out of a belief that homogeneous neighborhoods had the most stable property values, giving rise to what today we call redlining. These discriminatory practices kept many people out of the housing market, frustrating the desire to build equity and wealth for those individuals. But for those who stood to gain, this aid to distressed homeowners immediately became popular, and not just among its direct recipients. Even some affluent conservatives approved because they believed in the social benefits of home-ownership and saw it as a bulwark against radicalism. When FDR ran for reelection in 1936, one of the most common refrains heard from his supporters was "He saved my home!"[24]

To address the comparable mortgage crisis for family farms, FDR pushed forward the Farm Credit Act of 1933, to be overseen by the Farm Credit Administration (FCA), which he had created by executive order in late March of that year. This new law provided credit and mortgage refinancing for family farms that would have been deemed to be viable operations in more normal economic circumstances. Roosevelt's appointment of his trusted friend and neighbor Henry Morgenthau Jr. to run the FCA signaled how critical a priority it was for FDR. Indeed, by the end of the year, the tide of farm foreclosures had begun to recede, and family farming had stabilized. Like the HOLC, the FCA best served the needs of Americans in the economic middle. The most affluent farm owners gained little, as they were no longer able to snap up smaller foreclosed farms at bargain-basement prices. Bankers who catered to farmers also saw their profits fall, since the FCA capped the interest rates they were allowed to charge. Vice President John Nance Garner, a moneylender back in his native Texas, voiced those bankers' frustration at a cabinet meeting. Until the FCA came along, he said, "Mrs. Garner and I averaged sixteen percent on our money, and now we can't get better than five." And again, those at the bottom economically, the poorest subsistence farmers who were the greatest credit risks, were the least likely to be bailed out by the FCA, thereby making their poverty even more intractable.[25]

The lasting achievement of so many early New Deal programs was to restore some stability and security to the middle class, even if their compatriots at either end of the economic spectrum often felt cast aside. The middle class was now ascendant as a political and economic force, a phenomenon that drove major changes in America's social and cultural life during the 1930s. The end of Prohibition in 1933 provides a case in point. Repeal sparked raucous celebrations and was enthusiastically embraced in urban America and by beer-loving descendants of German-speaking immigrant families across the Midwest. In some other parts of the country, however, people strongly disapproved of the return of lawful booze. In the small towns and rural areas of the South and the West, for example, many people feared the drinking would only add to the social problems. But the New Deal, when it came to alcohol, found its greatest support from the majority of ordinary Americans who drank in moderation. Most Americans saw little harm in a cocktail or beer after a long day and were happy to see organized crime lose its biggest source of income.[26]

New Deal attitudes extended to what and how people ate. Herbert Hoover and his wife, Lou, had arrived in the White House in the last days of the Roaring Twenties, and every night they dressed formally for dinner and indulged in elaborate meals of continental cuisine, right through to the end of his unhappy presidency. By the time FDR took over, countless Americans were going hungry, often unsure of where their next meal might come from. Despite the Roosevelts' upper-crust backgrounds, Eleanor quickly put an end to the White House formal dining tradition.

With the help of her housekeeper, Henrietta Nesbitt, the new first lady was determined to set a new example. Out went the formal and the extravagant; in came the healthy, unpretentious, and bland. The new regimen emphasized nutrition and economy over enjoyment, which Eleanor and Henrietta dismissed as mere "flavor satisfaction." FDR obediently took his midday meal at his desk in the Oval Office rather than in the ornate dining room, and on his tray he found not Maryland terrapin soup and pâté de foie gras, but deviled eggs in tomato sauce with mashed potatoes on the side. If he was lucky, he might enjoy a dessert of prune pudding. Such would be the White House fare throughout his entire presidency.[27]

A cadre of mostly female home economists helped promote the new habits that Eleanor championed, supported by a flood of government pamphlets and even federally funded cooking classes. The "scientific eating" movement centered on finding the least expensive way to feed people healthily. Casseroles and combination loaves—meat loaf, peanut loaf, liver loaf, and bean loaf—became the rage, as dishes that both disguised leftovers and stretched ingredients. Canned foods and dried fruits, much cheaper and easier to prepare than fresh (and with more shelf life), filled kitchen pantries. Families experimented with unlikely mash-ups—peanut butter and baked onions, anyone?— that won points for nutrition, if not for taste. Milk and white bread, the epitomes of wholesomeness, became staples, as Americans came to accept bland food, which discouraged overeating, as the price to be paid for health and economy. People even began to think of the New Deal eating habits, so intensely focused on maximizing available food and avoiding waste, as benefiting the nation as whole.[28]

Before the Depression, Americans thought much less about the connection between food and health. In rural parts of the country and small towns, when people went out to eat, it was to all-you-can-eat buffets, with lots of meat, and treats such as pie served even at breakfast. City dwellers loved the fast food in their delis and cafeterias. But sweets and treats all but vanished after the crash, and meat became a once-a-week luxury, at best. Families ate in restaurants so rarely that, if they did, the experience made them feel like movie stars. The plus side of the new economic reality was the potential to improve people's health, and for households with adequate income, signs are that's what happened. The chief statistician of the Metropolitan Life Insurance Company was talking about that large middle-income demographic when he said in 1932, "As a people, we are normally given to overfeeding. . . . I would not be surprised if, under the present conditions of enforced moderation, many have enjoyed better health than ever before."[29]

The bottom third of the population did not fare so well nutritionally. The poor had so little access to food of any kind that their health seriously suffered. They simply didn't have the income to buy the food they needed, even staples such as milk, and many couldn't get enough assistance from relief programs to eat healthily. As paradoxical as it sounds, even farm families were going hungry. The poorest city dwellers didn't have the option of producing their own food and couldn't cobble together an adequate diet for their families out of meager relief payments and soup kitchens. For these poor families, the option of "scientific eating" simply wasn't on the menu. At the other end of the economic scale, those upper-income families that could still afford stylish three-course meals were the least enthusiastic about this economical new diet, seeing no reason why they should stoop to the bland and dreary diet of Middle America. People of middling income, whose economic circumstances tended to dictate moderate consumption, most readily adopted the new eating habits.[30]

In this era of rigidly defined gender roles, it fell mostly to American women to put this culinary sea change into effect. With more mouths to feed at home, and restaurants no longer an option for most families, unemployed men could have done more of their share of the kitchen work. But most were neither socially conditioned to think that way, nor did they necessarily know their way around a kitchen or a household budget. In upper-middle-class families, where "flavor satisfaction" expectations were higher, housewives tried to produce meals that were both tasty and economical. These conditions made a surprise bestseller out of Irma Rombauer's *The Joy of Cooking*, published in 1931, which offered an easy guide to making such meals.[31]

Moderation permeated all aspects of domestic life. People relied on sewing and knitting rather than buying new clothes—another burden borne by women more than by men—and learned to repair rather than replace anything that might break down in the household. A new product called Scotch tape appeared. Families turned to home-based entertainment, gathering around the radio each night as if it were the family hearth, to listen to their favorite soap operas, westerns, crime shows, and music revues. Even though radio was free, the networks, too, enforced moderation in their own way, signing off at a reasonable hour every night.[32]

The first family determined to set a public example of how affluent people could live a more frugal lifestyle, something memorably symbolized by Roosevelt's battered gray fedora. Wealthy Americans like them were to do less with more, in a manner of speaking, while middle-class people were being asked to do more with less. The poor, who had little, were simply expected to somehow scrape by until the anticipated economic recovery finally materialized. In domestic matters, as in so many other aspects of society, Americans from all walks of life were being gently nudged toward a middle ground of frugality, modesty, and sustainability.[33]

The New Deal's efforts to restore "law and order" also seemed designed to make neighborhoods safe for the middle class. The crime wave sparked by the Depression had strained state and local policing to the limit, and Roosevelt's new attorney general, Homer Cummings, responded by reorganizing the three major crime-fighting units in the US Justice Department into a single Division (later Bureau) of Investigation, with the secretive and largely unknown J. Edgar Hoover in charge. With the repeal of Prohibition, federal crime fighters shifted their focus from catching bootleggers to catching bank robbers and other dangerous criminals who operated across state lines. The success of Cummings's "G-men" in collaring such high-profile outlaws as John Dillinger, Pretty Boy Floyd, and Baby Face Nelson captured the public's attention, raising in their imagination the stature of the federal agents, and thus allowing the federal government to take on a bigger share of enforcement efforts. When, at the end of 1934, Roosevelt signed into law a long list of new federal offenses, including robbing any financial institution whose deposits were insured by the US government, it marked a major shift in American law enforcement. Like other functions of government, crime control became more concentrated in the federal government, a trend that aroused concern among civil libertarians about where it all might lead.[34]

This is not to say that state and local law enforcement faded from view. Public-sector jobs with the police, the prosecutor's office, or the judiciary offered the kind of stable, long-term employment that so many people longed for during the Depression. As prices fell, the real incomes available in these professions steadily rose, attracting more highly qualified applicants, and giving them reason to hold on to those jobs. These developments, too, served the needs of the middle class at the expense of those at the high and low ends of the economy. The proverbial thin blue line of policing thickened in the New Deal years, becoming more professional and more effective, which helped confine serious crime to the poorest neighborhoods. That result fueled resentment among the poor and among people who were not white, who viewed with suspicion the overwhelmingly white, male, middle-class members of the criminal-justice system now patrolling their communities. More affluent citizens also had plenty to grumble about, knowing that their tax dollars were footing the bill for more highly paid policemen who were driving down crime in neighborhoods where the middle class lived. The wealthy also felt more vulnerable, no longer as able to hide behind their power and position should they find themselves on the wrong side of the law.

Richard Whitney, president of the New York Stock Exchange, serves as a vivid illustration. Whitney had rejected New Deal efforts to reform the market when he testified before Congress in the 1930s, after which he was prosecuted for embezzlement and convicted by a young New York County district attorney named Thomas E. Dewey. Dewey's success in sending Whitney to Sing Sing prison put him on a path first to the New York governorship and eventually to the Republican nomination for president.[35]

Intentionally or not, the combined effect of the New Deal's changes in government and public policy was to cement the primacy of the middle class in America. It makes sense, then, that popular culture would follow suit and cater to the majority of the nation that was neither rich nor poor, neither uneducated nor elite intellectual, and who shared a common desire for stability and community. The filmmaking industry, for example, was encouraged to develop a code of fair competition under the National Recovery Administration. The resulting Motion Picture Production Code Administration would continue to enforce industry self-regulation even after the Supreme Court found the NRA to be unconstitutional. Studio heads, sensing pressure on all sides, could see the writing on the wall and came together to take an unprecedented step in what might be thought of as American cultural policy. By 1934, state film-censorship boards were forcing studios to reedit films at a cost of $500,000 (nearly $10 million in 2019 dollars) each year. In Congress, Dixiecrats seemed inclined to enact a rigid film code in response to the many morally traditional people in their southern constituencies. In the cities, too, where many morally traditional Catholics in favor of censorship lived, the drumbeat was getting louder for Hollywood to clean up the movies. Newspapers across the country were more than happy to jump on the bandwagon and paint the film industry in the worst light.[36]

While a number of mainline Protestants shared many of the Catholic objections to the more disturbing messages found in popular movies, many also had reservations about censorship. The majority of American Catholics objected even more to what they sometimes saw on the screen, and some were willing to take the lead when the NRA first determined that a code had to be established. The code was written by a Jesuit priest, Daniel A. Lord, with the help of a Catholic publisher, Martin Quigley, who edited a journal called the *Motion Picture Herald*. The deeply Catholic code that they produced reflected a universe in which the wicked come to a bad end, a moral order to which the movies had to conform. Sexual innuendo and activity were largely banished, as was graphic violence and even profanity, lest any of that should inspire imitation on the part of the young or the mentally unstable. Scenes of disrespect for immigrants or their nationality groups, and any that involved brutality, including cruelty to animals, were also out of bounds. Films would respect law, authority, religion, and the institution of marriage as pillars of right-living society.[37]

Moviemakers even hired a prominent Catholic layman, Joseph Breen, to oversee compliance with the new code when it went into effect in 1934. Breen was a broadly informed man of the world, but also the somewhat traditionally minded product of a Jesuit education. He spoke three languages and had worked as a newspaper reporter, a foreign correspondent, a US Foreign Service officer in Jamaica and Toronto, and head of Catholic war relief after World War I. For the next twenty years, Breen would serve as the final arbiter of the code's standards, wielding power in Hollywood that rivaled any of the fabled studio executives. Breen and his staff became deeply involved in the creation of films, offering commentary on scripts even before any scenes were shot. They were expected to impose the code's moral vision on those scripts, editing out anything that might be out of line. Breen practiced what he saw as "respectable censorship," steering clear of partisan politics. Over time, he built lasting relationships with filmmakers, creating an unlikely alliance of primarily Jewish studio heads and primarily Catholic censors, a unique team sprung from the wave of immigration around the turn of the century.[38]

The new films shepherded through the system by Breen and his panel quickly found favor with audiences, especially in the big cities, and the surge in ticket sales delighted the studios. Here were movies that reinforced what morally traditional middle-class parents were trying to teach their kids, particularly at-risk boys. The transition in American culture from the heady days of the Jazz Age to the wholesome probity of the 1930s is best illustrated by the two films that won the Academy Award for Best Picture in 1934 and 1935, both starring Clark Gable, the biggest star of the day. In 1934, he played opposite Claudette Colbert in the sophisticated comedy *It Happened One Night*, she the flighty heiress and darling of the society pages, he the world-weary newspaperman on her trail. Rich with both charm and satire, the film poked fun at the excesses of the nation's upper crust by following the little rich girl on her journey along the back roads between New York and Florida. The film was risqué for its time, with the mismatched couple uncomfortably sharing a motel room for a night and confronting the sexual politics with both candor and humor. In contrast, the next year's Oscar winner, *Mutiny on the Bounty*, with Gable as the heroic mutineer Fletcher Christian, took a high-seas adventure of raw passion, violence, and betrayal in exotic locales and turned it into an inoffensive, deracinated entertainment designed to appeal to the broadest cross section of the population. For instance, the bloody clash to wrest control of the ship was downplayed in the film, and the Polynesian women in the story who take up with the English sailors were portrayed by white actresses. Both films won praise from the critics, but while *It Happened One Night* brought in only modest ticket sales, *Mutiny on the Bounty* was a box-office smash.[39]

Not everyone liked the new films coming out of Hollywood. Americans who were less morally and religiously hidebound found the code-era films unrealistic, depicting people and lifestyles that existed only in Hollywood's collective imagination. They didn't recognize themselves or their communities in what they saw on the screen. Besides, they found these movies increasingly predictable and boring. Civil libertarians objected to the whole idea of government-mandated censorship. Even after the NRA ended and the industry assumed responsibility for censoring itself, the American Civil Liberties Union warned that the rigid control over creative thought and artistic expression was likely to go too far. Filmmakers, screenwriters, and on-screen talent, who were not always so morally traditional themselves, and who wanted to push the creative envelope, found themselves frustrated by the code's restrictions. Successful actors who had earned the right to pick and choose their roles and films grew frustrated by the boring goody-goody parts on offer.

The situation was far worse for African American actors, who objected to being marginalized and were all but invisible on-screen, except in the roles of slaves or servants. In Joseph Breen's primarily white and Catholic America, he had little or no contact with black people, which limited his understanding of their lives. Moreover, with the constant threat of direct government censorship mandated by a Congress dominated by Dixiecrats, studio heads knew better than to make films that promoted racial equality. Meanwhile, educated, forward-thinking women chafed at the patriarchal view of gender roles and sexual politics on-screen, as did gays and lesbians, who were excluded outright.[40]

More than anything else, the movies of the code era reflected the growing stature of the urban middle class, especially in the Midwest, during the New Deal's first phase. Typically, these films played more to the tastes and sensibilities of cities such as Chicago—heavily white, metropolitan, middle class, and Midwestern—than to those of more diverse and cosmopolitan places such as New York or San Francisco. Movies, like radio, were responding to the desperation felt by so many American families. People who lived with chronic insecurity welcomed the solace and reassurance they could find in these films and radio programs. If they felt that they had a significant stake in society, but were not always secure about their place in it, they could feel safe with entertainment that discouraged risky situations and behavior. The Jazz Age antics of F. Scott Fitzgerald's novels were relegated to a forgotten past.[41]

The middle class gradually came to dominate American life. The daily struggle to provide for life's basic needs had caused most Americans to turn their focus inward, a parochialism reflected and reinforced by a new government that had essentially turned its back on foreign affairs to focus on the Depression at home. Having taken up the flag of their own communities and their own nation, Americans choked up when they sang "The Star-Spangled Banner," which had become the official national anthem in 1931. With the nation's elite still more cosmopolitan in their outlook and sensibilities, and the poor growing ever more alienated from mainstream America, the middle class responded the most ardently to the growing patriotism embodied in that song.[42]

The New Deal's parochialism didn't play so well around the world. When representatives of the major world powers came together in London for a critical economic conference in June and July of 1933, Roosevelt and his advisers succeeded only in scuttling it. FDR knew he had to avoid Woodrow Wilson's mistake of failing to secure adequate congressional support for the deal negotiated at the Versailles Conference in 1919 and so appointed six well-liked Washington officials to represent his administration at the conference. That plan backfired when those six politicians, as popular as they were, proved dysfunctional as a team. Worse still, FDR alienated the other world leaders by refusing to commit to an effort to cancel debts related to World War I, knowing that wouldn't be acceptable to most Americans or to Congress. He also rejected the French government's proposal to freeze currency exchange rates, as that would have interfered with his efforts to raise prices. The French plan could have prolonged the Great Depression rather than helped bring it to an end, so FDR was probably right to reject it. But the cavalier and dismissive way he torpedoed it caused the effort to find an international solution to the Great Depression to collapse.[43]

Roosevelt fared slightly better in his efforts to lower trade barriers, although this would further sour international relationships down the road. In March 1934, Roosevelt asked Congress for the authority to negotiate new tariff agreements with individual nations. Congress approved the bill, but only over the objections of businessmen, who feared foreign competition, and of most congressional Republicans, who resented yet another New Deal transfer of power from the legislative to the executive branch. FDR delegated the work of lowering tariffs to his secretary of state, Cordell Hull, who, while hardly an ardent internationalist, did genuinely favor a change in American trade policy. Unfortunately, the agreements that Hull negotiated provided no remedy for the basic underlying problem of how complicated it was for debtor nations to trade with the United States, which had become the world's leading creditor nation after World War I. Since Hull's agreements made it easier for those nations to buy from American companies than to sell to them, the total amount owed to the United States only grew in the 1930s, which deepened the underlying imbalance in the global economy. Neither the American people nor their government seemed to notice or care. As it had during the earlier economic conference, the United States succeeded in hardening hostile attitudes abroad. The new administration had initially raised hopes around the world, but now the frustrated leaders in Europe and Japan began to move in more nationalist directions of their own.[44]

The United States took more meaningful steps to improve relations with its neighbors closer to home than with more distant nations across the Atlantic and the Pacific. While the steps taken in Latin America were more constructive than those elsewhere, they, too, were characterized by parochialism. Most important, in December 1933, FDR renounced the policy of armed intervention in countries of the Western Hemisphere, explicitly rejecting the precedent set by his role model, Teddy, of invading countries engaged in activities frowned upon by official Washington. The following May, FDR's administration acted on that intent by signing a treaty with the Cuban government giving up the legal right to intervene in Cuba, even though the United States had insisted thirty-three years earlier that such a right be written into the Cuban constitution. A few short months later, the United States removed the last of its marines from Haiti, after which no American armed forces were on the ground in any nation in the Caribbean or Latin America.

These first steps in what became known as Franklin Roosevelt's Good Neighbor policy greatly improved America's standing with our close neighbors, although that policy could just as easily be seen as a retreat from overseas engagement. Most Americans cherished the concept of community, and after their family, neighborhood, and town the most significant manifestation of community was their nation. By extension, Americans were prone to value the sovereignty of other nations as well. They liked the idea of avoiding direct conflict with our near neighbors by clearing out of their countries, while also keeping the rest of the world and its problems at arm's length. The danger of that kind of thinking lay in how it could blind Americans to important larger issues, such as the emergence of aggressive, militaristic governments in Germany, Italy, and Japan, and the perilous disparities of wealth both within other countries and among them. Americans, unfamiliar with the kind of world leader role that the British had historically played, simply didn't see any of those problems as their own, but they would eventually become everyone's problems.[45]

As the midterm election approached in the fall of 1934, the New Deal's first phase had begun to arouse both intense opposition and fervent support. Some urban workers and small farmers were increasingly angry. Although these Americans in the socioeconomic middle had been the primary focus of the New Deal's domestic policies, many of them felt that after five years of hard times, things weren't improving fast enough. Their hopes and desires were now hardening into outright demands. Workers in the cities and factory towns wanted better wages and working conditions, not to mention more direct relief from the newly activist federal government. Small farmers insisted on higher prices right away, not at some undetermined time down the road, and couldn't understand why the government wasn't doing more to prop them up.

But government resources were limited, even in the generous spirit of the New Deal. The economy, though no longer declining, remained weak overall, and tax revenues were lower than in the late 1920s. The federal government couldn't afford more relief or aid to farmers without running up what seemed to be a dangerously high deficit. Some people began to feel that the New Deal had promised more than it could deliver, and they were getting restless waiting for better days to come. Those raised expectations helped translate into a developing national strike wave, as angry workers, inspired by the NRA's pro-union section 7A, tried to organize unions. Newly politicized workers and farmers also put more energy into electing New Deal supporters, not only to Congress but also to state and local offices, in the hope that they could finish the work that Roosevelt and company had started.[46]

The result in November was a spectacular "wave election" that swelled the already wide Democratic margins in both the US House and the Senate. The Democrats would hold 322 House seats to just 103 Republican and 10 fringe-party seats, and more than a two-thirds

majority in the Senate. At least as startling was the shift in governors' mansions across the country, where now only seven Republicans
remained. Even in staunchly Republican Pennsylvania, where FDR
had lost to Herbert Hoover in 1932, New Deal Democrats won control of the key state government offices. A new national Democratic
majority was taking shape, bringing together urban workers—many of
whom had only just begun voting regularly—small farmers, southerners, and former Progressive Republicans, both urban and rural, from
the North and the Far West.[47]

This tectonic electoral shift aroused protests on both the left
and the right. Radicals on the left, heartened by the militant spirit
among workers and farmers that had helped produce those results
at the ballot box, began agitating in earnest for the redistribution of
national income and wealth, publicly funded old-age pensions, a big
federal public works program that would put the poor back to work,
and greater protections for workers trying to organize unions. On the
right, conservative business leaders, aghast at the decline of the GOP,
organized the American Liberty League to hold the line against the
rising wave of farmer-labor radicalism by promoting free enterprise
and denouncing the New Deal. (That group was so dominated by Wall
Streeters that even Hoover declined to support it.)[48]

The lot of the middle class had improved from 1933 to 1935, but not
always because of the programs and policies of Roosevelt's New Deal.
Many Americans fell back on more traditional sources of support in
their families and communities.

Let's look back again at Beatrice Bauch. By the spring of 1935,
she had married Howard Sindt, an industrious farmer and civil engineer in Davenport, Iowa, whom Beatrice had met when he lodged
in her parents' house. Howard had seen his income rise when the
farm price-supports program had gone into operation and had then
acquired more farmland through a foreclosure. The marriage, which
had already produced a baby boy, made Beatrice economically secure,
but also disqualified her from working as a schoolteacher, since state
law at the time prohibited married women from holding public-sector
jobs unless the wages were absolutely needed to support their families. She had held on to her teaching job for a while by not wearing her

wedding ring, but that ruse didn't last long. With her profession now off-limits because of Depression-era job rationing, Beatrice turned toward home and family. If the loss of financial independence and professional satisfaction bothered Beatrice, she could console herself with the knowledge that she remained much better off than those still submerged in the Great Depression's flood tide.

George Perkins's situation had also improved by 1935, and like Beatrice Sindt, as she now called herself, he'd had to take a step backward before moving forward. George and his family, now five after the birth of a third child, were still living with his mother in Providence, in the roomy old house where he had grown up, across the street from Brown University. George had spent six deeply frightening months out of work in 1932 and 1933 before finding a job through a combination of hometown connections, merit, need, and luck. A new Rhode Island office of employment security, a product of the New Deal at the state level, offered George a job helping unemployed people find work. Sensing that the hard times and joblessness would last, George signed on, eventually enjoying a lifetime of stability and security as a civil servant.

These two stories parallel the experience of so many middle-class Americans in the early years of the New Deal. Beatrice and George both had to lower their sights, but doing so enabled them to escape some of the trauma of the Hoover years. Their decision came with a cost, in abandoned dreams and ambitions. They saw their circumstances improve, but only because they were willing to return home, to rely on a network of family and community, and to make life choices that prioritized stability and security over independence and adventure. Both would remain in those hometowns for the rest of their long lives, their futures marked by limited choices but also by deep and lasting relationships.

The virtual sweep by New Deal Democrats in the 1934 election masked a continuing frustration among the least fortunate Americans. Dispossessed farmers and unemployed factory workers had allowed themselves to expect so much from the New Deal, but were still left empty-handed. Gone, however, was the paralyzing fear they had felt in the face of Herbert Hoover's inept and seemingly callous response to the national crisis. In its place came a new, populist assertiveness that shook the foundations of the American establishment. The pitchfork-carrying rebels in the heartland and the burly labor organizers in the working-class neighborhoods of the manufacturing belt had together turned from apathy to activism. They saw the New Deal as completely changing the terms of the existing social contract, whether upper-crust America liked it or not. Many of their specific solutions were still in the formative stages, and sometimes they conflicted with one another, but it was all held together by a larger logic, a greater sense of purpose and intention. Franklin Roosevelt had promised to give the dispossessed families of the country both work and security, the twin pillars of middle-class life, and those families would see that the promise was kept. The future would belong to people like them. In their minds, that's what democracy in America was supposed to be all about.

CHAPTER 3

Hour of Discontent

The rebuilding and expanding of the middle class got another big boost from the New Deal's second phase, which began in the spring of 1935 and lasted through the fall of 1938. This most turbulent phase mostly built on the accomplishments of the first two years of the administration's efforts. The introduction of major new innovations on top of what had already been accomplished transformed American society even further, taking the country into previously uncharted public-policy territory, which stirred both ardent support and intense opposition.

Many of those who believed that FDR and his supporters had reached the limit of necessary or possible reforms in 1933–34 found the New Deal's second phase thoroughly disorienting. In this, the most radical part of the New Deal era, Congress passed major new laws concerning relief, social insurance, labor unions, business regulation, taxes, and banking. Tensions worsened between the Roosevelt administration on one side and business and the wealthy on the other. FDR emerged as a spirited champion of the urban worker who dreamed of middle-class security. This polarizing turn, which deeply surprised seasoned pundits such as syndicated columnist Walter Lippmann, earned the new president a lasting, massive following in cities and factory towns.[1]

The American public grew exceedingly divided, with each side aggressively vilifying the other on the basis of politics and ideology. On the left, committed mainstream liberals cooperated with Communists to build unions while publicly decrying the evils of the existing American system. Many artists and intellectuals got caught up in the ferment, producing pathbreaking works in art, film, and literature. On the right, the New Deal's second phase prompted a conservative revival that defended free enterprise from growing restrictions imposed by government and labor and championed the courts as the last bulwark against New Dealish collectivism. That right-wing agenda attracted prominent members of both major political parties. FDR and his top advisers, as well as their primarily middle-class supporters, had to navigate the uncertain ground between those two poles. The future direction of American life was so fiercely contested during this phase of the New Deal that many had a hard time seeing where the nation was headed.[2]

Americans were just as confused about how to engage with the rest of the world. A large majority still couldn't shake off the memory of World War I, where military force—and the sacrifice and destruction that went with it—had failed to bring about a lasting peace. As aggressor nations such as Germany, Italy, and Japan expanded during the mid-to-late 1930s, many Americans concluded that greater involvement abroad would be just as futile and so resisted efforts to make the United States more of a factor in world affairs. That mix of pacifism and pessimism characterized American foreign policy in the New Deal's second phase, to the frustration of such long-standing allies as Britain and France. This was, in a way, not all that different from the New Deal's first phase, except for one important difference: the world was becoming a much more dangerous place in the mid-to-late 1930s, even as American isolationism persisted. The central problem was that most Americans simply didn't understand the menace of fascist regimes. Americans overwhelmingly preferred to avoid international conflicts altogether (rather than take sides) and focus instead on problems closer to home.[3]

In the clearest sign that Depression-era conditions still haunted the country, at least 10 million people were unemployed in early 1935. Roosevelt moved decisively and dramatically, requesting $4.8 billion for federal work relief, the single most expensive and immediately consequential undertaking of the New Deal's second phase. That huge sum, more than the total amount the federal government had spent in either of the two previous years, was intended to drive down the number of unemployed and turn them into consumers. As with other New Deal legislation, the temporary nature of the measure was built right in to the name, the Emergency Relief Appropriation Act. When Congress passed the bill in March 1935, it handed the president almost complete discretion in spending the money, in keeping with the New Deal emphasis on executive-branch leadership, although FDR moved quickly to delegate that authority. He bypassed Harold Ickes, whose Public Works Administration (PWA) had moved too slowly thus far to make a big dent in unemployment. Instead, Roosevelt tapped Harry Hopkins to run a new agency with a similar name: the Works Progress Administration (WPA). By choosing Hopkins, Roosevelt signaled his intentions that the first work-relief installment of $1.4 billion would go for smaller-scale projects such as the ones undertaken earlier by the temporary Civil Works Administration (CWA), which Hopkins had headed in the winter of 1933–34.[4]

The WPA quickly became more than just another of Roosevelt's alphabet agencies. In dollars spent during the Depression, it was the federal government's biggest domestic program, the public face of the New Deal. The WPA's emphasis on employing as many people as possible shaped the projects it sponsored. The cost of materials had to be kept down, so as not to cut too deeply into the money available to employ people. That ruled out construction of large-scale public housing complexes, despite the desperate need for more dwellings in the bottom third of the income distribution. The new relief law also included rules against competing with private industry or taking on work ordinarily done by existing government agencies, which further limited its activities.[5]

Despite these seemingly tight constraints, Harry Hopkins proved ingenious at putting the unemployed to work. Over its eight years of operation, the WPA built or improved over twenty-five hundred hospitals, almost six thousand school buildings, a thousand airport landing fields, and nearly thirteen thousand playgrounds. Hopkins also approved projects that employed idled artists, actors, and writers, who were hired to paint murals in public buildings, put on plays for the general public, and produce visitor's guides for all of the then forty-eight states. A related program, the National Youth Administration (NYA), gave part-time jobs to over six hundred thousand college students and over 1.5 million high schoolers. NYA also employed over 2.6 million jobless young people not in school, to do such things as build tennis courts, landscape parks, and renovate classrooms. Thanks to the speed with which Hopkins and the WPA worked, it had an immediate and substantial effect on the nation's economy. At least 3 million people, mostly male, earned desperately needed income during the WPA's first two years. The WPA's workers pumped what they earned right back into the economy, helping fuel a genuine economic upturn in 1935–37.[6]

The turnaround sparked by the WPA deflected attention away from some of its more troubling aspects. Like New Deal efforts to aid the unemployed, the WPA hired able-bodied people only. The new federal relief law turned the problem of caring for the permanently disabled back to the states, many of whose governments remained largely indifferent to those "unemployables." The WPA's emphasis on employing male breadwinners likewise excluded other segments of the population. African Americans struggled to gain equal access to the WPA, despite needing it more than many white citizens. True to New Deal form, the program tended to work best for the average unemployed person rather than the unusual one. Additionally, work relief, by its nature, siphoned off some of the funds for supplies, tools, and materials, leaving less available for wages. (An outright dole of the sort Britain possessed would have allocated all of its funds to the unemployed.)

In many places, especially in cities controlled by Democratic Party machines such as Chicago, Jersey City, and Kansas City, partisan administration of the program limited its reach. Registered Democrats in those places usually had the best odds of getting a WPA job. Grateful recipients were also sometimes expected to donate to the party and support its candidates, giving rise to endless Republican charges that New Deal relief was essentially a way of buying votes. Some WPA projects could also be faulted as make-work of little lasting value. The WPA functioned as a Rorschach test about the New Deal as a whole: Did people see mostly the benefits or mostly the problems?[7]

Harold Ickes always thought Harry Hopkins named his agency the WPA to confuse people into thinking it was the same as Ickes's Public Works Administration (PWA). While two sides of the same coin, the programs were fundamentally different. PWA built much bigger infrastructure projects than WPA, such as major bridges, dams, and highways, including the Triborough Bridge and Lincoln Tunnel in New York, the Golden Gate Bridge, and the Hoover Dam. Those kinds of ventures relied much more on heavy capital expenditures and exemplified the New Deal's commitment to promoting economic recovery by spending on needed infrastructure projects that promised to contribute significantly to long-term economic growth. Roosevelt decided, however, to steer the bulk of work-relief money to the WPA, shifting the focus toward putting money into as many workers' pockets as possible so as to stimulate consumption. Under "Honest Harold" Ickes's careful direction, PWA accomplished its economic goals, although once again earning criticism by limiting employment mostly to white, male breadwinners in the hard-hit construction industry. In some big cities, most notably New York, black protests eventually opened a limited number of such jobs to people of color. The PWA also drew criticism for concentrating its projects in a limited number of places—with Roosevelt's New York the single biggest recipient— rather than spreading them out evenly across the national landscape. Thus, the appearance of regional favoritism gave even the honestly managed PWA a partisan image.[8]

Other unintended consequences made a fair assessment of the New Deal even more difficult. For example, Hopkins's decision to create federal theater, arts, and writers' projects under the auspices of the WPA meant the federal government was for the first time subsidizing artistic expression. Given that one of the fundamental purposes of the arts is to challenge people to think differently about life and its problems, these WPA initiatives soon became controversial, both within the artistic community (for potentially limiting creative freedom) and outside it (for potentially using artists to produce pro–New Deal propaganda). Some critics also worried about Hopkins's emphasis on employing as many people as possible, fearing that it could conflict with the goal of producing high-quality work. And it did not sit well with many that government bureaucrats now controlled some cultural purse strings, deciding what kinds of art ought to be funded.[9]

Most of what was produced with WPA funding could best be described as "middlebrow art." The Federal Theatre Project, for example, sponsored productions of canonical works such as Shakespeare's plays in ways that made them more accessible to audiences without a lot of formal education. The overall reach was impressive: 30 million people attended these performances between 1935 and 1938. The Federal Art Project focused on the creation of murals and paintings that were representational rather than abstract. Even someone without much of a background in art could understand and relate to these images. The Federal Dance Project similarly emphasized canonical works that were seen as most likely to appeal to people least familiar with the art form. The Federal Music Project emphasized performances of such well-established genres as classical music and jazz. The Federal Writers' Project's highly popular state visitor's guides were likewise aimed at the person of average education and experience, out to see the most popular sights. At times, the various WPA arts projects did break new ground, by staging plays that addressed contemporary social problems from a moderately left-wing perspective, but that was very much the exception rather than the rule. The more avant-garde work, such as Clifford Odets's rousing pro-union play entitled *Waiting for Lefty*, tended to attract more attention, though, not to mention more controversy. Conservative critics in Congress denounced such works as partisan attacks on traditional American values. The more typical WPA art forms, however, were as patriotic as they were populist.[10]

In the New Deal's second phase, middlebrow began to arrive as the dominant mode of cultural expression, a shift that the WPA contributed to and also influenced. Middlebrow took many forms. The number of "respectable" tabloid newspapers gradually grew, spreading from big cities to smaller ones. These papers succeeded largely because they relied heavily on illustrations and simple prose to convey news of interest to the average reader. The advent of *Life* magazine in 1936 was another marker of that shift. *Life* accomplished with photographs what *Time* had earlier done with words, which was to paint a picture of the world easily understood by readers with an ordinary amount of schooling. By the end of 1937, *Life's* circulation had reached 1.5 million, more than triple that of any previous new magazine.[11]

The success of *Reader's Digest* (which began its first international edition in 1938) signaled a similar shift. This monthly periodical culled material from more high-powered publications, shortened and simplified it, and presented a fresh version in language readily accessible to someone with no more than a grade school education. The Book of the Month Club (BOMC), which targeted a "middle class" of literary consumers, rose to prominence around the same time. BOMC offered its members inexpensive hardbacks written to appeal to readers without advanced formal education. Earning a place as a Book of the Month Club selection all but guaranteed commercial success for a new book.[12]

Something similar went on in the world of children's literature, where easy-to-read formula fiction starring such characters as the Hardy Boys and Nancy Drew became highly popular. What such work lacked in literary distinction and racial and ethnic sensitivity, it made up for, to some extent, by encouraging a wider swath of kids to read more. Such books, set in nondescript towns and peopled by generic character types, also introduced the less affluent youth to a sanitized and idealized version of life for the more privileged, thereby reinforcing the assimilating effects produced by radio and the movies. Comic books also offered an exciting alternative. The single biggest milestone in that realm came in June 1938 when Action Comics published its first issue, with Superman, a hero whose exploits soon engaged millions of young readers. These graphic adventures were mostly aimed at boys, whose commitment to reading (and formal schooling) had usually been substantially less than girls'. That, too, was characteristic of New Deal–era middlebrow culture, which provided exposure to skills and a broad base of common knowledge that would help boys achieve success as adult breadwinners.[13]

The music industry, in the mid-1930s, followed the lead of WPA's Federal Music Project, taking often complex and esoteric musical genres and making them more accessible to popular audiences. NBC achieved great success by creating a symphony orchestra under the disciplined direction of the European conductors Pierre Monteux and Arturo Toscanini to perform weekly classical concerts on the radio. From the first broadcast on November 13, 1937, the emphasis was on raising the cultural standards of average American listeners, which meant lots of Beethoven, Mozart, and the like. Listeners already familiar with the canon of Western music likely found such selections overly familiar; those who had never been exposed to classical music may well have found them overly formal. These broadcasts found greatest traction with that middle class of listeners who had been taught to think of such music as "important" and maybe even enjoyable, but had seldom if ever heard it performed live.[14]

Another landmark in the emergence of middlebrow music was the domestication of jazz into what became known as swing. The leading exponent of that change was the clarinetist and bandleader Benny Goodman. Born in Chicago in 1909, he was the ninth child of poor Jewish immigrants from eastern Europe. Goodman's early influences were New Orleans jazz clarinetists such as Johnny Dodds, Leon Roppolo, and Jimmie Noone, who were all working in Chicago then. By age fourteen, Goodman was performing in a band led by the Iowa-born cornetist Bix Beiderbecke.[15]

By the spring of 1935, Goodman had organized his own band and started performing on NBC's *Let's Dance*, a weekly three-hour radio show that featured a variety of dance music. Goodman's distinctive contribution was blues-inflected jazz transformed by African American musician and bandleader Fletcher Henderson into something much more upbeat, which was just what Depression-era America craved. Breakthrough performances on the road in California during the summer of 1935 gave rise to a new dance form—the jitterbug—which young listeners began performing spontaneously in the aisles whenever Goodman and his band played. This dance, a high-energy jazz variation of the two-step—with couples swinging and twirling and tossing each other around acrobatically—soon became a national craze, helping propel Goodman and his band to stardom.

The King of Swing reached the pinnacle of success on January 16, 1938, when Goodman's band took the stage at New York's Carnegie Hall, the great bastion of classical music. That concert has been described by music critic Bruce Eder as "the single most important jazz or popular music concert in history; jazz's 'coming out' party to the world of 'respectable' music."[16] Goodman's band played to the moment by performing in black tie, which made them look more like classical performers than traditional jazzmen. Many purists bemoaned what Henderson and Goodman had done—taking an art form rooted in African American sorrow and turning it into something so upbeat that middle-class whites could embrace it enthusiastically. But as with the changes in art and the printed word, the advent of swing brought a kind of jazz to a vastly wider audience. The most flexible jazz tradition-alists, Louis Armstrong especially, adapted to the change and profited from it. Such was the fundamental nature of the artistic compromise at work in the emergence of middlebrow during the mid-1930s.[17]

As the number of public-sector jobs grew under the New Deal, ever more lower-middle-class office workers and upper-working-class man-ual laborers found themselves with money in their pockets. As their ranks swelled, so did their influence in the marketplace of ideas. A new mass audience was taking shape. Artists, performers, producers, and programmers who aimed straight at the middle of that big diverse crowd secured their spot in the emerging popular culture. This wide swath of the population that was now moving out of poverty, but still were by no means rich, were happy to spend money on newspapers, magazines, books, and phonograph records, as long as they weren't expensive or hard to understand. All those new consumers of culture made a much bigger impact in the United States than they could have in Europe, given that the American government had not been in the habit of subsidizing arts and culture as had been the tradition across the Atlantic. By funding and organizing so many cultural projects, while creating jobs that enabled people to become consumers for that culture, the New Deal became the driving force behind a great shift toward the middlebrow in literature, art, and music.[18]

The dominance of the middlebrow didn't mean that all highbrow or lowbrow culture went completely underground. In the world of litera-ture, for example, the 1930s saw the publication of an extraordinary list of important books. Serious readers flocked to such novels as Ernest Hemingway's *To Have and Have Not*, with its characteristic focus on a rootless drifter; John Steinbeck's sophisticated if sometimes cynical depictions of working-class life in *Of Mice and Men* and *In Dubious Battle*; Richard Wright's collection of short stories entitled *Uncle Tom's Children* and Zora Neale Hurston's *Their Eyes Were Watching God*, which thoughtfully explored the place of race in American life.

Lowbrow entertainment likewise endured. Traveling circuses and carnivals still made their way across the country. Blues singer Bessie Smith and folk musician Woody Guthrie relished playing to enthusias-tic crowds of the poor and dispossessed whose stories they told in song.

But changes in income and wealth distribution drove the greater visibility and popularity of middlebrow culture. As the real wealth of upper-class Americans sank well below what it had been in the mid-to-late 1920s, sales of expensive hardback books and attendance at pricey Broadway shows and other, similar upscale cultural offerings remained depressed. As the poorest Americans struggled just to afford life's basic necessities, many less expensive cultural offerings just couldn't stay afloat without paying customers. Still unclear in 1935–38 was whether this shift to the middle marked the beginning of a long-term trend in American cultural life, or simply a temporary aberration.[19]

Meanwhile, uncertainty hung over the rest of the other major initiatives of the New Deal's second phase. Roosevelt's proposed Social Security law, which he formally sent to Congress on January 17, 1935, was, after the relief spending bill, the most costly and controversial. The handiwork of a cabinet committee headed by Labor Secretary Frances Perkins, this measure contained a slate of programs through which the federal government would support the financial and physical well-being of citizens, including: contributory pensions for the elderly; cost sharing with the states for the indigent elderly who were not covered by the pension system; unemployment insurance for those unable to find work; aid on a matching basis to the states to help them assist poor, single-parent families headed by women and aid to the disabled and the blind; and funds to support public-health programs.

All of this was to be financed by payroll taxes on workers and their employers, with participants (and their families) reaping benefits related to their contributions. The financing mechanism and approach to calculating pension benefits together gave Social Security the outward appearance of a publicly run insurance system not unlike private-sector models. By making the funding dependent on worker and employer contributions, rather than general federal tax revenues, Social Security cleverly gave people a sense that all they were getting back in old age were their own contributions, plus accrued interest. Thus, to the average person, Social Security represented nothing more than a new form of saving, mandated by the federal government. The reality was somewhat more complicated because the pensions paid would be somewhat more generous than what a private bank or insurer would have thought actuarially appropriate. The intent was to ensure at least a minimal livable income to low-wage contributors and to people who had reached middle age by the time Social Security began, and who had usually saved less for old age.[20]

As well-intentioned as it was, Social Security as proposed in 1935 met with plenty of resistance. Its approach to financing pensions required accumulating reserves that could generate interest before any benefits could be paid, which meant that most people would receive nothing until the system had been up and running for a time. Only as the years went by and contributors accumulated substantial pension benefits would Social Security mature into a major source of income for the elderly. Some critics believed that the system would be unfair and regressive in income distribution. Contributors would all pay the same flat rate up to a certain level of overall income, then nothing beyond that, which would place the least burden on those who earned the most. Social Security's financing mechanism also threatened to depress overall consumer activity during the program's early years because far more money would be going into the system than would be paid out in benefits. The pensioner movement, headed by California doctor Francis Townsend, objected to the administration's proposal primarily because of that potential negative impact on the economy. What Townsend and other left-wing populists called for instead were immediate, generous pension payments to the elderly, funded by the federal government's general revenues.[21]

Others objected that not all Americans would be covered by Social Security. Farm laborers and domestics were excluded, supposedly due to the difficulty of estimating their real wages, given that many were paid at least partly in room and/or board rather than actual wages only. That so many of these kinds of workers in the USA were African American made Social Security more acceptable to the mostly conservative southern Democrats running Congress, without whose support the measure would likely not have passed. The Dixiecrats also pushed for as much local administration of the act as was possible so as to strengthen the ability of Social Security offices in the South to exclude other kinds of black workers as well. Other low-wage workers, and people employed by the smallest businesses (defined as ten workers or less), would also be ineligible. Social Security, then, had nothing to offer in the way of pensions to those who would have the least in old age. Even some white citizens from middle-class backgrounds, most notably women, could find fault with the measure because it assumed a male-breadwinner model in calculating pensions for widows. By making the pension system more generous for women married to male earners than for single women, Social Security put pressure on women to conform to that model.[22]

The proposal for a joint state and federal unemployment insurance system drew fire as well. Roosevelt's Social Security law gave each individual state the power to determine the amount and duration of unemployment compensation it would make available. Given the disparities in wealth and resources among the states, such a program could perpetuate and even exacerbate regional inequalities.[23]

Like so many things FDR tried to do, the proposed Social Security law incensed many of the richest Americans, led by the du Pont family and the American Liberty League it had helped found. To them, the whole idea smacked of state paternalism at odds with the American tradition of individual responsibility. They claimed that the proposed bill also infringed on the prerogatives of the states so as to benefit some but not all Americans, which seemed a kind of illegitimate "class" legislation. Using the power of the federal government to *require* workers and employers to fund old-age pensions also struck upper-class Americans such as the Liberty Leaguers as an unconstitutional interference with the free-enterprise system. What really got under the skin of the wealthy was that the whole scheme had nothing to do with them. They just didn't need it, since most of upper America tended to accumulate sufficient wealth for old age without government intervention. Why sit still for a massive, costly expansion in the federal government's role that would primarily serve the needs of the middle class?[24]

Plenty of upper-class Americans had already developed a healthy distrust of government. Now they expressed serious doubts about whether that government could handle the administration of such a huge and complicated program. Could Roosevelt's people develop a workable system for recording all of the various payroll contributions, making the requisite pension calculations, and sending payments to what would eventually be millions of recipients? Many conservatives, from the business world especially, thought of the American government as small and staffed mostly by second-rate people and so could not imagine Social Security actually delivering on its promises.[25]

That last point was actually a valid concern, as Frances Perkins discovered when she went to Britain to see how its government handled administration of the British social insurance system. To her consternation, she discovered that it depended on entries made by hand in ledgers kept by civil servants at a public-records office housed in a building that was not fireproofed. Perkins concluded that such an approach, while feasible in the much smaller and more homogeneous society of the United Kingdom, would likely never work in the very different United States.[26]

The solution, she and FDR agreed, was to go see his neighbor in New York, IBM CEO Thomas Watson Sr., who had supported the New Deal from the start. Even though IBM was still a small firm at that time, it specialized in making and servicing the kind of recording and tabulating machinery that would be needed to make Social Security possible. Watson, perceiving that doing good in this instance could also mean doing well as a businessman, agreed to develop prototype machinery. No one could know for sure, in the spring of 1935, whether Social Security would ever function as promised, even with this new technology.[27]

Despite all of the objections, Social Security moved through Congress during 1935, propelled by widespread support from middle-class Americans and the congressmen and senators they had swept into office the previous November. The trauma of the Great Depression, and especially the many bank failures of the early 1930s, drove middle-class demands for a new system that would make it easier and safer to save for old age. That same quest for greater economic security also explained the broad popular support for the bill's other parts, which would at least partially protect people against disaster stemming from unemployment, family breakup, poverty, disability, and blindness. Even the official opposition of the US Chamber of Commerce, which passed a resolution against Social Security at the Chamber's annual convention in May, could not derail the bill. It finally emerged from Congress on August 14, 1935, and was signed into law the next day by a beaming Franklin Roosevelt. For all its initial faults, Social Security nonetheless marked the start of a fundamentally new and improved social contract between the government and the people, one that better fit the conditions of an America in transition, newly dominated by the population centers of the major metropolitan areas.[28]

The third major legislative initiative of the New Deal's second phase, the National Labor Relations Act, sparked an even bigger firestorm. The measure was the brainchild of New York senator Robert Wagner, who had immigrated from Germany with his family in 1886, at age nine. When he arrived in New York City, the nine-year-old Wagner spoke only German. His family had little money, but Wagner made his way through City College by working as a bellhop at the New York Athletic Club, whose membership included many of the city's power brokers. Interested in politics, he gravitated, like so many immigrants before him, to the Democratic stronghold of Tammany Hall. His mentor there, Tammany leader Charles F. Murphy, encouraged Wagner to open a law practice in the heavily German American neighborhood of Yorkville, located around East Eighty-Sixth Street in Manhattan. At age twenty-seven, Wagner won that district's seat in the New York General Assembly, beginning a storied political career. He came to the US Senate in 1926, owing his unlikely victory to a third-party, Prohibitionist candidate, who siphoned off enough votes from the Republican to make Wagner the winner.[29]

Robert Wagner was an emblematic product of the heavily urban and industrial part of America, where support for labor unions was strongest. His humble origins and immigrant status surely contributed to his sympathy for the workers' cause. Upon his arrival in the Senate, Wagner assembled what became the first modern congressional staff, hiring such stars as Simon Rifkind, a brilliant lawyer who later became a distinguished federal judge, and Leon Keyserling, who would go on to head the Council of Economic Advisers under President Truman. These men helped Wagner develop his labor-relations bill, which would, if enacted, extend broad legal protection to union organizing, collective bargaining, and striking. What was revolutionary about the measure was its applicability to the private sector as a whole. Prior to the 1930s, unions in the United States had emerged only in a limited number of industries, such as construction, mining, printing, and railroads. The typical trade unionist then was an exceptionally skilled working-class person, who was hard to replace if on strike. The

American Federation of Labor (AFL), founded the same year Wagner had arrived in the USA, existed primarily to support the needs of those specialized workers. Wagner's innovation was to enable workers with no more than ordinary skills to form a union, which would help make unionization much more the norm than the exception, in heavy industry especially.[30]

Wagner believed the spread of unions would benefit American society as a whole, even management. The Great Depression had taught him that the ability to support oneself financially went hand in hand with the ability to buy the things one needed. Wagner saw unions as a way to raise workers' wages, making them more self-reliant and also more active consumers, and thus agents of a broad-based, lasting economic prosperity. His proposed labor law also promised to reduce workplace conflict by establishing rules of fair play during strikes, and by helping give workers more of a say in how the work was to be done and how their workplace was managed. Better wages and working conditions also had the potential to increase worker productivity, by giving employees a more positive outlook and motivation to work hard, even when the foreman wasn't around. Better treatment would also reduce the likelihood of great big work stoppages that could harm the entire economy. The result would be a more prosperous, peaceful, and productive American workforce. Wagner firmly believed that even business leaders would come to prefer these more personally invested workers to the underpaid and strike-prone industrial laborers so typical in 1930s factories.[31]

Wagner's first small step, in 1933, had been to insert into the National Industrial Recovery Act a provision known as 7A. That provision endorsed forming unions as a way to halt declining wages and had raised expectations among labor leaders, organizers, and ordinary workers that their efforts to build unions would now enjoy the protection of federal law. When management resisted 7A's implementation, workers began going on strike in huge numbers beginning in the second half of 1934. That strike wave encouraged Wagner to introduce his proposed National Labor Relations Act in February 1935. The new bill went far beyond what 7A had supposedly provided, but did not at first win the endorsement of the White House, which led many experienced observers to believe the proposed measure would not pass. To their surprise, rising labor unrest combined with the Supreme Court's ruling on May 27 striking down the National Industrial Recovery Act, including section 7A, converted Roosevelt into a reliable supporter of the bill. Suddenly a legislative proposal viewed as a long shot moved swiftly toward passage, despite firm opposition from the overwhelming majority of business leaders. On June 27, 1935, Congress approved the Wagner Act, as it became known, which Roosevelt signed into law eight days later.[32]

Labor leaders such as John L. Lewis of the miners (the one major AFL union that admitted all workers regardless of skill) and Sidney Hillman of the garment workers (who believed that organizing the less skilled could strengthen the union movement) hailed the new law as labor's "Magna Carta." It emboldened them in October 1935 to reject the AFL's narrow focus on highly skilled workers in favor of unions for workers regardless of skill level in such key industries as steel and automobiles. Pressure for unionization in such places had already been building both from alienated workers and radical organizers. The Wagner Act encouraged experienced and more moderate trade unionists such as Lewis and Hillman to commit more fully to the movement and help expand its reach.[33]

By the spring of 1937, both US Steel and General Motors, the two biggest industrial firms in the country, had signed agreements with unions, illustrating the rapid and improbable transformation in American industry. In steel, the process proved fairly calm. US Steel had earlier established an in-house workers organization, which purported to represent the firm's nonmanagerial employees, although it had no real bargaining power. As more and more units (called locals) of that "company union" voted to affiliate with the new United Steelworkers of America (USWA), headed by Lewis's lieutenant Philip Murray, management gave in rather than risk a strike. At General Motors, management fought a pitched and at times violent battle against unionization, but surrendered when neither the Roosevelt administration nor New Deal Democratic governors would provide any help in breaking the organizing strike, as federal and state officials had so often done in the past. The United Automobile Workers (UAW), like the Steelworkers, soon became part of a new labor federation: the Congress of Industrial Organizations, or CIO for short. Almost overnight, the new federation became a major force in the economic life of American workers, which gave it significant political influence. Its first president, John L. Lewis of the Mine Workers union, became a major national figure, to the astonishment and consternation of many wealthy conservatives and the delight of many working-class Americans. Still unclear, however, was whether this change would quickly be swept away (as union gains during World War I were after it ended) and whether it would spread into other important areas of private industry.[34]

The largely conservative community of business leaders also pushed back against Roosevelt's proposals for regulating business more strictly, the leading targets of which were the giant utility companies that provided electric power. A merger wave in the 1920s had led to the creation of vast corporate electric-utility empires called holding companies, many of which collapsed during the early years of the Great Depression. Roosevelt had demonstrated his inclination for public power utilities by pushing to build plants along the St. Lawrence River as governor of New York. He and his advisers tended to view electric power as a natural monopoly that needed to be reined in and thought smaller firms in that sector would be easier to regulate than great big ones. They proposed to break up the electric-utility empires into smaller units subject to stricter government regulation, much as FDR's role model, TR, had favored breaking up Standard Oil a generation earlier. As with the relief, Social Security, and labor measures, FDR let everyone know that he considered the proposed Public Utility Holding Company Act essential legislation (a "must," in his words) and pushed it through Congress in modified form by the summer of 1935. It led to the breakup of most big utility companies, to the fury of many conservative businessmen.[35]

Along with creation around the same time of the Rural Electrification Administration (REA), which Harry Hopkins set up to bring electricity to isolated farmers, and the Tennessee Valley Authority's public power stations, this new measure permanently expanded the presence of government into the growing electric-power-generation industry. Many consumers welcomed those developments, resenting the utility companies' stranglehold on the electricity that was fast becoming a necessity of modern life. The results were more access to electric power (in the countryside especially), more government regulation of how much that power cost customers, and increasingly polarized views about the implications for the nature of American society.[36]

Roosevelt's fifth piece of "must" legislation in 1935 was a tax bill aimed squarely at the wealthiest Americans. Partly intended to head off pressure from left-wing populists such as Louisiana senator Huey Long for "soak the rich" taxation, Roosevelt's bill raised federal-income and inheritance taxes to heights unprecedented during peacetime. Given how depressed even the top-end incomes were at the time, the bill wasn't expected to produce a lot of immediate revenue, but it enraged affluent Americans just the same. To them, it symbolized the administration's commitment to more progressive federal taxation of incomes and inheritances. Upper America grew even more alarmed about the longer-term implications of the proposed Revenue Act of 1935—the potential to extract a lot more in taxes from the upper-middle class and truly rich when their incomes rebounded after the end of the Depression. Despite outraged protests from some elements of the country's upper crust, the measure passed Congress that summer.[37]

Roosevelt had pushed hard, putting the full weight of his office behind the legislation he thought the country needed most desperately. While he was just as committed to the final major new law of the New Deal's second phase, he put less direct effort into getting it passed. The bill, the Banking Act of 1935, was pushed by Federal Reserve Board head Marriner Eccles. Eccles, a Utah banker, held the unorthodox view that an expansion of the nation's money supply could help revive the economy and lift the nation out of the Depression. Eccles argued for a more centralized American banking system that could promote a uniform national policy of lower interest rates. He helped draft the proposed Banking Act of 1935, which gave the president more control over appointments to the Federal Reserve Board, and the board more control over appointments to regional federal reserve banks. The measure also increased the Federal Reserve's control over monetary policy and required all of the big state banks to join the Federal Reserve system by July 1, 1942, if they wished to continue to participate in the federal deposit insurance program. Eccles drummed up support for the bill in Congress and among other maverick bankers. When Roosevelt finally signaled his support in June 1935, the measure moved toward passage that summer. When Roosevelt signed the measure into law on August 23, he committed the nation to effective federal government control nationwide over currency and credit policies.[38]

Franklin Roosevelt and the Democratic majority in Congress pushed through an enormous amount of transformative legislation during the second phase of the New Deal. The long-term future of that legislation, however, stood very much in doubt. Those laws would still have to pass muster with the US Supreme Court, where a conservative majority seemed more than willing to strike them down as unconstitutional. From 1934 to 1936, a majority of the justices voted to strike down more such laws for that reason than had been struck down in the Court's entire previous history. If that pattern continued, the Court's strongly conservative majority would likely rule against some if not all of the most important new measures by 1937. Four of the justices most inclined to reject the New Deal policies were elderly, however, which suggested change would be possible if Roosevelt won reelection in 1936 and got the chance to appoint some replacements. So the struggle to make the New Deal's second phase stick, like the previous struggle to make the first phase last, soon moved from the halls of Congress and the state legislatures to the realm of electoral politics.[39]

As the country headed into the election year of 1936, no one could say for sure exactly which way the wind of public opinion was blowing. Public-opinion survey research, now better known as polling—and even the social science behind the measuring of public attitudes—was just in its infancy. "Scientific" pollsters such as George Gallup, Archibald Crossley, and Elmo Roper were only just beginning to develop the kind of representative national population samples needed to make polling consistently accurate. Most existing surveys, such as the nationally known ones conducted by the *Literary Digest*, did not rest on statistically representative samples and failed to account for crucial, but sometimes subtle, factors that could even further skew their unscientific results.[40]

One of the biggest mistakes made during 1936 by the editors of the *Literary Digest* was to poll potential voters by mail-in survey only, using addressees drawn from telephone books and automobile-registration lists. That technique had been effective in the mid-to-late 1920s, when voter turnouts were low and the electorate was disproportionately upper class, but surveys of that sort became less reliable in the middle years of the Depression, when voting increased overall, and especially among the middle three-fifths of the income distribution. Despite their greater share of the electorate, many middle-income households, in cities especially, could not, or could no longer, afford their own telephones and cars. Even if they did own cars or phones, these voters completed mail-in surveys at a markedly lower rate than upper-class Americans did, due to language and literacy barriers and the cost of postage. Gallup, Crossley, and Roper dealt with that problem in 1936 by using in-person surveys in urban neighborhoods, which generated much more reliable results. The data showed Roosevelt and the Democrats with a consistent and sizable lead, albeit smaller than their final margins, thanks to the difficulty of predicting actual voter turnout among urban workers, who historically had not voted consistently in large numbers.[41]

Other, less accurate polls, including the *Literary Digest*'s, pointed toward a landslide victory by the Republicans. The resulting confusion was greatest in upper-income neighborhoods, where few outright supporters of Roosevelt's New Deal, its second phase especially, could be found. The irony was thick in 1936: the seemingly natural leaders of the community, those in positions of influence with the most formal education and access to official information, tended to lack understanding of what was going on politically, at least on the nation's proverbial Main Street. Workaday Americans with more ordinary backgrounds, in cities and larger towns especially, were more likely to see the signs of Roosevelt's popularity and so had a better sense of how the election would play out.[42]

The emerging labor movement made that affection for Roosevelt tangible with contributions of cash and campaign volunteers. John L. Lewis committed $469,000 of the Mine Workers' member contributions to Roosevelt's reelection. Other major unions also gave heavily, beginning a lasting pattern of strong financial support from labor unions for Democrats of a New Deal bent. Labor's efforts to get out the vote in cities and factory towns also propelled Roosevelt's campaign forward, along with those of like-minded candidates farther down the ballot.[43]

But nobody had ever sold FDR to the public as well as he sold himself. He was simply a natural on radio and in person, an enthusiastic and articulate spokesman for his administration's accomplishments. His natural gifts as a campaigner stood out even more when contrasted with those of his ineffective GOP opponent, Kansas governor Alf Landon. Roosevelt confounded the pundits who insisted that a disabled person could not campaign as well as an able-bodied one in a strongly contested election. In some ways even more surprising was the gusto with which the aristocratic Roosevelt publicly denounced the wealthy Liberty Leaguers who opposed his program, calling them "economic royalists" and "the forces of entrenched greed." Sophisticates then and later understood that Roosevelt's condemnation of such people stemmed from an upper-class paternalist perspective, which saw the avaricious businessman as the unwitting tool of the radical leftist. When Liberty Leaguers denounced the New Deal, the most thoughtful upper-class people understood, they played into the hands of the radical Marxists by contributing to a simplistically negative view of the privileged and the powerful.

Instinctively opposed to what we would today call the wing people of American politics, Roosevelt presented himself in 1936, as had his cousin Theodore a generation earlier, as the leading example of the socially responsible rich in politics. Not that FDR needed it, but a surprisingly large number of voters in upper-class neighborhoods responded positively and added their support to what he already had from northern, urban workers (both white and black), small family farmers, and the solid South. FDR ran away with the election and the Democrats won even wider margins of control in Congress and the states than before.[44]

FDR's decisive victory even had an unexpected effect on the Supreme Court. Chief Justice Charles Evans Hughes and Associate Justice Owen Roberts, usually the swing votes on the Court, began to side more often with decisions that favored New Deal legislation, reducing die-hard opposition on the Court to an aged minority. In the spring of 1937, the Court began finding all major New Deal laws constitutional, usually by votes of five to four with Hughes and Roberts consistently in the majority. FDR's push to increase the number of justices on the Court—and thus pack it with supporters—ultimately went nowhere in Congress, but apparently encouraged Hughes and Roberts to stick with their newly regular practice of finding New Deal laws constitutional. In addition, other elderly opponents on the bench began to retire, allowing Roosevelt to appoint replacements he thought would view the Constitution as he did. As resistance from the bench began to fade away, it seemed that the New Deal's most revolutionary legislation was here to stay.[45]

This is not to say that things went smoothly or easily for the forces of change during the last few years of the New Deal's second phase. The biggest factor working against progress was the ongoing economic decline—a recession within a depression that began in the summer of 1937 and continued through the end of the following year. A complex convergence of separate policies combined to depress the economy much more than anyone expected. First were the substantial cutbacks in federal government spending. (FDR was making good on his promise to the fiscally conservative southern Democrats who mostly ran Congress that he would reduce spending—and the budget deficit—once reelected.) And the Federal Reserve Board, worried about inflation as the economy moved forward rapidly, pushed member banks to lend less.[46]

While those factors caused the economy to begin contracting, the Supreme Court ruled on May 24, 1937, that the new Social Security law was constitutional. The decision surprised conservatives in both parties. The federal government could now start collecting Social Security contributions from workers and their employers. This sudden, massive new revenue stream, combined with cuts in federal government spending, led the Treasury to take in almost as much as it paid out by June 1937. While a balanced budget was usually seen as desirable, in the highly unusual conditions of the mid-1930s, private consumption and investment were still too limited to power the economy forward without the stimulating effect of federal deficit spending. When the WPA contracted as federal spending fell, those it employed became jobless again and could no longer afford to buy much. Once these changes in taxes and spending converged, the economy collapsed. The stock market both reflected and contributed to the economic about-face by crashing again in late summer. Other major economic indicators did much the same. What made this new downturn especially frightening was how much steeper its angle of descent was than the one that had taken place from 1929 to 1933.[47]

All of a sudden, Roosevelt and his New Dealers found themselves on the defensive. Much of what they had accomplished during 1935 had spooked conservatives in Congress, including the influential southern Democrats who chaired most of the major committees. So, too, had FDR's unsuccessful quest to pass legislation to pack the Supreme Court with administration supporters. Roosevelt further alienated the Dixiecrats by going after some leading conservative Democrats in the 1938 party primaries. Now, to make matters worse, his popularity took a significant hit because of what was being called the "Roosevelt recession." The president could no longer count on the unwavering support of Congress.[48]

The only truly new reform measure that got through Congress in 1937–38 was the Fair Labor Standards Act, or FLSA. It mandated an eight-hour day and forty-hour workweek, above which employers would be required to pay 50 percent more for overtime. FLSA was intended to impose a standard of moderation for workers, which was believed to be what was best for them both physically and psychologically. It marked a drastic departure for a work culture often characterized by workaholism (among family farmers and other kinds of small-business people) in good times and idleness (among wage laborers) in bad ones. FLSA's overtime penalty was also intended to fight unemployment by pressuring companies to hire more employees when business was good, rather than trying to make existing employees work longer hours. FLSA also established a federal minimum wage, which was intended to mitigate to some extent the common practice of paying less than what a male breadwinner and his family could live on decently. One consequence was to shrink substantially the number of low-paying jobs. In a related move, FLSA also banned child labor (defining anyone under the age of sixteen as a child). Many of the lowest-paying menial jobs had previously gone to children.[49]

To get the measure passed, Roosevelt agreed to exclude from its reach the farm-related employment categories most common in the heavily rural southern and Mountain West states, whose leaders were determined to maintain a low-wage system as a way to attract more employers to those regions. Thus FLSA helped create a "first-world" set of labor standards for the major industrial states of the Northeast, Midwest, and West Coast and allowed the "third-world" labor standards in the South and the Mountain West to continue. In the short run, the country became predominantly first-world, for the simple reason that many more people lived in the major industrial states than in what would, in time, become known as the Sunbelt.[50]

In the short term, FLSA proved detrimental to some workers. In the major industrial states of the North, for example, the lowest-paying jobs had historically been disproportionately held by women, children, and men of color. Establishing a floor for wages threatened the already meager economic prospects for many of those workers. The exception would be women who got married (and stayed married) to a male breadwinner, and men of color who could find jobs that paid enough to support a family. The sharp uptick in overall unemployment during 1937–38, when 4 million people lost their jobs, made the big picture that much more bleak.[51]

In light of the erratic performance of the federal government's economic policies, voters could hardly be blamed for doubting the New Deal's ability to stem the tide of unemployment. Roosevelt and his advisers did resume heavy federal government spending in the spring of 1938, having decided it was the only realistic way to spark a revival. Turning on the federal tap, while the Federal Reserve Board eased credit and currency policies, halted the new economic decline of the moment, but was not nearly enough to end the Great Depression. When surly swing voters punished the Democrats that fall by electing a lot of Republicans to Congress and state offices (outside the South), it became a lot harder for the administration to keep the federal dollars flowing. Most of the newly elected Republican officeholders, state and federal, were fiscal conservatives who resisted more public spending to fight the Depression. They had been elected not so much for their economic philosophy as for the simple fact that they weren't Democrats, who had to shoulder the blame for the 1937–38 recession. The chief consequence of the off-year elections in 1938 was to bring about a sometime alliance in Congress between conservative southern Democrats and Republicans, with respect to domestic spending issues especially. Thus, as the New Deal's second phase came to a close in the fall of 1938, a sense of economic and political gridlock developed.[52]

• • •

Meanwhile, at home in Iowa and Rhode Island, both Beatrice Sindt and George Perkins felt the reverberations of all that tumult in their own lives. For Beatrice, the recession that began in the second half of 1937 seems to have deepened the psychic scar left by the earlier crash of 1929. That the crash of 1937 came just as her family acquired another mouth to feed (her daughter Carol was born in September of that year) heightened Beatrice's fears for her family's economic security. Beatrice's life didn't change radically as a result of the new recession; she didn't suffer the sudden, sharp drop in social status as she had before. But the reminder of just how fragile her circumstances were ensured that anxiety was her constant companion. Like so many of her contemporaries, Beatrice could only tighten her grip on whatever tiny promise of stability she had secured for her family.

George Perkins felt the impact of the New Deal's second phase more in his work than in his personal life. The upsurge in labor-union organizing complicated his work in the unemployment office. The competing AFL and CIO unions sometimes insisted on hiring only their own members, rather than those of the other federation, or newcomers to the workforce who had not yet joined either organization. Like so many middle-class people, George Perkins basically sympathized with labor's efforts to give workers a better deal in the workplace, but sometimes resented the way trade union leaders seemed to enjoy flexing their muscle, picking fights with government officials, employers, and each other. As it became clear that neither the AFL nor the CIO would prevail, nor would they come together anytime soon, their rivalry began to look like a long-term problem, to the frustration of those such as George Perkins who had to work with them. The sharp rise in unemployment and the wage cuts during 1937–38, which were heavily felt in the factory and mill towns of Rhode Island, made George's job that much harder.[53]

The Roosevelt recession and the sense of political stalemate in Washington gave rise across the country to the feeling that the nation was stuck, like a car furiously spinning its wheels in the mud. After almost ten years of the Depression, millions were still without work. The early optimism for FDR and the New Deal had all but evaporated. People no longer argued about when or how the problems would be solved, but if they could be solved at all. Leading economists such as Harvard's Alvin Hansen spoke of the American economy as having reached a "permanent plateau." They predicted slow future economic growth that would do little or nothing to reduce the ranks of the unemployed. Contributing to that pessimism was a world economic system moving steadily away from free trade, as aggressor nations such as Germany, Italy, and Japan expanded their commitment to nationalistic trading blocs. Even the leaders of Britain and France went along with that trend by protecting their imperial economic systems from outside competition. Still more depressing by 1937–38 were the clear signs that those same aggressor countries intended to realize their economic vision at least partly by foreign conquest. In the summer that the Roosevelt recession began, Japan's armed forces officially invaded China. By the fall of 1938, Germany had annexed Austria and the German-speaking parts of Czechoslovakia. The smell of wider war was in the air.[54]

CHAPTER 4

The Good War

It almost goes without saying that the coming of World War II altered the political, economic, social, and cultural life of America in both profound and enduring ways. The three years after the election in the fall of 1938, leading up to the US entry into the war in 1941, and then the war years themselves, until 1945, marked the third, final, and most transformative phase of Franklin Roosevelt's New Deal. This final phase eventually recaptured the spirit of national unity that had flourished during the first phase, with people from every corner of the country and from all along the socioeconomic spectrum rallying to meet a major crisis. As he had when he first became president, Roosevelt once again recruited businessmen and less partisan Republicans to hold key jobs in his administration. That change of tack went a long way toward defusing the tense, confrontational relationship between the White House and the conservative-leaning business community. The massive federal spending on the war effort during this third phase dwarfed domestic New Deal expenditures during the 1930s and helped bring about a rapid end to the Great Depression. The United States witnessed a major advance in income and wealth equality, and an expansion in the size and influence of the middle class so great as to signal the arrival of a whole new era in the nation's history.[1]

In the fall of 1938, the dominant mood across the country was resignation, if not outright gloom, not only about the likelihood of ending the Depression, but also about the chances of restraining foreign aggressors. The New Deal's third phase unfolded in two distinct parts. During the first, a period of transition that ran from the fall of 1938 through the end of 1941, the economy grew fairly steadily but slowly, while unemployment remained high. What good economic news there was stemmed mostly from growth in arms manufacturing; Britain and France bought more munitions from American companies, and so did the US government. However, resistance within the country to getting involved in the conflicts abroad limited the public's appetite for a military buildup. Only after the Japanese military's shocking attack on Pearl Harbor in December 1941 did the New Deal's third phase kick into high gear. As America, and the world, hurtled toward a terrible conflagration, no one could predict what the coming years would bring. Only with the passage of time would the events of the late 1930s through the mid-1940s come to seem destined to play out as they did.[2]

If anyone doubted that the New Deal had entered a new phase, they only had to look at the rise in military spending. Up until the fall of 1938, Roosevelt had practiced only austerity with military spending, except for the navy, for which he had once served as assistant cabinet secretary. That approach reflected a conception from an earlier time of how best to defend the USA during peacetime. Rather than maintain a big standing army or an air force (then considered part of the army), the US government, emulating long-standing British tradition, favored instead having a vast and powerful navy. By the late 1930s, that kind of military posture had become dangerously outdated. First, advances in military technology in such areas as aviation, rocketry, and submarines had reduced the protection afforded America by the Atlantic and Pacific Oceans, and the US warships that sailed upon them. Second, the small size of the American army, which was hardly bigger than that of tiny Belgium, did little to deter such potential aggressors as Germany and Japan, which had huge and highly skilled ground forces.[3]

Only after the shocks of the initial offensives of the Axis powers did the United States rally itself to reconsider its national security policy, and even then, change came slowly, with the first step coming shortly after the Munich conference of September 1938. In Munich, the French and British governments agreed to accept Germany's annexation of the heavily Germanic part of Czechoslovakia known as the Sudetenland, the possession of which would add to Germany's military strength. The Sudetenland was a major arms-manufacturing center, and the Czechoslovak army housed most of its advanced equipment there. American politicians and generals had counted on France and

England to check Hitler's designs on Germany's neighbors and were taken aback when those two major powers rolled over at Munich. When Hitler announced a major German military buildup only a few days after the signing of the Munich agreement, Roosevelt responded on October 11, 1938, by calling on Congress to approve another $300 million for national defense.[4]

Congress responded warily. The US government spent approximately $1 billion on the military in 1938, about the same as two years earlier. The increase in the number of American military personnel from 1936 to 1938 was similarly modest, from 291,000 to 334,000. When the German government annexed the rest of Czechoslovakia the next March, making it clear that it had no intention of honoring the Munich pact, Congress got behind FDR's request. Germany's flagrant defiance of the Munich agreement showed a complete disrespect for diplomacy as a means to resolve disagreements over territorial boundaries. As Europe began sliding toward war in the spring and summer of 1939, Roosevelt became convinced of the need for a truly major American military expansion.[5]

At first, neutrality laws passed by Congress in the mid-1930s posed the main obstacle to making those arms and munitions available to America's informal allies, Britain and France. These measures essentially prohibited arms sales to warring nations, so as to prevent the United States from becoming gradually invested in one side of another big European war. Roosevelt's rearmament program depended on revising those laws, but through the fall of 1939, Congress stubbornly resisted, convinced that such a change would likely put the country on a path toward military involvement in whatever conflict broke out in Europe.[6]

In September 1939, the start of what became World War II, when German and Soviet armies jointly invaded Poland, changed attitudes in Congress—but not completely. The most Congress would agree to was to end the arms-embargo policy and replace it with one requiring foreign nations to pay cash for what they bought and to carry it away in their own ships. The "cash and carry" policy set real limits on what Britain and France could buy because they simply didn't have the needed financial resources. Still believing that this European war would be like the previous one, when French and British armed forces had successfully checked Germany's military advance for years, many members of Congress rejected direct American military aid to Britain and France as unnecessary and provocative. Many also took a dim view of British morale and resources. The mood in London seemed weary, even defeatist, to many American observers, including the US ambassador there, Joseph P. Kennedy Sr. He and other experts knew that World War I had been an extraordinary drain on British wealth and had concluded that Britain could not afford to fight another war with Germany. Even the bigger and stronger French military was still reeling from the terrible losses of World War I and seemed unable to rouse itself from its defensive crouch. In Washington, the prevailing attitude was that pouring more aid into those beaten-down nations might well be pointless.[7]

Americans had more than enough reasons for putting the brakes on any military buildup. Many pointed to the wastefulness of manufacturing armaments that we didn't intend to use or to sell. They also worried that such a buildup might backfire if it was perceived as a sign of aggressive American intentions. Some argued that making the United States more prepared to fight also would make it more willing to fight, thus increasing the possibility that simple momentum would take us into war.

Americans' anxiety arose directly from nightmarish memories of World War I. Even within the civilian government, few people understood how the development of modern tanks, trucks, and military aircraft had restored the ability to go on the offensive. Most Americans assumed that any new European war would be fought like the previous one, with its horrific slaughter of ordinary infantrymen immobilized in trenches.[8]

Perhaps the most obvious deterrent to a big American arms buildup was the enormous cost. A buildup would only perpetuate, and perhaps even accelerate, the increased federal government spending, higher taxes, and persistent budget deficits that had come to define the New Deal. And if the expense wasn't bad enough, civil libertarians expressed the concern that the kind of repression visited upon German Americans, antiwar radicals, and pacifists during World War I could return with a vengeance if the nation had to get behind another war effort. Some worried, too, about a decline in traditional American conceptions of freedom and democracy if the military and the rest of the government grew much bigger and more powerful.[9]

All of these mutually reinforcing objections combined for a while to stymie Roosevelt's efforts to take American national security policy in a new direction.[10]

Only the swift and stunning fall of France, in just six weeks, to Germany's invading army in the spring of 1940 began to change minds. No longer could anyone assume that military conflict in western Europe would produce the same kind of long-term stalemate seen in World War I. It wasn't as though the American people had their heads in the sand about the reality of Nazi aggression. The militarism and imperialism, persecution of Jewish people, and earlier attacks on much smaller and weaker neighbors had already turned most Americans against Hitler and his followers. George Gallup's ever more sophisticated polling operation had reported shortly after the start of the war in September 1939 that 84 percent of Americans surveyed favored an Anglo-French victory, and only 2 percent backed Germany, with 14 percent undecided. The critical effect of the French collapse on American public opinion was to put to rest the naively confident view that a Nazi Germany victory over all of its adversaries, Britain included, could not happen.[11]

German military victories in the spring of 1940 also completely upended American presidential politics. Until the French collapsed and the British withdrew their army at Dunkirk, the upcoming presidential election that fall looked likely to proceed along customary lines, with the Republicans choosing a nominee from the ranks of career GOP politicians and the Democrats nominating a successor to Roosevelt. But as the Republican National Convention opened in Philadelphia on June 24, word arrived of the French government's formal surrender. That unwelcome news, like the earlier French reverses on the battlefield, thoroughly disrupted the GOP's selection of a presidential nominee. The two leading contenders—New York prosecutor Thomas E. Dewey and Ohio US senator Robert Taft—had both staked out foreign-policy stands that almost overnight seemed thoroughly wrongheaded. Both Dewey and Taft had fallen into the trap of assuming that France and Britain would check Germany's advance in 1940, a belief shared by a large number of GOP partisans, in the Midwest especially, who had opposed greater American involvement in the conflict. When the basic assumption underlying that stance crumbled, so, too, did the convention delegates' willingness to nominate either Dewey or Taft.[12]

Instead, the Republicans surprised even themselves by nominating a genuine outsider, New York businessman and former Democrat Wendell Willkie. He alone among the major candidates for the GOP presidential nomination had argued that the United States was truly threatened by Nazi Germany's ascension, and that Britain deserved immediate American aid. Willkie had also staked out moderately conservative positions on Roosevelt's most popular domestic programs such as relief, bank-deposit insurance, farm price supports, and Social Security. Rather than attacking the principles behind those programs, Willkie found fault with the way New Dealers had gone about implementing them. Willkie warned that overly centralized federal programs had created a danger to the republic, redeploying the phrase he had used to condemn FDR several years before: "big government." Major print publications such as *Time*, *Life*, the *New York Herald Tribune*, and the Cowles newspaper chain, whose owners shared Willkie's views, heavily promoted them and his candidacy. The exposure made Willkie into a genuine media star and helped him win over swing voters, who preferred his moderately conservative approach to the more rigidly anti–New Deal stance so popular with the GOP establishment. Willkie emerged as the thoroughly unexpected victor on the Republican convention's sixth ballot. In his acceptance address to the delegates, many of them still furious that he had won, Willkie pledged to work for "the restoration of democracy in the world . . . and here at home."[13]

The fall of France had a similarly profound effect on the Democratic Party's presidential nomination contest. Nazi Germany's victory in western Europe underscored the need for a nominee with a firm grasp of foreign-policy issues. Believing that after two terms in office he had unique and unrivaled experience and expertise, Franklin Roosevelt decided to seek an unprecedented third term as president. Most leading figures in the four major power blocs that dominated the Democratic Party (big-city mayors, Dixiecrats, organized labor, and reform-minded members of the middle and upper classes) went along, in part because no plausible alternative ever emerged.[14]

No president, even including George Washington, had served more than two terms, and FDR was sensitive to how many Americans would be unsettled by such a significant break with tradition. Theodore Roosevelt had run up against that resistance when he had unsuccessfully sought to return to the White House in 1912, and FDR had no wish to emulate his cousin in this regard. The second President Roosevelt understood that Americans would likely react more positively to a third-term bid if it appeared to be the party's idea rather than his own ambition. Accordingly, FDR insisted on a draft, or at least the appearance of one, and got it from the Democrats at their convention held in Chicago during July 1940.

To strengthen the ticket's appeal in the face of a strong challenge from Willkie, Roosevelt chose a new running mate, onetime Progressive Republican Henry Wallace of Iowa. Unlike the sitting vice president, John Nance Garner of Texas—who had, like other Dixiecrats, become more hostile to Roosevelt's leftward drift—Wallace was an outspoken New Deal liberal. As agriculture secretary Wallace had presided over the creation of the popular federal subsidy program for farmers, which promised to win votes from traditionally Republican farmers in the nation's heartland. To soothe the hurt feelings of the delegates, who had little real say in selecting either Roosevelt or Wallace, FDR dispatched Eleanor, whom no one blamed for the way the delegates had been manipulated, to make the first-ever address by the spouse of a nominee to a national-party convention.[15]

The ensuing presidential election was close, exciting, and unpredictable, influenced in part by unforeseen external events. Nazi air marshal Hermann Göring's decision to order the heavy bombing of London in September–October 1940, and the overall Battle of Britain waged by the German and British air forces that summer and fall, signaled that Nazi Germany's military aggression would continue. The air war over England reinforced the sense among swing voters that the nation couldn't take the risk on a foreign-policy novice as president for the next four years. But for a variety of reasons—Roosevelt's lack of success in ending the Depression, the third-term issue, Willkie's ability to rally swing voters, and a long-standing bias in the electoral college in favor of the Republicans—the outcome remained in doubt to the end. (Had FDR finished only two points ahead of Willkie in the national popular vote, Roosevelt would likely have lost the electoral college tally by a margin of 225 to 306.)

The high voter turnout on Election Day revealed an electorate divided more sharply along class lines, outside the essentially one-party South, than was typical. Roosevelt was carried to victory, by a margin of 55 percent to 45 percent in the national popular vote (and 449–82 in the electoral college), by the worsening foreign news, falling unemployment (due to the emerging military buildup), and the combined support of upper-working-class and lower-middle-class voters in cities and factory towns, small farmers in the Middle and the Far West, and the solid South. But in a larger sense, what mattered most was that both major parties had chosen presidential candidates committed to aiding Britain in its fight with Nazi Germany.[16]

The emerging bipartisan support for changing course in foreign policy allowed for broader growth of the national security state to go along with the increased military spending of the late 1930s. Observers could see the first clear sign of that in 1938, when the US House of Representatives created the House Un-American Activities Committee (HUAC). The committee targeted radical leftists believed to be associated with the Communist Party USA and its Soviet sponsor, and pro-Nazi groups were also viewed as potential fronts for spies and saboteurs. After Stalin and Hitler signed a nonaggression pact in August 1939 and then carved up Poland between them, the belief grew that Communists and Nazis posed a joint threat to American national security. Many in official Washington believed that espionage must have played a role in Germany's stunning defeat of France. That suspicion kicked the expansion of the internal security apparatus into high gear. Congress quickly passed and Roosevelt signed the Smith Act of 1940, which required aliens to register with the US government and outlawed conspiracies aimed at its overthrow.[17]

Also telling was the rapid growth of the FBI that began around that same time. From 1933 to early 1940, the total number of FBI agents had risen from 391 to 898, but in 1940 alone that number doubled, then doubled again in 1941. By adding so many more agents, the FBI was able to greatly expand its indexes of dangerous citizens and resident aliens, its infiltration of suspicious political groups, its wiretapping of suspected subversives, and more generally its surveillance of those deemed disloyal. FBI director J. Edgar Hoover clung tightly to the reins of all those operations, cementing his stature as a major player in the US government. Hoover publicly urged state and local police forces around the country to be on the lookout for spies and saboteurs, and to communicate all relevant findings to the FBI. FDR also spurred the expanding role of the FBI by authorizing it in June 1940 to carry out counterintelligence and security operations in Latin America, from where Nazi spies were known to be operating. The United States lacked a national intelligence agency at the time, and such steps solidified the FBI's authority in that area. Inexperienced with extensive foreign operations, Hoover quickly formed a working relationship with British intelligence officials.[18]

The most controversial matter related to the growth of the national security state in the summer of 1940 was the effort to institute military conscription. Some private citizens such as the contingent of World War I veterans headed by prominent New York lawyer Grenville Clark, as well as *New York Times* general manager Julius Ochs Adler, favored greater military preparedness and lobbied for a draft to enlarge the US Army, but until France fell, Congress had refused to act on the idea. It gained traction thereafter, though in highly restricted form. The proposed Selective Service Act of 1940 mandated only one year of service, and the entire measure would be subject to annual review by Congress. It also prohibited deploying draftees outside the Western Hemisphere. When first Roosevelt and then Willkie endorsed the measure, it gained sufficient momentum to pass on September 16. In the following month, 16 million men between the ages of twenty-one and thirty-five registered. Like the Social Security system in 1937, the swift start of this newest New Deal program was made possible, on an administrative level, by IBM tabulating and recording machines.[19]

Like many earlier New Deal initiatives, the draft in 1940–41 tended to affect most the lives of average men. Women were excluded entirely; they could serve as volunteers, if they wished, but ought never be compelled to do so (the thinking went), given how dangerous and physically and mentally demanding military service could be. Most Americans also accepted that military training and combat would likely leave women even more unsuited for a return to domestic life than was true for men.[20]

The emphasis on filling the enlisted ranks with "healthy, normal young men" tended to screen out those seen as deviant in any way, especially in sexual orientation and/or criminal behavior. Some of the most religious were granted conscientious-objector status if their faith called for pacifism. The poorest eligible men, who were disproportionately black, tended to have serious health problems and were rejected as unfit for service at a much higher rate than middle-class draftees. Half of all men who underwent a military examination for the draft during 1940–41 were deemed unable to serve. Ninety percent were rejected for health reasons, and the rest for illiteracy. The large fraction barred for poor health reflected the poor diet and lack of medical care so common in the bottom third of the income distribution, made worse by the Depression. Upper-class draftees, who could obtain college deferments, were also underrepresented compared to those from more middle-class households. Well-connected parents found other ways to keep their sons out, at least for a while, such as by arranging for their enrollment in the local National Guard unit or by helping them obtain jobs in government or at defense plants that exempted them from military service altogether. Affluent young men could also more easily afford to marry and start families, and many did just that in 1940–41, which usually shielded them from conscription. Thus, the advent of the draft contributed to the New Deal's promotion of male breadwinning even as an indirect consequence of an unrelated effort.[21]

The officer corps of the standing army and navy similarly reflected the disproportionately ordinary middle-class roots of their enlisted ranks. Both branches of the service had long served as a means to a free college education at West Point and Annapolis, respectively, which helped make the officer corps somewhat more diverse socioeconomically than civilian college graduates. The Reserve Officers' Training Corps (ROTC) program, created after World War I, heavily subsidized the cost of attending a participating civilian college or university, putting a military career, and a college degree, within reach for many more young men. Intelligent, ambitious, lower-middle-class men, who could not otherwise afford higher education, took advantage of that opportunity in large numbers. Even some of the US military's most influential senior officers, most notably Dwight D. Eisenhower, had a background such as that. The navy's officer corps was somewhat more elite in social background than the army's, in part because sailing was viewed as an upper-class pursuit, but the two corps were more alike than different. And both, like the enlisted ranks, being so heavily made up of white men of middling social background, were striking in their outward homogeneity prior to Pearl Harbor.[22]

Roosevelt fought an uphill battle to win support for his plans to expand the army via the draft, and to help the nations fighting Nazi Germany. When the renewal of the draft came up in the House in August 1941, it passed by just one vote. The year before as well, FDR had met with resistance to his decision to exchange fifty older American destroyers for military bases in British possessions in the Western Hemisphere. The "destroyers-for-bases" deal, as it became known, proved highly controversial because it drew the United States even closer toward some kind of alliance with Britain.

Sure that Congress would not endorse the plan but believing that Britain's vulnerability to invasion made it imperative, Roosevelt took the legally questionable step of approving the transfer on his own presidential authority. FDR had never been shy about exercising executive muscle to drive New Deal domestic policies, and now, as the country edged closer to direct involvement in World War II, the executive branch of the federal government claimed more and more power in the national security realm as well. Roosevelt rationalized his taking matters into his own hands, claiming that the urgency of the situation demanded it, but others argued that he tended to exaggerate the threats posed by Germany and Japan and worried that extending the reach of his office in that way set troubling precedents.[23]

Britain's gritty defense of its home island under the inspiring leadership of Prime Minister Winston Churchill validated Roosevelt's faith in Nazi Germany's main enemies and allowed him to continue steering foreign policy as he saw fit. The German air force was forced to abandon daytime attacks over England in mid-September 1940 because the Royal Air Force was shooting down too many planes that could not easily be replaced. German air force head Hermann Göring shifted thereafter to less militarily significant nighttime bombing raids, and with that step the threat of Nazi invasion began to fade. By the end of 1940, Americans had started to believe, rightly, that Britain had won its first real victory. That inclined a majority of the American public to support Roosevelt's call for the United States to become "the great arsenal of democracy."

The shift in public opinion, and the related reelection of Roosevelt, helped smooth the path for FDR's Lend-Lease aid program in 1941. The idea was to enable the British government, which had nearly run out of funds, to obtain more munitions by promising to return them later, and to pay for their use only when it was able. Roosevelt proposed an initial $7 billion appropriation to fund the program, which obliged him to seek congressional approval. After a stormy national debate, Congress did so by wide margins in March, and heartened by this aid, the British government's leaders vowed to go the distance against Nazi Germany even as bombs continued to fall on London.[24]

A second major unexpected development ultimately strengthened Roosevelt's hand over national security policy. In June 1941, Hitler unleashed a massive military invasion of the Soviet Union. Lacking the protection of a great surrounding ocean such as Britain had, the USSR seemed likely to fall, or so Roosevelt's senior military leaders believed. They advised against extending Lend-Lease aid to Stalin's government. Roosevelt felt he needed a more informed assessment of the situation on the ground in the Soviet Union before making a decision and sent Harry Hopkins on a fact-finding tour. When Hopkins returned, he reported that he thought the Soviets would hang on with some assistance, a view strongly seconded by the deeply anti-Soviet Winston Churchill and by Roosevelt's civilian advisers. The president was persuaded and got Congress to include the Soviets in Lend-Lease. As the Red Army continued to retreat steadily in the second half of 1941, the wisdom of that decision remained very much in doubt. But unlike France in 1940, the disastrous early military defeats did not lead to the outright collapse and surrender of the Soviet Union. The specific nature of Soviet aid requests also signaled Stalin's determination to wage a protracted resistance, thus making the logic of FDR's action more supportable for American senior military leaders.[25]

By the fall of 1941, a solid majority of Americans, as measured by polls, favored what Roosevelt called "aid short of war" to the UK and

USSR. A majority likewise favored the ongoing American military buildup as a sensible precaution that might well, in itself, deter an Axis powers' attack on US overseas territories and shipping. America now found itself in a highly precarious and unpredictable situation, having become a major participant in World War II without formally entering it. Roosevelt's decision to help protect American arms shipments to Britain and the Soviet Union—by ordering US air and naval vessels to "shoot on sight" German submarines and surface warships trying to obstruct the flow of Lend-Lease aid—might well have provoked Nazi Germany's government to go to war with America eventually. So, too, might have his successful push in October–November 1941 for legislation allowing US merchant vessels carrying Lend-Lease supplies to be armed and given freedom to operate in combat zones.

However, the third big national security surprise since the spring of 1940—Japan's attack on December 7, 1941—brought America into the war as a full-fledged combatant. Critics charged then and afterward that Roosevelt's economic sanctions against Japan, intended to deter its unfolding military conquest of East Asia, had provoked the heinous attack. The more common view, however, was that it had confirmed the wisdom of FDR's position that America needed to become more involved in a global war that would sooner or later come to its shores. When that became the reality, the shift to the New Deal's third phase (1938–45) became plain for all to see.[26]

So the second stage of that third phase abruptly began. It lasted from December 1941 through August 1945, a period that would reshape America and the wider world. With formal entry into World War II, the United States didn't change course completely, but moved faster and farther along a path it had already laid out. Under the Roosevelt administration's leadership, the USA waged war for three and a half years. Throughout it all, the country stuck by the practices that had defined the New Deal. The size, cost, and reach of the federal government mushroomed, especially its executive branch.

To pay for that massive growth in the national state, the federal income tax system expanded greatly, not just in the fraction of households it touched and the amounts collected from them, but also in the effective redistribution of income and wealth. Unemployment, which had in 1941 fallen below 10 percent for the first time in over a decade, essentially vanished by early 1943, as the draft, the military, and war production plants put millions to work. That change, as disorienting as it was welcome, helped labor unions, with the encouragement of the Roosevelt administration, enroll huge numbers of new members in the mass-production industries. In just four years, organized labor, as economists often called it, emerged for the first time as a durable major factor in America's economy and society.[27]

The enormous demands of the war effort tilted the American social structure in favor of the vast middle—economically, politically, socially, and culturally—and transformed it even more than earlier phases of the New Deal had done. A greatly expanded federal bureaucracy meant lots of new jobs for lower-middle-class office workers. War and Navy Department contracts for the manufacture of tanks, trucks, planes, and ships likewise increased greatly the number of jobs for highly skilled and semiskilled blue-collar workers. In marked contrast to what those kinds of middle-class factory jobs were like during the 1930s, employment tended to be full-time and year-round for the duration of the war. Many industrial laborers found themselves in such demand that they were regularly required to work overtime. Wages were also high by peacetime standards, in part because the government's contracts typically pledged to pay all production costs plus a fixed profit.

These "cost-plus" contracts, as they became known, meant that employers could pass their labor costs on to the taxpayer, something that reduced management's resistance to paying high wartime wages. Even the 16.5 million people who served in the US armed forces were well paid by the standards of other countries, most notably Britain. As England gradually filled up with young American GIs who would eventually take part in the Normandy invasion, some envious residents quietly grumbled that their new guests were "over-sexed, over-paid, and over here."[28]

All of this income could not, in itself, increase the wealth of the middle three-fifths of American households. If lower-middle-class and upper-working-class Americans had spent most or all of their wartime windfalls, distribution of wealth would not have changed. But the combination of much higher incomes with the wartime regime of taxation, war financing, and rationing produced the only major shift in the distribution of wealth—toward more equality—in modern US history. The income tax system hit upper-middle-class and more affluent Americans much harder than those with ordinary wages and salaries, despite that more people at all economic levels were paying federal income tax than ever before. As recently as 1939, only 7 percent of the American labor force had paid federal income tax, in part because household incomes were still severely depressed and because the existing federal income tax targeted only a small fraction of people at the high end of the income scale. By 1944, that number had skyrocketed to 65 percent as household incomes rose and the reach of federal income taxation was extended by law to a much bigger fraction of income earners. The arrival of the mass federal income tax was facilitated by the introduction in 1943 of the modern system of deducting estimated taxes out of workers' paychecks. In short order, federal income taxation regularly touched a majority of the working population.[29]

The progressive tax rates introduced during World War II produced results that today seem remarkable. A reasonably well-paid factory worker was contributing around 12 percent of his or her income in federal income tax by the war's end, having paid nothing in the prewar years. A married professional person without dependents usually paid almost 20 percent by then, almost ten times more than what he or she had paid before the war. The richest were paying nearly 70 percent of their income by war's end. Most Americans were willing to go with the program, understanding the national emergency, and believing that the tax burden was being equitably shared. Even those hit hardest by taxes sensed that complaining about it would appear unpatriotic. The much higher federal income tax revenues, when combined with excise and corporate taxes, paid for about 45 percent of the total cost of the war, a much greater fraction than during either the Civil War or World War I.[30]

The rest would be financed through borrowing, for which FDR's Treasury Department came up with a novel scheme it called "war bonds." Those bonds, when combined with wartime rationing and shortages of civilian goods, would also generate growth in middle-class wealth. Most Americans with ordinary incomes had never bought bonds before, so Treasury officials quickly organized patriotic advertising campaigns to persuade them to "invest in victory." To make the new war bonds more appealing to average people, Treasury Secretary Henry Morgenthau Jr. emphasized the issuing of small-denomination bonds registered in the bearer's name and so replaceable if lost. Thus was born a bond that an inexperienced investor could easily afford and understand. Americans in the emerging middle-class majority, having grown accustomed to the sensibilities of the New Deal, responded in large numbers, which meant more middle-class wealth accumulation and less consumer spending for the duration. By 1944, Americans as a whole were spending about as much on war bonds—which paid interest—as they were contributing in federal income taxes, which made their wealth grow substantially.[31]

Other factors also contributed to the accumulation of middle-class wealth. The wartime rationing of meat, butter, cheese, sugar, coffee, tires, gasoline, and other staples did much to keep down middle-class spending. So, too, did the lack of new cars to buy, once the automakers shifted to producing tanks, trucks, and warplanes. Shortages of materials meant less construction of new housing, making it easier for the middle class to choose saving or investing instead. Psychological factors were also at work. Vivid memories of hard times in the thirties were still fresh in the minds of most Americans. Uncertainty about what economic conditions would be like after the war made people reluctant to spend money carelessly. Thus, even as factory workers' real average income rose by 27 percent from 1940 to 1945, their rate of spending grew much more slowly. That same combination of pressures turned lower-middle-class office workers as well into cautious spenders.[32]

As in the New Deal's earlier phases, not everyone grew wealthier at the same rate. By war's end, households in the middle three-fifths of the income distribution had gained the most when compared with those above and below them. Middle-class households had typically acquired a substantial nest egg by then, many for the first time. Less consumption also promoted middle-class wealth-building by helping keep down wartime inflation, which if unchecked could have greatly eroded the value of what ordinary people were putting away at the bank and in war bonds. Upper-class households grew wealthier, too, but more slowly due to the higher taxes they paid, and to the drafting after Pearl Harbor of many more upper-class men, which sharply lowered their incomes. The poorest Americans enjoyed income gains during World War II, but not nearly as much as more skilled factory and office workers did. Those in the bottom fifth were also much less likely to buy war bonds or to accumulate much wealth in other ways, given how low their incomes still were. The results conformed to the New Deal pattern of tending to help those with ordinary incomes the most, and narrowing the social distance between them and more affluent people.[33]

Much the same could be said for the war's consequences for diet and overall public health. Rationing helped perpetuate the Depression-era regime of moderate intake of food and drink. With Eleanor Roosevelt leading the way, the White House made such economies as serving the president salt fish for lunch four days in a row, which the first lady insisted was only fitting during wartime. She also cut coffee from the after-dinner ritual. Eleanor Roosevelt also took the Home Front Pledge to always pay ration points in full, rather than try to game the rationing system, as some did by buying mislabeled goods that cost less in ration points than they should have.

Nutritionists used the wartime school-lunch program, overseen by anthropologist Margaret Mead, to promote healthy, bland lunchtime meals. By regularly reaching so many of the nation's impressionable youngsters, the school-lunch program became a significant force in homogenizing Americans' diet and discouraging overeating. Similar meals fed to those serving in the armed forces produced the same results. Food consumption did rise along with incomes, but more exercise during the war helped keep excess weight off. With auto factories now churning out military vehicles, limited gasoline for civilians, expanding employment, and the lack of new suburban houses keeping people in cities, Americans spent more time walking and using mass transit. Mandatory exercise regimes in the armed forces likewise kept the prevalence of obesity low. Those wartime conditions promoted better diet and health for all social classes, but made the biggest difference for the middle one. They were the ones whose real incomes and wealth rose the most when compared to what they had been during the Depression.[34]

• • •

Once again, the economic and political developments helped shape the kinds of popular culture that Americans enjoyed, reinforcing trends that had emerged during the mid-1930s. As middle-class incomes grew, so did the market for accessible music, radio shows, plays, and movies with themes that appealed to mainstream audiences. One of the more common themes was patriotic nationalism, of the sort the WPA arts project had promoted during the mid-1930s. Congress had voted to abolish the Federal Theatre Project in 1939, and the entire WPA four years later once mass unemployment vanished, but commercially supported media and other parts of the government took up from where the WPA left off.

Perhaps no piece of popular culture signaled that patriotic fervor as clearly as the song "God Bless America," which Kate Smith first sang on November 11, 1938, during an Armistice Day broadcast of her popular radio show. The advance of Nazi Germany's anti-Semitism that same year had prompted songwriter Irving Berlin to update an earlier version of that song, which became one of the most heavily played tunes of the entire 1938–45 period. In 1940, both the Willkie and the Roosevelt presidential campaigns had adopted it as their official song, a sign of how increased patriotism in response to growing outside threats had become bipartisan. In 1942, Kate Smith again performed "God Bless America," this time in the highly successful Broadway musical entitled *This Is the Army*. A Hollywood film version with the same name appeared one year later, by which time the US Treasury Department had deployed both "God Bless America" and its most famous performer to promote the sale of war bonds. As with so much of the New Deal's third phase, this cultural artifact of it proved to be remarkably durable, outliving the war by decades.[35]

Kate Smith and her famous song embodied other themes that became more pronounced in the popular culture then, thanks to the growing affluence of middlebrow consumers. One of those themes, albeit somewhat double-edged, was populism. Smith's success in promoting war bond sales stemmed in no small part from her matronly image. She symbolized sincerity and generosity and, in marked contrast to the high-fashion glamour of most Hollywood starlets and Broadway leading ladies, Smith looked and spoke like someone who might live around the corner. The point may seem obvious, but it nonetheless reflects one of the most striking changes in popular culture during the war years: the much greater prevalence of performers who looked like everyday Americans, rather than photographers' models. People of other backgrounds, and African Americans in particular, did not fare well in an era that placed ever more emphasis on culture of, by, and for the mostly white middle class. (Kate Smith had earlier recorded racist southern songs with titles such as "That's Why Darkies Were Born" and "Pickaninny Heaven," the second of which she performed in the 1933 movie *Hello, Everybody!*) To the extent one's background was unusual, the pressure to look and perform in ways familiar and pleasing to Middle America became ever greater.[36]

"God Bless America" reflected another major double-edged theme in popular culture: mainstream religiosity. Historically, the theological mainstream in America had been defined as mainline Protestantism. The New Deal's third phase helped bring about, in popular culture especially, the beginning of including Catholics and Jews in that definition. Here was a massively popular song, almost an unofficial American anthem, written by a Jewish immigrant from Russia, and performed most famously by a woman who grew up Protestant and later converted to Catholicism. The start of a redefinition of the religious mainstream to mean the "Judeo-Christian tradition" built on earlier phases of the New Deal, when Roosevelt's administration had given unprecedented attention and numbers of government posts to Catholic and Jewish people. Increased voting by those descended from newer immigrants, whose support helped put—and keep—FDR in the White House, increased their influence and visibility in American society, which helped begin this redefinition of the religious mainstream. Hitler's monstrous anti-Semitism also contributed, in a way, by making public expression of anti-Semitic attitudes less socially acceptable.[37]

America's entry into World War II and the loss of life that inevitably followed nourished a revival of mainstream religious belief and observance. As more and more households became more concerned about matters of life and death, and better able to afford the weekly contributions on which America's houses of worship so heavily depended, the popular audience for "God Bless America" in song, play, and film (and other forms of popular culture) steadily grew.[38]

Those closely related shifts in income distribution, popular culture, and religious practice were powerfully reinforced by the way the US military operated during wartime. Its leaders decided to organize and promote mainstream religion for the millions of impressionable young men serving as soldiers, sailors, and marines, who could choose between Protestant, Catholic, and Jewish Sabbath services. Organizing a Protestant service was especially challenging given the many different denominations of American Protestantism. Methodist clergy designed a service for the military with the broadest appeal, thereby helping to set in motion what would become known after the war as the nondenominational movement.

Like the populist theme to which mainstream religiosity was related, the promotion of a religious observance that would include the broadest spectrum of believers also made some American soldiers feel somewhat more emphatically excluded. Many observant Catholics and Jews welcomed the start of a shift that embraced their faith traditions as part of the theological mainstream. However, the most secular citizens, including many radical leftists, became more conspicuous and ostracized by that change. So, too, did the most devout, who had committed their lives to a specific ritual practice and theology, during a time when mass culture began to emphasize what Christians and Jewish people of all kinds had in common rather than what set them apart.[39]

Moral traditionalism, the natural companion of mainstream religiosity, also tightened its grip on the popular culture during the New Deal's third phase. America's houses of worship served, then as now, as engines of traditional family values. As church and synagogue affiliation and attendance grew, so, too, did the influence of their views on how best to live one's life. The change was most palpable in the vast middle of the society, much of which had become disconnected from organized religion during the Depression. From the late 1930s through the end of the war, that trend reversed itself. But the war also put tremendous stress on families, as some family members went into the armed forces while others moved, often great distances, to find work in war plants and government offices. The two historical episodes, economic depression and war, overlapped most closely in their tendency to increase middle-class desire for a stable domestic life.

Popular culture both reflected that reality and contributed to it, typified by such highly popular and sentimental songs as the Andrews Sisters' rendition of "Don't Sit Under the Apple Tree (With Anyone Else but Me)," and Bing Crosby's "I'll Be Home for Christmas."[40]

Patriotic nationalism, populism, mainstream religiosity, and moral traditionalism all went hand in hand with another main theme of mass culture during the New Deal's third phase: optimism. This was, to a degree, simply a continuation of an official government message from the New Deal's beginning. In the final phase, that optimism took on a new intensity, so as to keep up morale both in the armed forces and on the home front, and a greater degree of legitimacy, as the economy boomed and the news from the various combat fronts began to favor the Allies. Even before American soldiers joined the battle, Judy Garland's rendition of the dreamily hopeful "Over the Rainbow" helped make a box-office hit of the movie version of L. Frank Baum's *The Wonderful Wizard of Oz*. "Over the Rainbow" won the Academy Award for best original song, and the recorded single became a chart-topper. Its extraordinary durability mirrored many other aspects of the New Deal's third phase. The song remains first on the list of "Songs of the Century" compiled by the Recording Industry Association of America and the National Endowment for the Arts. The American Film Institute has likewise ranked it the greatest movie song of all time.[41]

That optimism also infused the exhilarating big-band music that made the Glenn Miller, Gene Krupa, and Dorsey Brothers' ensembles famous. Like so many of the art forms of that time, big-band music was intended, at least in part, to boost morale. Some listeners and critics found the pervasiveness of this upbeat dance music unsettling, and even inappropriate, in the face of history's most violent and destructive war. But the music provided a desperately needed escape from the constant anxiety of that war. Cultural escapism had become popular during the Depression; in wartime, it became an absolute necessity. The theme of optimism both as a description of reality and an escape from it resonated most strongly with middle-class people, whose situation materially improved the most during the war, and who were the most likely to have family members serving in that conflict.[42]

· · ·

Wartime changes proved more problematic, even devastating, for racial minority groups, most notably those of Japanese and African ancestry. The Roosevelt administration's decision to order those of Japanese descent—citizens included—removed from the Pacific Coast region into internment camps as Japan's armed forces moved steadily eastward during early 1942 was the single most notorious example of a hardship endured by a segment of the American population outside the majority. The US Supreme Court, having begun to show essentially uniform support for New Deal initiatives, offered little resistance to that decision. The Court upheld it overall, but ordered the immediate release of those US citizens of Japanese ancestry who they determined had followed the military's rules with respect to removal and detention and posed no threat to national security. Even that ruling, in a case known as *Ex parte Endo*, came late in 1944, by which point it made little difference to these internees, who were already being released. For those who had violated the relocation rules in some way, such as the plaintiff in *Korematsu v. U.S.*, the Court offered no escape from confinement.[43]

For African Americans, the war tended to reinforce the ugly patterns of official segregation and discrimination. Black men were drafted, but at such low rates early on that, as late as January 1943, the US Army was less than 6 percent African American, even though black people comprised 10.6 percent of the nation's population. Their participation grew steadily thereafter, but was mostly confined to noncombat roles, which were not necessarily safer but were certainly less prestigious. For northern black Americans subject to military service, basic training for it—like the larger military itself—remained segregated to a degree that many of them had never before known. That so much of the training took place in the South only made matters worse. For black civilians living in the urban North and Far West, access to defense-related jobs grew faster than access to decent housing near those jobs. More and more African Americans crowded into urban ghettos, pushing their outer boundaries, and becoming the targets of racist reprisals.[44]

The war did drive down unemployment for African Americans to unprecedented lows, which helped working- and lower-middle-class black people move forward economically. Mass movement out of the

South and the border states also strengthened black political power because so many new black northerners settled in the most populous states, which had the most clout in American presidential elections. This stood in stark contrast to the time when African Americans, even if they represented a majority of a state's population, were effectively disenfranchised by whites in power, who denied them the vote. Socially and culturally, however, the war years brought only marginal gains, thanks to the growing dominance of middle-class white people.[45]

The way the rise in their influence eclipsed African Americans and their problems in the popular culture could clearly be seen in how Hollywood approached the explosive issue of lynching in the 1939 film *Young Mr. Lincoln*. In it, Abraham Lincoln, played by the young Henry Fonda, faces down a lynch mob in front of an Illinois jail, arguing that the intended victims deserve a trial to determine whether they had committed murder. Lincoln's bravery and eloquence shames the crowd into dispersing, allowing for a trial to take place, and the two defendants are found to have been wrongly accused. This true story, the focal point of the entire movie, argued powerfully against the evil of lynching. At this time the National Association for the Advancement of Colored People (NAACP) was persistently lobbying Congress for passage of a bill to make lynching a federal crime because most lynchings were of a black victim by a white mob.

But in *Young Mr. Lincoln*, almost everyone in the story is white, including the two men accused of murder. The only black character in the film is a servant in the home of wealthy residents of the town, and he appears only briefly, waiting on guests at a party Lincoln attended. That approach arguably had a greater impact on white people because it showed the practice as wrong without introducing the explosive issue of the victim's race. But that depiction of lynching denied the reality of its close tie to race.[46]

For women, wartime conditions brought similarly mixed results. Women did have access to an unprecedented number and range of paying jobs, but mostly factory and low-level clerical ones. Many of those jobs were clearly intended to employ women only for the duration of the war. Throughout the war, employers, government officials, and popular culture continued to send women clear signals that once it ended, they would return to domestic life. These temporary jobs appear to have appealed to upper-working-class and lower-middle-class women the most, rather than those above or below them on the socioeconomic scale. Women of the middle three-fifths moved most easily into the kinds of jobs the war created for them, but those jobs, typically menial and routine, provided less satisfaction than what more elite women with formal education could sometimes obtain. Women of a middling social status could also readily imagine relying on a husband, unless the Depression returned, to be the breadwinner. That was in marked contrast to poorer women, who lived in a world where neither men nor women typically made enough by themselves to support a family.[47]

The consequences of expanded employment options for middle-class people can be seen in how Beatrice Sindt and Emily Perkins (George's spouse) responded to the wartime boom. For Beatrice, the low unemployment of the war years did not mean that she went back to teaching school, a career option that remained closed to married women whose husbands had steady work. With three young children to look after and sufficient household income from Howard's work as a civil engineer and farm owner, she had neither the time nor the need to earn money. The closest she came to a paying job during the war was selling eggs from her family's farm to people in the Davenport area who could now afford them.

Emily Perkins, who lived in the much more urban Providence, had more employment options than Beatrice did, but that didn't make for an easy transition to the world of paid work. The highly favorable labor market of the wartime years (for middle-class women) produced an opening for a telephone switchboard operator at Brown University, and Emily, eager for more independence and social contact, applied. She got the job, but George erupted in anger, convinced that her acceptance of a paying job would send a message to their friends and neighbors that he wasn't earning enough. When Emily refused to back down, an irate George gathered a bunch of her things and put them out on the sidewalk. Emily, both tactful and tenacious, simply brought them back inside and went on to work at Brown for the next thirty years. George made his peace with his strong-willed spouse's decision. However it might have been perceived, it certainly eased the financial pressure he felt in trying to support a family of five on a public employee's salary. Even more than for Beatrice Sindt, wartime economic conditions gave Emily more freedom—though she had to fight for it—to earn money and hold certain kinds of jobs, but still did not produce a genuine revolution in gender roles.[48]

If the war had gone on a lot longer and/or killed many more men, as was the case in Germany, Japan, and the Soviet Union, it might have led to a more lasting change in American women's status. Instead, the war came to an end with unexpected suddenness in the summer of 1945. Germany's earlier defeat in May 1945 had signaled the end of the fighting in Europe and had turned Americans' attention to an anticipated invasion of Japan. When the US Air Force's massive, deadly bombing of Japanese cities, capped by atomic bomb attacks on Hiroshima and Nagasaki, forced Japan's government to surrender in August 1945, the typical reactions were surprise, relief, and sometimes even elation. Not even Franklin Roosevelt's death four months earlier—the result of a cerebral hemorrhage—which had shocked much of the nation, lastingly disrupted the majority's optimistic mood that spring and summer. FDR's death even contributed to the ascendancy of the middle class, by making former family farmer and haberdasher Harry Truman the new president. Thus by the time Japan's government surrendered, America's new first family didn't just support the middle class, it exemplified it in ways the Roosevelts never had.[49]

The intensity of the rejoicing in America at the Axis powers' surrender reflected how differently the war affected the nation, compared to the other major combatants. Unlike the countries where the war had been fought, and whose war-related deaths numbered in the millions, the total number of Americans who died was just over four hundred thousand. And almost all of these were combat deaths of soldiers, sailors, and airmen, not defenseless civilians. Even more striking, those in American uniform who died accounted for just one out of every forty of the 16 million who served in World War II. Yes, many of the men who went overseas came back with problems—but they mostly survived. Still more remarkable was the contrast in terms of wartime damage done on the home front. Alone among the major

PROMISED LAND

fighting nations, America's main homeland—the continental USA—
suffered no significant attacks, from aerial bombardment or other
sources. To many, but certainly not all, Americans, World War II was
a "good war," not just because the Axis powers needed to be stopped
by force but also because the war did so much less harm, when compared with what other nations suffered, to America itself. Instead, the
war had transformed the country, benefiting many in the short and
long terms.[50]

CHAPTER 5

Postwar Fog

The celebratory spirit at the end of the war in August 1945 soon gave way to an uneasy apprehension about the future that lasted for the next five and a half years. In the fall of 1945, public-opinion surveys indicated that many, perhaps most, Americans feared a return to the dreary economic conditions of the 1930s once the 12 million people (mostly men) currently serving overseas came home. That's just what had happened two years after World War I, when the American economy had sunk into a deep postwar recession. Government spending fell drastically, and unemployment rose sharply (to 20 percent) as millions of soldiers and sailors once again became civilians. Intense public pressure in 1945–46 to "bring the boys home" as soon as possible seemed likely to create a similar situation, given how many former GIs would be looking for work as military spending wound down.[1]

Fully a year earlier, Roosevelt and his supporters in Congress had sought to head off an unmanageable glut of postwar job seekers by pushing through the last major piece of New Deal–era legislation: the Servicemen's Readjustment Act of 1944. That measure offered aid to veterans wanting to do such things as obtain medical care, get more schooling, start a business, and/or buy a home and gave them a weekly allowance of $20 for up to one year after leaving the service. The bill also mandated that employers give veterans preference when hiring, which soon became a powerfully effective form of what we would later call affirmative action. The GI Bill, as everyone soon called this measure, would in time achieve characteristically New Dealish results: expanding the middle class and promoting its economic security through persistent reliance on the male-breadwinner model. But the law had been drafted to accommodate a steady, gradual return of veterans, not the sudden deluge of the entire fighting force from both Europe and Asia.[2]

Many Americans also missed the reassuring presence of Franklin Roosevelt in the White House. Harry Truman's middle-American ways appealed to many people, but his lack of stature made some of them nervous about the future. Truman owed his ascension from Missouri senator to vice president and then president in 1944–45 more to his acceptability to the Democratic Party's various factions than to his qualifications to serve as FDR's successor. Truman's predecessor as vice president, Henry Wallace, had alienated the Dixiecrats with his uncompromising liberalism, and they responded by denying him the chance to return as Roosevelt's running mate. James Byrnes, the former South Carolina senator, Supreme Court justice, and head of the wartime mobilization effort, had been viewed by many party officials as the likely alternative to Wallace, but Byrnes had alienated the powerful union leaders with his antilabor views. Truman, an honest and able public servant brought to the Senate by corrupt machine politicos in Kansas City, had conventional New Deal views that made him acceptable to Democratic Party chieftains of all kinds. The "new Missouri Compromise," as the press soon dubbed him, helped the Democrats win a fourth straight presidential election in November 1944, but when Roosevelt died suddenly five months later, the nation acquired a new leader who was out of his depth, especially with foreign policy. The critical next two years saw unpredictable and confused presidential policies and actions, which only heightened people's fears of a postwar recession.[3]

Some of that anxiety grew out of a lack of understanding that the economic conditions in the United States after World War II differed from those after World War I. Waging war for almost four years according to the principles of the New Deal had enabled the broad middle class to achieve unprecedented prosperity, which had the potential to drive the economy forward even as military spending fell. Twelve years of economic depression prior to the war, followed by four years of wartime shortages, had left the newly comfortable middle class with an enormous pent-up demand for such durable consumer goods as cars, houses, furniture, and appliances, and they were inclined to start spending. State-of-the-art plants and equipment, built during the war with government money, were now passing into the hands of private industry at a fraction of their true cost and were being retooled to produce those goods in great quantities. Those new manufacturing facilities also meant solid jobs for middle-class workers. Just as important, the wartime work ethic, that patriotic commitment to quality and efficiency and duty that had helped carry the nation to victory, led to large and lasting gains in worker productivity in many industries. The economy, like the nation, was gathering momentum.[4]

Misguided fears about a return to the Depression helped feed that momentum. Ongoing public support for such New Deal innovations as farm subsidies, Social Security, and heavy government spending in general all stimulated consumer spending. So, too, did the New Deal's pro-union policies, which had helped make organized labor big and strong enough to secure for its members even higher wages and better benefits after the war ended. The heavy damage to farms and factories overseas, along with restrictive US trade policies, allowed American workers' incomes to rise without the immediate threat of low-cost foreign competition. The nation's strict limits on immigration, enforced by tighter border controls imposed during the war, discouraged foreign competition of another sort, as immigrants, legal or otherwise, would likely have been willing to work longer and harder for a lot less. The newly progressive and greatly broadened tax structure also promised to help equalize incomes in America.[5]

All of these legacies of the New Deal would help power mass production and consumption on a much larger scale and in a more egalitarian way than had existed after World War I. And World War II had left the United States with a greatly altered role in world affairs, and that change in stature would, itself, become an engine of increased prosperity. The pressures on the federal government to maintain a large national security state were much more intense on V-J Day than on Armistice Day in 1918. By August 1945, the national security apparatus had emerged as the biggest and most expensive part of the federal government, which presumably meant continued spending in that area for the foreseeable future. The situation was unlike any previous period in the United States, making it difficult to imagine the magnitude of the postwar boom that was to come.[6]

• • •

It took five and a half years for that outcome to become clear. Some Americans simply could not have imagined such a future, or perhaps could, but couldn't bring themselves to believe in it. It wasn't pessimism that people were feeling. It might be better described as competing kinds of optimism in the afterglow of the successful conclusion of the war, which together bred a feeling of uncertainty about what was to come next. Business leaders found themselves on much firmer footing by then. The biggest firms, the so-called Fortune 100, which had won most of the wartime government contracts, generally experienced enormous growth and high profitability during World War II. Their share of the gross domestic product grew from less than half to two-thirds, a shift that proved to be long-lasting. The success of the wartime "production miracle" also helped restore, to a degree, the prestige the business community had lost during the Depression. They had chafed at wartime government controls, high taxes, and bigger, stronger unions—but once the war ended, the leaders of big business tended to feel a renewed confidence in the private sector's ability to lead.[7]

That confidence was buoyed by the understanding that many people had accumulated substantial savings and were eager to spend that money. Thus, business leaders were inclined to believe that private consumption would be enough to ward off another Depression. They assumed, too, that fighting World War II had so devastated the nation's potential future adversaries, most notably the Soviet Union, as to allow America to fall back on the older model of a small, inexpensive peacetime military. As these tycoons and executives looked ahead, they tended to share a "back to the future" vision of a federal government that taxed, spent, and regulated much less, providing more individual freedom even as prosperity reached new heights.[8]

Many of those on the political left, including the heads of the newly powerful unions, imagined a different future. They heralded the founding of the United Nations in the fall of 1945 as the dawn of a new era of world peace. In their vision, high progressive taxation would persist, but the huge sums of money previously spent on the military could mostly be redirected to domestic use, providing the United States with the kind of expansive social insurance programs of the sort found in northern Europe. A public health-care system, better schools, laws against racial segregation and discrimination, and a strengthened social safety net would promote a more egalitarian society. Eventually, poverty would become a thing of the past in a nation where every individual would have the opportunity to develop his or her full potential.[9]

The heads of America's enormous national security establishment took a view different from that of both the businessmen and the liberals on the key question of what providing for the country's defense would entail. The military services chiefs saw a return to the small prewar army as unacceptable and sure to lead to another Pearl Harbor, sooner or later. They favored instead a continuation of the draft; a big and heavily equipped army, navy, and air force; and the high taxes needed to pay for them. Senior military leaders firmly believed that a powerful military in constant readiness would more certainly deter the kind of aggression that had brought on World War II.

Top intelligence people, such as William Donovan of the Office of Strategic Services, and FBI director J. Edgar Hoover, endorsed this peace-through-strength approach. They were more worried than either the business community or the liberals about the intentions and capabilities of potential foreign adversaries. The leaders of the national security state saw the Soviets in particular as likely to try to expand their system after the war, and to be in a good position to do so unless the United States resisted. Senior military and intelligence officials tended to share in the postwar optimism in their sense that a large and permanent national security apparatus could cope with any challenges while preserving the bulk of traditional American rights and freedoms despite conscription and higher taxes.[10]

Those differing visions of the future helped define the programs of the nation's two major political parties. Partisan Republicans expected to regain control of Congress and the White House, and to bring the New Deal era to an end. The GOP had swept back into national office after World War I and seemed likely to do so again. Roosevelt's death had deprived the Democrats of their most popular national leader, making the Republicans even more confident, as had the Republicans' recent success in electing several prominent new governors with national appeal, most notably New York's Thomas Dewey and California's Earl Warren. Leading Democrats, having dominated the nation's political system for over a decade, and having led the efforts to end the Depression and win the war, were just as optimistic. They saw themselves as the new majority party, which would preserve a greatly enlarged role for government in the years ahead.[11]

Factions within each party, however, held different views about the specific policy steps needed to achieve the party's greater goals. Republican voters and officeholders in the Northeast were generally pleased with America's new place in the global order, especially in western Europe, and liked the idea of wielding that influence into the future. Midwestern Republicans seemed to prefer a more modest role, perhaps limiting American involvement to the Western Hemisphere. Western Republicans, and especially those in the Pacific Coast states, tended to focus on America's role in Asia. The three factions, then, could not agree on how big a national security state would be required to support an enlarged foreign-affairs role, which related directly to the future size and cost of government. Within the party were also rifts on such important domestic programs as Social Security and farm price supports, which would also help determine the future size of the federal government and the appropriate levels of taxing and spending. Most leading Republicans in the fall of 1945 seemed committed to a smaller, less expensive, and less intrusive federal government, and to curbs on union power, but remained seriously at odds with each other about how to accomplish that.[12]

The Democrats were divided as well. The two major segments of the population supporting the party, the cities and the South, were almost mutually exclusive. Northern urban Democrats, for the most part, saw no reason to upset the New Deal status quo. They favored a permanently big federal government, an expansion of government-sponsored social programs and labor unions, high and progressive taxation, and a much smaller military. However, most southern Democrats disagreed. The Dixiecrats remained dominant in Congress, where they often sided with the Republican minority on such issues. The Dixiecrats also emphatically rejected the push by African Americans and their northern white liberal allies (and some Republicans) to use the federal government's power to dismantle legally sanctioned racial segregation. The Dixiecrats mostly looked after their own, frowning upon an activist, costly federal government unless it somehow benefited their mostly impoverished home turf, as military installations often did. All this infighting among Republican and Democratic politicians reflected similar struggles being waged elsewhere in American society.[13]

The factional discord in Washington reverberated around the country, dividing ordinary Americans and playing out publicly in the mass media. The fog of war had given way to the fog of postwar. But a series of seismic developments in the outside world would force people to start seeing beyond their squabbles at home and make clear what the future would bring for the middle class.[14]

The main instigator behind most of those outside-world events was the Soviet Union, which would become the primary focus of America's international attention for most of the next fifty years. First, the Soviet leadership declined to withdraw the Red Army from Austria, Czechoslovakia, Hungary, and Poland, the countries it had liberated from Nazi Germany's rule. Those on the far left who were sympathetic to the Soviets tended to see that decision as essentially defensive, and those who were inclined to be suspicious saw it as proof of the USSR's aggressive designs. Harry Truman tried at first to use the carrot of a big postwar American loan for rebuilding to induce the Soviet Union to bring its armies home. When that didn't work, Truman tried the stick of trying to intimidate the Soviets into leaving, but "getting tough with the Russians," as he called it, proved similarly unproductive. Frustrated throughout 1945 and 1946, Truman and his advisers spent the next two years moving toward a formal policy of using American power to contain any further expansion of Soviet influence. When high postwar inflation, labor unrest, and Truman's rocky start as president allowed Republicans to win control of both houses of Congress in 1946, containment became, of necessity, a bipartisan policy. Truman found a partner on the other side of the aisle who shared his pessimistic views about Soviet intentions and capabilities: Michigan senator Arthur Vandenberg, the head of the Senate Foreign Relations Committee for the next two years. These two native sons of the Midwest worked together in 1947–48 to lay the first cornerstones of containment.[15]

More unwelcome news from abroad made it easier for Truman and Vandenberg to persuade a doubtful Congress to go along. In February 1947, Britain's government determined that the drain on its wealth brought by World War II meant that it could not afford to provide substantial financial support to the existing governments in Greece and Turkey, both of which were menaced by left-wing political movements. Unable to play a role on the international stage of the sort it had before World War II, the British government in effect passed the baton to the United States. Seeing the potential openings for Soviet expansion, Truman called for Congress to provide $400 million in aid to those countries' governments, which was approved. Fearful that the weak economy in western Europe could provide Stalin more openings, Truman called next for Congress to approve much more money to fund a European Recovery Program (ERP), devised by his secretary of state, George Marshall. The Marshall Plan was intended to help provide badly needed food and investment capital. The high price tag of the Marshall Plan, which ultimately totaled $120 billion of today's dollars, met with much more congressional resistance than the aid package for Greece and Turkey. Only when Communists in Czechoslovakia, backed by the Soviets, overthrew the lawfully elected government in February 1948 did Congress become alarmed enough to approve the Marshall Plan.[16]

The Czech coup also prompted Congress to pass the Selective Service Act of 1948, which restored the draft that had lapsed a year earlier. The draft's swift return meant that policies established during the New Deal's third phase would be extended, reshaping American life as they had during and just after World War II. In particular it ensured that the GI Bill of Rights would continue to touch the lives of young American men, especially with its powerful employment preference. So, too, would the new draft law's system of deferments and exemptions, such as for married men, those in college, and those who entered such socially valuable fields as teaching and medicine. All of these powerfully affected the life choices of those men and the building of a bigger, more prosperous middle class based on the male-breadwinner model.[17]

Growing tensions between the United States and USSR encouraged the Truman administration and Congress to double down on their commitment to the big national security state that had emerged during World War II. The first major step, what some have called the permanent national security state's "Magna Carta," was the National Security

Act of 1947. Developed primarily by Truman administration officials and military leaders rather than by members of Congress, it did away with the separate cabinet Departments of War and Navy, consolidating them into a new Department of Defense. The act also created a new national intelligence agency: the Central Intelligence Agency (CIA), which gathered and evaluated information of use to those responsible for foreign policy. The act also created a new National Security Council (NSC), staffed by both military and civilian personnel, to advise the president on these areas, reflecting a view that serious national security challenges had become essentially permanent, and that the president would always need a team of specialized advisers close at hand. The advent of the NSC reduced somewhat the State Department's influence over the making of foreign policy and the emphasis on diplomacy that was the State Department's stock-in-trade. Sent to Congress in the late winter of 1947, the proposed act was hotly debated for the next five months before being signed into law.

Those tensions with the Soviets also prompted another historic departure from precedent for the United States: its participation in a permanent military defense alliance with other nations. The North Atlantic Treaty Organization (NATO) grew out of the Treaty of Brussels, signed in March 1948, and envisioned cooperation by western European countries, the USA, and Canada to deter common threats. The related NATO pact was a collective-security alliance, rooted in the principle that an attack on one member is an attack on all. The hope was that the prospect of a massive collective response to aggression would act as a convincing deterrent. Support for the idea grew in the spring and summer of 1948, when the American, British, and French governments clashed with the Soviets over Germany's future. In June of that year, leaders of those three Western powers, which along with the USSR had divided Germany among them for military occupation, signaled to the Soviets an intention to unite the American, British, and French sectors of the country into a new Federal Republic of Germany (FRG). As part of that plan, they intended to circulate the new FRG currency in their parts of Berlin, which would effectively make those sectors of the city part of the FRG, too. The Soviet government responded the next day by terminating road and rail links into those areas, which became known collectively as West Berlin. That part of the city was entirely surrounded by the Soviet sector of occupied Germany and thus seemed about to become a permanent hostile outpost in Soviet-dominated eastern Europe.

The clash over the future of West Berlin became the Cold War's first potential hot spot. Any attempt by the United States and its allies to resupply West Berlin by force had the potential to spark an armed conflict. Truman and his advisers responded instead with the Berlin Airlift of 1948–49, a huge logistical undertaking to resupply the western part of the city. The fear that the Soviet government would try to block the movement of American planes over Soviet-controlled airspace around West Berlin made the possibility of a third world war seem real for the first time, but the Western allies completed their mission without interference.[18]

The Berlin crisis stoked the growing Cold War between the USA and the USSR, with major ramifications for American electoral politics and the future of the middle class. Before the blockade of Berlin, Truman appeared to have little chance of winning the 1948 presidential election. He had lost support at both ends of his own party. Left-wing Democrats had defected, throwing their support behind Henry Wallace's bid as the candidate of a newly created Progressive Citizens of America (PCA) party, whose more conciliatory policy toward the Soviets gained it the support of American Communists. The most conservative southern Democrats, determined to preserve racial segregation in the face of Truman's growing hostility to it, organized a States' Rights Party, which was headed by its presidential candidate, Governor Strom Thurmond of South Carolina. The emergence of these splinter groups seemed to dash Truman's reelection hopes.[19]

As the threat of confrontation with the Soviets grew, however, Truman's electoral prospects began to improve. Much as FDR had owed his reelection victories in 1940 and 1944 largely to his greater foreign-policy experience, Truman benefited in 1948 because his main opponent, GOP governor Thomas Dewey of New York, was a relative novice in national security matters. The Republicans running Congress unwittingly helped Truman's cause by alienating both labor (by passing a new law restricting union power) and farmers (by reducing farm price supports even as farm incomes were falling). Truman won support from black voters in major northern cities by endorsing civil rights legislation and ordering the military desegregated. Those four factors, enhanced by Truman's energetic campaigning and the lift provided by a slew of strong Democratic candidates for statewide office around the country, gave his party its fifth consecutive presidential election victory. The Democrats triumphed as a political force, rather than Truman alone; they had won not only the presidential race but control of Congress. With that change, the most significant New Deal policies and the growth of the middle class acquired genuine staying power.[20]

Any confusion about whether the United States would fundamentally alter its national security stance was put to rest in late August 1949, when the Soviet Union conducted its first successful atomic bomb test. The alarming news that the Soviets had joined the United States as a nuclear power immediately made the USSR a more threatening adversary on the world stage. Global tensions ratcheted up even further only a little over one month later, when a successful Communist revolution in China marked a sudden and stunning surge in the spread of Communism. With the ascension of Mao and his supporters in Beijing, East Asia clearly emerged as another major area of East-West tension. What had earlier been thought of as mostly a European problem now looked more and more like a global concern.[21]

The Truman administration responded by developing a plan to further ramp up its military buildup as a deterrent to Communist expansion worldwide. Distilled into a formal proposal known as NSC-68, the plan envisioned restoring the US fighting force to World War II levels, and for the long term. The army in particular had shrunk a lot, even with the restoration of the draft, from what it had been in 1945. Not only would a multimillion-man (mostly white male), combat-ready army be hugely expensive to maintain and equip, the country would have to bear the cost of veterans' benefits for generations to come.

This commitment to a massive governmental enterprise would prolong the influence of the New Deal in America, with all that it meant for the future of the middle class. It would, for instance, extend the reach of the veteran's preference in employment, strengthening the promotion of the male-breadwinner household. Building more modern naval vessels and warplanes, and expanding the nation's nuclear arsenal, would likewise be enormously expensive and influential, given that big business and research universities would likely be the recipients of most of those government contracts. Expanding the nation's intelligence agencies and the national security state more generally would further add to the expense, and limit traditional freedoms, as had happened during World War II, which tended to sit well with the mainstream majority but not nearly as much for others, those on the far left especially.[22]

Thus, taking the path NSC-68 proposed would likely mean putting these World War II–like patterns and practices of an enormous federal government in place for the long term. It would require huge rivers of federal government money, being spent year after year, and the high taxes needed to keep it flowing. With the Democrats once again in control of Congress, and Truman still in the White House, that broadened and progressive tax system would continue its New Dealish pattern of strengthening and expanding the middle class.[23]

The heavy cost and far-reaching implications of NSC-68 delayed a decision about it until another distant upheaval influenced political decisions in the United States, again with long-lasting implications for American society and the middle class in particular. A major military conflict boiled over in Korea, between the Communist-dominated North and the pro-US government in the South. The success of the Chinese Communist revolution had emboldened North Korea's leaders to seek China's support for its military invasion of the South. China's new leaders grudgingly agreed in June 1950. (The Soviets did so as well, but mostly stayed on the sidelines during the fighting.) If successful, that aggression promised to reunify Korea under Communist control, making the Chinese Communist revolution more secure. Underestimating the Truman administration's commitment to defend a non-Communist South Korea, the army of North Korea attacked in force, quickly driving back much weaker South Korean units. The Truman administration viewed this as a Cold War confrontation between the West and global Communism and called for a substantial military response to meet it. Both sides found themselves, suddenly and unexpectedly, on a path to a vastly more deadly and destructive conflict than either had wanted or expected.[24]

By the end of 1950, most of those fighting on one side were Chinese and most of those on the other were American, making what had earlier been a Korean civil war into a kind of Chinese-American one fought on the Korean peninsula. The alarm produced by those developments persuaded Congress to approve the kind of heavy military spending that NSC-68 had earlier envisioned. With that step, the fog of uncertainty about what postwar America might look like finally lifted.[25]

The lasting influence of the New Deal on American society was by now a given. Throughout the 1930s and 1940s, New Deal policies had fundamentally altered the economic lives of all Americans, but had most profoundly affected that middle three-fifths of the population (with respect to income). People in that range may have come from a multitude of backgrounds with an enormously wide variety of life experiences, but they now tended to share a deep-seated commitment to security and believed that the future, while always uncertain, held some promise. Less than a decade removed from the desperation of the Depression, that sense of cautious optimism persisted even as America waded deeper into another distant war.

Once again, the prevailing mood in the nation helped to shape social and cultural trends. The clearest manifestation, no doubt, was the pronounced shift toward early yet stable marriage and the conception of lots of kids—the postwar baby boom. Historically, a high percentage of Americans had always chosen marriage. What changed in this era was their propensity to marry early, to stay married, and to have more children. After a brief surge in the divorce rate, as many couples that had separated during the war broke up once it ended, the divorce rate fell off sharply and remained low for the next twenty years.[26]

The average age at which Americans married dropped into the early twenties, and the number of young married couples who chose to have three or four children rose. These trends had begun to emerge as early as 1946 and were most pronounced in the broad middle class. Helping make that possible were the steadily rising real wages and salaries of the men in that group, veterans especially, who received heavy government subsidies and an employment preference thanks to the GI Bill. It's important to remember that as the 1940s drew to a close, that dream of middle-class security was still something of a work in progress. Having weathered the storms of the Great Depression and World War II, young adults were not suddenly ready to have faith in good times to come. Comfort and stability were the goals, and settling down into safe domesticity seemed to be the logical first steps in that direction. The marriage and family boom that resulted was dominated by lower-middle-class and upper-working-class people who were predominantly white; risk averse; and organized into households in which the husband earned most if not all of the income, and his wife mostly stayed home and focused on the household.[27]

Another crucial factor behind that trend in the later 1940s was a boom in house construction in the burgeoning suburbs. Most good jobs then and afterward were found in major metropolitan areas, and so a housing boom in the near suburbs was unsurprising. What made this remarkable was the enormous amount of construction, primarily of houses priced for families with ordinary incomes, and located considerably farther from downtown than in the past. Americans had long preferred more space, more privacy, and more greenery than most city apartments offered, and now the conditions were just right for the population to spread out into what would become mass suburbia. Middle-class incomes had grown and were backstopped by huge government subsidies. On top of that, given the advent of the Cold War, concerns that the massive aerial bombardments of city centers that had ravaged Europe and East Asia during World War II might someday happen in America made the average young couple more receptive to moving out to a safer distance.[28]

Responding to that kind of consumer demand for middle-class housing, the Levitt brothers, William and Alfred, harnessed the assembly-line techniques and prefabrication that had powered wartime manufacturing to create huge numbers of modest-size houses quickly. The first of their iconic Levittowns, a trendsetting, planned suburban community, was built on Long Island in the late 1940s, about thirty miles from New York City. Residents began moving in on October 1, 1947, and construction was mostly finished by the end of 1950. At the peak pace of construction, a new house was put together every seventeen minutes. The result—a community of over eighty thousand residents living in about seventeen thousand houses—was the biggest single housing development by one builder in American history. Levittown featured not just houses but also village greens, playgrounds, swimming pools, bowling alleys, and a town hall. The Levitts also encouraged the construction of other kinds of communal spaces by selling land at cost for schools and donating space for such things as houses of worship and fire stations. Buyers flocked to Levittown. Its immediate success encouraged the Levitts to build more and spawned a bevy of smaller-scale imitators across the country.[29]

What was living in such a place like during the early years of the baby boom? To the upper-middle-class and more well-to-do Americans who had mostly populated suburbia before the later 1940s, the houses looked too small and had a depressing, cookie-cutter sameness. To the Levittowns' less affluent inhabitants, who had mostly been living with relatives or in apartments, a house of their own of about 750 to 900 square feet on a 6,000-square-foot lot felt almost grand. A *new* house of that sort, complete with appliances, for two and a half times the median household income, struck potential homeowners as quite a bargain. If the buyer qualified for the GI Bill, it was an even sweeter deal, with no down payment, a low mortgage interest rate, and a repayment schedule that stretched for twenty-five years. While the uniform exteriors and still-barren landscapes seemed starkly dull and conformist at first, as residents began to add personal touches to the houses, and the greenery grew and matured, the aesthetics of the town became more inviting.[30]

The typical Levittown house had four rooms, with a partly open layout that encouraged interaction more than privacy. As a space to raise small children, the design made a lot of sense, enabling busy mothers to keep one eye on their offspring. The war years had disrupted family life for a generation of young adults, and for all the shared national spirit, many had been anxious and lonely. The togetherness fostered by the open-plan interiors, and having neighbors so close at hand, seem to have helped restore a comforting sense of belonging.[31]

Most Levittowners started out as strangers to one another, highlighting the need for community at home. The shared class backgrounds of most residents also helped bring them together. The upwardly mobile families in Levittown during the early years didn't stay long, often leaving when dad was promoted at work. Fairly quickly, Levittown acquired an overwhelmingly lower-middle-class/upper-working-class population. For that demographic group, whose members in those days had not usually gone beyond high school and labored in fairly routine jobs, the central focus of life—and its chief satisfaction—was raising kids and building a happy family. Here was a new kind of suburbia, one designed, inside and out, to help people of modest education, income, and aspiration to achieve those dreams.[32]

Social critics soon started to complain about the uniformity of the suburban population, but even that critique failed to recognize the family emphasis that attracted people to places such as Levittown. What middle-class people raising lots of small children typically want are safe communities with neighbors—and peers for their highly impressionable kids—who share similar values and behavior. The tightly knit urban enclaves that many new homesteaders escaped had all of those qualities, which could now be replicated in a less confined suburban setting. Having grown up with the Depression and the war, many of these young parents remained risk averse and typically wanted neighbors cautious in spending, morally traditional, focused on child-rearing, and committed to maintaining the exteriors of houses and yards so as to protect the value of the other houses on the block.[33]

That last point is crucial. To these suburbanites, houses were more than places to live; they were their single greatest financial asset. The resulting fixation on protecting that investment led these new parents and homeowners to sort themselves into like-minded communities, as had happened, for one reason or another, throughout human history. That tendency became especially acute during the baby boom, both because of the greater number of children involved, and the perceived fragility of this stable new life for people with only a slim financial cushion. They generally remained more focused on parenting and less open to different kinds of people and experiences than their more affluent contemporaries, especially in the years right after the Great Depression and World War II.[34]

The interplay of economics and prejudice is complex here. Some, probably many, middle-class white people were racist, meaning that they harbored prejudiced views about black people that led them to object to black residents in the new suburbia. Other middle-class white people, determined to maximize the value of their main asset, resisted black residents to protect the resale value of their homes. Both of these attitudes could coexist to varying degrees in people's heads. To the outside observer (and to many in later generations), all of these kinds of white homeowners seemed essentially the same because the result surely was: rigid resistance to black neighbors.

That attitude, and the developers' belief that it was more or less universal among middle-class white people, led to the exclusion of African Americans from this great suburban expansion to an extent that many outside observers, then and later, found disturbing. William Levitt, when asked about the unfairness of the situation, stated publicly that he harbored no animus against "Negroes," as African Americans were then usually called. His hardheaded view was that to have permitted black residents early on would have undermined the appeal of the community for most whites, making it essentially a non-starter. Levitt couched this as a business decision stemming from a belief that white people with ordinary middle-class incomes were too risk averse and too committed to living with people like themselves as to allow a multiracial population, but such a decision is premised entirely on the assumed racism of the white population. The result was that *all* Levittown residents in the early years were white, in a country in which, according to the 1950 census, just over 10 percent (mostly African Americans) belonged to racial groups outside the majority one. Levittown *did* have a good deal of diversity in ethnicity and religion, which partly reflected a broadened conception of who was considered white, but none of that greater openness applied to black people.[35] Levittown, in its racial exclusiveness, wasn't all that different from earlier New Deal initiatives to encourage and subsidize new housing. The Roosevelt administration's housing policies, most notably assistance to mortgage lenders, assumed that racially homogeneous communities fostered stable property values, again taking for granted the endemic racism of the white population. Those policies had fairly limited reach until 1945, however, because so little housing was built during the Depression and the war. They began to make a big difference, though, in the suburban construction boom of the later 1940s. The mass suburbia that spread across the American landscape in the later 1940s would remain almost entirely white for the next twenty years.[36]

The exodus of middle-class white people from urban neighborhoods to the new suburbs increased the amount of available housing stock within cities. That flight opened up more housing for immigrant groups and populations of color within central cities while such places remained—at least for the time being, before retailers and services followed the whites to the suburbs—economically vibrant. Urban neighborhoods, where people were unlikely to need a car, made sense for most within these groups, given their generally lower household incomes. The much greater availability of rental housing in cities also better suited their financial situation.

The postwar baby boom phenomenon extended to the black population as well, and white Americans simply assumed that black people, too, would want to raise their families in racially homogeneous communities, rather than live as a minority among mostly hostile or indifferent neighbors. White citizens tended to assume that even black Americans prominent enough to have established a positive place in white consciousness and culture, such as Brooklyn Dodgers second baseman Jackie Robinson—who in 1947 became the first African American to play for a major-league baseball team—would rather reside within the black community than outside it.[37]

That same mix of attitudes, policies, and assumptions also greatly affected new home construction within cities. Even though suburbs grew faster, a substantial amount of new housing also went up within city limits in the late 1940s. In the urban environment, the homogeneous groups that people fit into were defined as much by income and ethnicity as by race. Chicago, then the nation's second-largest city in population, continued to grow into a series of urban small towns, contained within the larger city, where residents mostly shared similar backgrounds, values, and social status. Critics in the intelligentsia and within the black community expressed outrage over the stark segregation, but many of the people who lived in those neighborhoods saw them as highly functional, reinforcing what parents were teaching their children about the values of family and community. Those children were also absorbing the inherent racism and segregationist attitudes that gave rise to those neighborhoods in the first place. White Americans saw those separate enclaves as reducing social tension and promoting order and stability. In the long run, such separation actually provoked resentment and conflict, but for anyone who had lived through the upheavals of the Depression and the war, the security they offered overshadowed any underlying injustice.[38]

Whatever moral qualms some people may have had about the evolving system, it seemed to be working, although better for whites in the suburbs, where resources were more abundant, than for urban populations. People, especially those who existed in some way outside that conforming mainstream, faced other drawbacks as well. The compartmentalizing of society increased the distance, literally, between different kinds of people. This was especially vivid in the suburbs, which usually had no black residents and hardly any elderly people, to offer only two of the most extreme examples. Greater distance might reduce tension, but it could also create a fertile breeding ground for prejudice. When different kinds of people don't experience one another in their daily lives, any group can become abstract to any other, making it easier for myths and misconceptions to remain entrenched. Even within the world of young white adults were outliers of other kinds. Not everyone was prepared to reflexively conform to the values and behavior of the group into which he or she had been born; not everyone wanted to marry early, to stay married, and to raise two to four children in a suburban tract home. Like so much else associated with the changes brought by the New Deal, the postwar baby boom and the housing patterns it helped foster tended to work best in the later 1940s for unexceptional young adults and their families. Those factors also increased the number of young adults who gravitated toward that lifestyle even if it didn't suit them.[39]

It was a time to "stay in your lane," except there just weren't that many lanes to choose from—and in the late 1940s, the widest lane in popular culture was the middlebrow one. It took some time, in the confusion immediately after the end of the war, but eventually, most moved in that direction. The movies, as popular as ever, reflected as well as any other cultural form middlebrow's growing strength, along with hints of uncertainty as to where American society was going. In 1946 came the highly acclaimed film *The Best Years of Our Lives*, which followed the return home (to a thinly disguised Cincinnati) of three veterans. One was working class, one lower middle class, and one upper class. The movie's frank acknowledgment of the difficulties the men faced in readjusting to family life and work resonated with many Americans. The film was fundamentally optimistic, but neither unrealistic nor cloying. Especially effective was the casting of a disabled veteran, Harold Russell, who lost his hands during the war, as a character facing that challenge.[40]

Although a perceptive piece of social commentary, which helped it win several Oscars including Best Picture, *The Best Years of Our Lives* also shared some of the limitations seen in earlier code-era films. All three veterans were white, and except for a fleeting glimpse early on of one black servant and one black serviceman, so were the movie's other cast members. Reaching as wide an audience as possible meant accommodating white southern audiences, who would not have abided making a black veteran a central part of the story unless depicted in a subordinate way that would likely have offended both black people and white liberals. The film is also at times sentimental, in keeping with the sensibility of so many ordinary Americans at the time. The outcome as well is limited by the mores of the period, as all three men by the movie's end are on track to join or rejoin married life, parenting, and domesticity, which are presented as the only appropriate path for them.[41]

Three years later, the film *Adam's Rib* did try to push the middlebrow envelope a little, but never strayed too far beyond acceptable societal norms. A childless married attorney, played effectively by Katharine Hepburn, takes as a client a woman who shot and wounded her husband for having an extramarital affair. Hepburn's character is married to the opposing lawyer in the case, the local prosecutor, played by Spencer Tracy. Her attempts to turn the trial into an indictment of sexual double standards creates so much tension in her own marriage as to endanger it.[42]

The most memorable scene, from a modern feminist perspective, has Hepburn's character calling three extraordinary women (a scientist, a construction supervisor, and an acrobat/weight lifter) to the witness stand, offered as proof that women could achieve as much as men outside the home and therefore ought to be treated equally in law and life. Here was a welcome reminder that the abilities of other kinds of women than full-time homemakers would be squandered in a culture that rigidly confined them to that one role.[43]

Adam's Rib was very much a film of its time. It posed a kind of limited challenge to motherhood and homemaking as the best choice for women, and to the male-breadwinner model, in an era when decisions about national policy and programs increasingly presumed an adherence to those gender roles. In the three years prior to the film's release, Congress gave serious consideration to a proposed Equal Rights Amendment (ERA) to the US Constitution, which would have required equality before the law regardless of sex. The ERA was more of a Republican issue in the 1940s, while the Democrats chose not to support it. The push to pass the ERA petered out in the late 1940s, just as the film's challenge to New Deal–era gender roles ultimately collapsed. The female defense attorney is persuaded by her prosecutor husband that her client acted wrongly. She reconciles with him, saving their marriage. One could argue that the movie never had the courage of its feminist convictions. Even the women put forth as exemplars of strength and competence were played to some degree for laughs, softening the impact of the film's message.[44]

Another popular film genre of the late 1940s revealed some of the lingering uncertainties about where life in America was heading. The moody crime dramas characterized as film noir often featured gritty urban settings and central male characters who seemed poorly suited for middle-class domestic life. The action-oriented, sometimes violent, and essentially independent lives led by the detectives at the center of these stories likely appealed to the many men of that generation who felt a dim nostalgia for the quicker pulse of city life. The Depression or the war, or most likely both, had deprived many men of a quiet family life and led them to seek that out afterward. In the shadowy world of film noir, they perhaps felt something more authentic. The genre's popularity is a reminder of the doubts that returning veterans would easily adjust to domesticity or could relate to it on the screen. Their military service had taken them out of that world, exposing them to places and experiences both terrible and beautiful. It had scarred and hardened them, but also expanded their horizons. The terrible loss of life brought by the war, and fears of another, more devastating nuclear world war, made traditional values even more suspect, a moral ambiguity that lay at the heart of film noir.[45]

As much as the middlebrow continued to dominate postwar popular culture, works in every medium were being produced that subtly challenged that sensibility or at least offered some tiny glimpse of other possibilities. Radio, television, print publications, music, and painting all reflected that zeitgeist. Of these cultural forms, the newest, television, had the most far-reaching potential, promising to bring all manner of entertainment and information directly into people's homes, but had not yet established itself as a mass phenomenon. Although basic TV technology had been developed by 1940, World War II delayed its emergence. The major TV networks, spun out from the established national radio networks, didn't begin operating until the late 1940s. The audience was limited mostly to major urban centers in the Northeast, given TV's reliance on transmission technology that had yet to reach most of the rest of the country. Not surprisingly, the TV programming that resulted was New York–centric, in which variety shows with an urban and urbane middle-class, white sensibility dominated the airwaves. Network television, like radio before it, was based in the country's most populous city, which reinforced New York's place at the center of the cultural life of the nation. The earlier New Deal pattern of encouraging the growth of big institutions, such as the TVA, the US Army, the Fortune 100, labor unions, and the like, was felt in the cultural realm, too, and grew more pronounced during the later 1940s.[46]

Highbrow art reflected that same centralizing trend, with New York becoming a mecca for modernist painters. Before the war the movement had been led by Europeans working in a variety of places; in the immediate postwar years Willem de Kooning, Lee Krasner, Joan Mitchell, Jackson Pollock, and the other leading abstract expressionists living and working in New York first emerged as major figures. The city was the first destination for most new immigrants, but especially for talented artists, many of whom were fleeing from a war-torn and impoverished Europe. As middlebrow spread, seeping steadily into all the visual and performing arts, many artists who considered themselves more serious or intellectual created works that challenged it. Middlebrow culture, somewhat paradoxically, spurred perceptive and skillful artists to confront it directly in their work. Middlebrow's main themes, such as patriotic nationalism, populism, mainstream religiosity, moral traditionalism, and optimism, struck many artists of that time as blinkered and suspect. Hadn't patriotic nationalism done much to bring on the devastation of World War II? Did "average people" understand best the complex questions of the postwar world, such as race relations and foreign policy? Wasn't mainstream religion more focused on reassuring people than explaining the central issues of human existence? Did moral traditionalism, with its focus on domesticity, meet the most deeply felt needs of cosmopolitan people shaped by depression and world war? Above all, did middlebrow's persistent optimism square with the doomsday scenarios threatened by the Cold War and the new nuclear age? That kind of questioning of middlebrow's basic premises led artists such as Pollock and de Kooning and many others in innovative directions, even as traditional painters and illustrators such as Norman Rockwell dominated the mainstream media and, seemingly, the artistic consciousness of most middle-class people.[47]

Some cultural critics also began to voice their concern about the rising tyranny of the middlebrow. For example, after about a decade of broadcasts, critics began to grumble about the classical music presented by Arturo Toscanini, the conductor of the highly popular NBC Symphony Orchestra. They argued that Toscanini's highly disciplined and technically correct direction lacked spontaneity, creativity, and vitality. To the German émigré philosopher and sociologist Theodor Adorno, Toscanini provided slick and satisfying classical music that appealed most to conventional middle-class tastes. David Sarnoff, the president of NBC's parent corporation, RCA, defended Toscanini, arguing that the maestro was providing "the average man" with an introduction to classical music, so that interested listeners might later dive deeper into it on their own. To critics and theorists such as Adorno, however, the increasingly greater influence of middlebrow was just encouraging people to accept bland and unchallenging artistic expression such as Toscanini's as the ideal.[48]

The world of literature had its parallels. The kind of middlebrow books associated with the Book of the Month Club and *Reader's Digest* became more affordable to middle-class people after the war and typically sounded middlebrow's main themes. But reading a novel required a much greater investment of time and effort than listening to music on the radio or looking at a painting, which skewed the book-publishing market upward. Books aimed at intellectually sophisticated highbrow readers could still be found. Norman Mailer's novel about American military service during World War II, *The Naked and the Dead*, was perhaps the single most influential example. Instead of simply celebrating the heroic teamwork of the somewhat mythically diverse US military units, Mailer's book pointedly described the tensions among GIs who served in them. Mailer was not alone. Even as the influence of middlebrow spread through the literary world as it had through music and art, a cadre of talented and dedicated writers such as Saul Bellow, Gwendolyn Brooks, John Cheever, Langston Hughes, Flannery O'Connor, J. D. Salinger, and Truman Capote would buck the tide with serious works of fiction and journalism.[49]

Critical protests against middlebrow grew in the later 1940s as the middlebrow cultural juggernaut, fueled by growing middle-class incomes, pushed highbrow and lowbrow perspectives further to the margins. Most intriguingly, it seemed that—regardless of the particular cultural medium—the more the middlebrow sensibility spread, the louder and more vigorous the critical backlash became, especially in artistic and intellectual circles.[50]

The relentless march of the middlebrow mind-set distorted Americans' perceptions of key issues and trends. Patriotic nationalism was still pervasive, for example, and that affected the way people understood income inequality. Although the population had, in the postwar years, begun to sort itself out more distinctly into communities of ethnic, cultural, and economic similarities, most Americans also maintained a powerful sense of belonging to the overarching national community. That binding national identity tended to strengthen support for such existing policies as restrictions on trade and immigration, which, at least for a time, made for a more egalitarian outcome in the United States as a whole, if not globally. By the late 1940s the American economy, already the world's largest, was growing faster than those of most other nations—which meant that globally income inequality was growing, not shrinking. That was especially true when one compared the richer northern nations of the globe with the poorer southern ones.[51]

Thinking about how critical issues affected the nation as a whole also tended to obscure and distort the different ways in which discrete parts of it, regionally and demographically, might have been experiencing those issues. Patriotism had to coexist with the strong sense of identity people derived from their regions, communities, and neighborhoods. In the first five years after World War II, the already wealthier and more populous states of the Northeast, Midwest, and West Coast moved forward faster economically than the poorer and less populous ones of the South and the Mountain West. The same was true for certain kinds of social groups. Middle-class white people living in the Northeast, Midwest, and West Coast saw the gap between them and the more affluent narrow, but the gap between the middle class and the still poor bottom fifth widened. Disproportionately composed of black people and dispossessed rural white people such as those living in Appalachia, that bottom fifth was becoming ever less visible to the ever more prosperous middle class. Thus, stability and security blossomed for those who already had a taste of it, but also widened the distance between them and those who had less. These inequalities based on region and demographic group were to some extent related. For example, a national perspective obscured that black people, who were then disproportionately southerners, typically moved forward economically more slowly than their white counterparts.[52]

Still, to people who thought in national terms, the almost unconscious assumption was that the number of people living on the outer edges of the mainstream would shrink as a fraction of the total population. Over time, more and more Americans would gravitate toward the vast economic and social middle. From that perspective, the long-term declines in the South's share of the US population as people migrated north, and in African Americans' share of the population as heavy immigration by whites during the nineteenth and early twentieth centuries altered the country's racial mix, suggested that the majority's experience would become ever more the norm. That kind of thinking made it easy to forget that some people would always remain institutionally marginalized.[53]

Things were toughest for those people furthest removed from the middle and the middlebrow. As patriotic nationalism grew more fervent, Americans whose politics fell to the radical left were increasingly marginalized, branded by the mainstream as "un-American" and "disloyal." By February 9, 1950, when Wisconsin senator Joseph McCarthy launched his anti-Communist crusade with a speech in Wheeling, West Virginia, a national campaign against leftists associated with the American Communist Party and/or suspected of sympathy for the Soviet Union was already well under way. Those sorts of people were not, however, the only ones affected by the rise of an ever more myopic middle-class America. Women who opposed the trends toward early marriage, motherhood, and a focus on domesticity had likewise come under sustained and mounting attack from middle-class leaders. So, too, had gays and lesbians, whose orientation challenged typically rigid middle-class views on traditional gender roles, including heterosexuality. Middlebrow's tendency toward anti-intellectualism also led to more suspicion of academics and teachers who seemed to possess unorthodox ideas.[54]

The intense marginalization of these kinds of outliers had immediate and significant consequences for politics and culture. Fringe people in American politics, and those on the far left especially, found themselves after 1948 increasingly on the outside. By the end of 1950, many of the most advanced New Deal liberals, who seemed to have bright electoral futures just five years earlier, had been voted out of office. In the mass culture, TV and the movies, which had the greatest influence, followed that trend and reinforced it. New York intellectuals could decry middlebrow's limitations, and bohemian artists such as Jackson Pollock could create dissenting works freely because they did so in relative obscurity, but the much more visible TV and movies were subject to strict censorship. A new set of industry regulations for film and then television adopted in the later 1940s drove out entirely, or pushed into the background, many radicals and dissenters who worked in those industries. In their place came more mainstream artists, writers, and directors who were more content to create middlebrow culture. That shift, like the larger ones in politics and culture, had a regional aspect, in that the overall sensibility of film and television became even more Midwestern than it had been before, with its focus on white, native-born, middle-class family life.[55]

Back in the Sindt and Perkins households, the Cold War and the domestic political pressures it produced were palpable. In the later 1940s Howard Sindt became a hawkish anti-Communist, a position he maintained for a long time. For George Perkins, the change was more subtle, in part because serving in the army during World War I, though never in combat, had helped make him unenthusiastic about war and warmongers. For George, the real change was a rightward shift in his views on domestic politics. As his more liberal younger daughter, who grew up in the intellectual milieu of the academic community at Brown, later complained, "He hit fifty [in 1947] and turned conservative."

These kinds of shifts on foreign policy and domestic issues pleased many in the broad middle of the population, politically and geographically, while making outliers feel both more isolated and targeted. As had been the case with the critiques of middlebrow in arts, the open hostility toward dissent and nonconformity in some ways strengthened the power of those perspectives, in part because repression has a way of focusing the response to it. The origins of gay and lesbian community activism lay in that trend. So, too, did much of the innovative work of dissenting artists and musicians. The late 1940s saw a growth in discrete social spaces where the more independently minded creative people could do their work and were ever more inspired to do so by middlebrow's growing dominance.

Thus, as the fog over postwar American life lifted, middlebrow and predominantly white, middle-class perspectives moved more to the forefront, while outliers increasingly organized themselves into like-minded subcultures. In time, those dedicated communities of dissenters would begin to have more influence on the wider society. For the next seven years, however, the mounting progress of mostly white Middle America would render them more and more invisible.[56]

CHAPTER 6

The Middle-Class Model

The predominantly middle-class country that Herbert Hoover had promised in 1928 finally became a reality during the 1950s, although it took a different form from what he had envisioned. A look back at the odyssey of Hoover and political conservatism during the Roosevelt and Truman years does much to explain why the middle-class model of the fifties took the shape that it ultimately did.

After leaving the presidency in 1933, Hoover had effectively exiled himself through more or less constant travel for the rest of the decade. Hoover had no doubt that Roosevelt's presidency would end after two terms, and that in the ensuing Republican revival in 1940, the New Deal would be laid to rest. So certain was the former president that the New Deal would be a temporary aberration rather than a lasting change in American life that he made plans to move back into the home he still owned in Washington, DC.[1]

Even though he had turned sixty-five by early 1940, the official retirement age mandated by the new Social Security system, the vigorous Hoover soon busied himself with promoting the Republican Party, with the utterly unrealistic hope of emerging as its presidential nominee in the event of a deadlocked convention. If that plan failed, he would support the presidential candidacy of his protégé Ohio senator Robert Taft. Taft's first job in Washington was as an assistant to Hoover during his stint there overseeing American aid to Europe after World War I. Taft had impressed Hoover as highly intelligent, principled, service oriented, and like-minded in political philosophy. The two men remained close as Taft entered politics and won his Senate seat in 1938. Hoover apparently hoped that Taft could be elected as FDR's successor in 1940 and revive Hoover's agenda of voluntary cooperation to end the Depression, while also avoiding American involvement in World War II and the expansion in federal government power that would inevitably follow. When Wendell Willkie's upstart campaign with its more centrist message prevailed over Taft's at the GOP convention that year, Hoover was deeply disappointed, but not defeated. Even as the federal government mushroomed in size throughout the war years, Hoover refused to give up on his dream of a Taft-led conservative restoration.[2]

Hoover never made the move back to Washington, choosing instead a suite at the Waldorf-Astoria Hotel in New York City, where he would live for the rest of his life. He wanted to associate himself with America's financial capital as he worked to return the country to a much smaller, cheaper, and less activist federal government, both at home and abroad. He employed four full-time secretaries to help him produce a seemingly endless series of letters and public statements intended to spread that message. Hoover spent the rest of the 1940s trying to develop a pool of talented new anti–New Deal Republicans who could advance his agenda, while also working hard to keep himself in the public eye. Among his most important finds, besides Taft, were three men who all achieved national prominence. One was General Douglas MacArthur, whose hostility to Roosevelt's domestic policies, gifts as a public speaker, and war-hero status had led the GOP's old guard to consider him as a possible presidential prospect. Hoover thought MacArthur might make a fine running mate for Taft, but nothing came of that plan in either 1944 or 1948.[3]

The other two Hoover discoveries both achieved notoriety as anti-Communist crusaders. One was an obscure Los Angeles metropolitan area lawyer named Richard Nixon, whom Hoover and his son, Herbert Jr., helped recruit to enter politics. The Hoovers and other wealthy California conservatives in the Pasadena area backed Nixon's pair of successful races against New Dealers serving in Congress. His first victory, in 1946, was over incumbent representative Jerry Voorhis. Four years later, Nixon advanced to the US Senate by beating Congresswoman Helen Gahagan Douglas in a nationally watched race. Nixon had come to national attention during his service on the House Un-American Activities Committee when it investigated New Deal diplomat Alger Hiss for spying and perjury. The third of

Hoover's best-known protégés was Lewis Strauss, a businessman who became a member of the Atomic Energy Commission under Truman, and who played a major role in the development of atomic weapons and nuclear power. Strauss waged a successful campaign to revoke the security clearance of prominent atomic scientist J. Robert Oppenheimer on the grounds of his left-wing associations. As was true for Nixon, Strauss's triumph raised the ire of liberals as much, if not more, as it pleased conservatives.[4]

In addition to his writing and recruiting, Hoover also sought to mold conservative opinion during the 1940s by giving many talks to elite groups on the state of the nation and the world. He found the ideal forum at the Bohemian Grove, a rustic retreat for wealthy West Coast conservatives located in Northern California, which hosted an annual survey of public affairs.[5]

Hoover saw his own star rise as well in the later 1940s, when Harry Truman asked him to head a commission studying ways to reform the federal government's administrative structure. Hoover's effectiveness in that role helped rehabilitate his public reputation, which encouraged him to keep working toward a right-wing Republican revival.[6]

As 1951 opened, Hoover busied himself again on behalf of Bob Taft's presidential aspirations, convinced that 1952 would finally be Taft's year—and by extension Hoover's. At first, the signs appeared promising. Truman's mishandling of the Korean War had by then soured the broad middle of the electorate on his administration. Truman had tragically blundered, raising the stakes in Korea in the elation that followed MacArthur's successful landing at Inchon in mid-September 1950. A more cautious commander in chief would have stuck with the original American military and political objectives, which were to defeat the invading North Korean army and restore the previous government in Seoul. Those missions had largely been accomplished by early October 1950. If the United States had brought its forces home at that time, the Korean conflict would never have escalated beyond a "police action," the official American label that would become more of a misnomer the longer the fighting continued.[7]

Instead, encouraged by an overconfident MacArthur, Truman expanded the original goals to include invading North Korea so as to unite the entire country under a pro-US government. When MacAr-

131

thur's military forces marched northward, however, they provoked a massive Chinese intervention that soon turned the police action into a full-scale war, and eventually a bloody stalemate. The Truman administration's heavy military spending in support of that increasingly unpopular venture produced high wartime inflation that took away most if not all of the wage and salary gains that middle-class Americans were enjoying. The president could not afford to lose the support of that huge voter base.[8]

Other developments undermined Truman's popularity. The public worried that his administration hadn't taken the problem of Soviet espionage seriously enough, which had led to the loss of atomic secrets to the Russians. Also, a pattern of misconduct by several lower-level Truman administration officials, who couldn't resist the temptation to profit personally and illegally from their time in public office, was exposed. Truman's standing in the polls collapsed and, with it, his hopes to run for reelection in 1952. The contest for the Democratic presidential nomination became long and drawn out and threatened to split the party. Thus it seemed, to Hoover, Taft, and other conservative Republicans, that their hopes for a comeback would finally be realized.[9]

As in 1940, however, Taft's bid for the White House in 1952 was derailed by another newcomer to presidential politics. This time it was the much more formidable figure of Dwight D. Eisenhower, the former five-star general who had served as supreme commander of the Allied forces in western Europe in World War II and then as president of Columbia University. Ike, as his friends called him, had been born in Denison, Texas, in 1890 and grew up in the small town of Abilene, Kansas. The single most salient fact about Eisenhower's upbringing was that his family had suffered a sharp drop in social status, from securely middle-class to just barely so, when his father's business failed. Even though that happened long before the Great Depression, living through sudden, lasting downward mobility helped Eisenhower understand the trauma that so many millions of Americans experienced during the 1930s.[10]

Eisenhower's lower-middle-class roots probably explained his unpretentious manner and moral traditionalism, not to mention his lifelong fondness for middlebrow art and culture. His favorite bedtime reading during the 1950s was the western novels of Zane Grey. The middle-class majority found him easily relatable. He was so outwardly friendly that almost no one disliked him, even as he rose from an obscure West Point graduate to the very top of the US Army. The success of the Normandy invasion and the ensuing American military triumphs in western Europe convinced many people of Dwight Eisenhower's leadership ability. He could decide what needed to be done and find people to do it.[11]

After the war ended, Eisenhower appeared to be a natural presidential candidate for either party. He was a household name, well liked and respected. He appeared to have centrist views, a middle-class everyman persona, a lack of a partisan edge, an easy grin, and a voice that sounded like Clark Gable's. But no one knew if he had any interest in politics. IBM head Thomas Watson Sr. recognized Eisenhower's political potential and tried to move him along that path. He arranged to have Columbia University's board of trustees, of which Watson was the most influential member, offer Eisenhower the university's presidency, which he accepted in 1948. Watson's plan was to get Eisenhower out of uniform, introduce him to the right people in New York (in the business world especially), and prepare him to run for president.

Eisenhower was initially unenthusiastic about entering the political fray, but by the fall of 1951, his attitude had changed. By then he was living in Paris, having taken leave from Columbia to become NATO's first supreme military commander. Eisenhower worked tirelessly to convince America's allies that the nation was committed to the defense of western Europe. He was disheartened by Robert Taft's opposition to NATO and disgusted by Taft's support for Joseph McCarthy's demagogic crusade against Communist spies. Eisenhower was dismayed, too, by the mess Truman and MacArthur had made of the Korean conflict, and the way the war had increased anti-Communist hysteria in America. In response to all of those developments, several nationally prominent and moderately conservative Republicans, such as Massachusetts senator Henry Cabot Lodge Jr., Pennsylvania senator James Duff, and Time/Life publisher Henry Luce had begun beseeching Eisenhower to come home and challenge Taft in the upcoming Republican presidential primaries.[12]

Characteristically, Eisenhower opted instead for a middle path. On October 14, 1951, his sixty-first birthday, he wrote a letter to his friend Jim Duff, declaring an adherence to "liberal Republican prin-

ciples" and a willingness to accept the 1952 GOP presidential nomination if it was offered to him. Declining to abandon his NATO duties
prematurely, Eisenhower remained in Paris and in effect gave his
political supporters permission to mount a draft presidential bid. To
Eisenhower's surprise, a highly organized and effective Eisenhower for
President campaign suddenly materialized, seemingly out of nowhere,
due in large part to the backing of New York governor Thomas Dewey.
The campaign focused on New Hampshire, the site of the nation's first
primary, on March 11, 1952. The stunningly decisive victory there by
the pro-Eisenhower forces persuaded the general to come home and
fight for the nomination against the GOP's old guard, which had lined
up solidly behind Bob Taft.[13]

The ensuing effort marked a sort of second coming of Wendell
Willkie and his moderately conservative ideas. Willkie had died in
1944, but the appeal of his critique of the New Deal's excesses had
not. The twin failures of Thomas Dewey's presidential campaigns in
1944 and 1948 also worked to Eisenhower's advantage. Dewey occupied an ill-defined place on the conservative spectrum, somewhere
between Willkie and Taft. He had been able to snare a pair of GOP
presidential nominations but couldn't muster enough support among
influential middle-class voters to win the White House. Dewey firmly
believed that old-guard Republicans in Congress such as Taft had
undermined Dewey's previous presidential campaigns, and that, more
than anything else, persuaded Dewey to throw his support behind
Eisenhower in 1952. He handed the political novice and his band of
eager supporters something close to a fully operational national presidential campaign organization.[14]

Dewey's maneuver evened up the odds between Eisenhower and
the old guard. The intensity of that struggle was apparent in the voter
turnout for the GOP primaries in 1952, which tripled over what it
had been just four years earlier. Legions of newly affluent, middle-
class people responded to the emergence of a Republican presidential candidate they liked by flocking to the polls and making lots of
modest-sized campaign donations. At the end of the process, the 1952
Republican National Convention looked like a replay of 1940, with the
late-starting Eisenhower forces, like Willkie's twelve years earlier, narrowly prevailing over the old guard's choice.[15]

There the parallel ended because in 1952 Eisenhower's run in the general election proved much stronger than Willkie's had. For the first time in twenty years, the GOP's nominee would not be facing a popular Democratic incumbent. The other party's candidate this time was a newcomer to the national political scene, Illinois governor Adlai Stevenson, an unapologetic liberal. Eisenhower's candidacy also benefited from the well-organized campaign machinery that Dewey had provided, and from Eisenhower's own unrivaled national security credentials, both of which had been sorely lacking in Willkie's campaign. Unlike Willkie, Eisenhower and his aides succeeded in uniting the old guard behind his candidacy, by selecting Richard Nixon as his running mate, and by trying hard to mollify Bob Taft, Joe McCarthy, and their supporters by keeping disagreements with them private. At least as important, voters in 1952 appeared more dissatisfied with the status quo than they had been twelve years earlier.[16]

Eisenhower also made good use of the new medium of television, which Stevenson disdained. Rather than try to communicate with the rising middle class mostly through speeches, Eisenhower and his aides opted instead to broadcast short commercials featuring the candidate answering questions of concern to ordinary voters in simple, accessible language. These TV "spots," as they were called, were as straightforward and memorable as the campaign's overall slogan: "I like Ike."[17]

Derided by many upper-middle-class liberal intellectuals as dumbed-down campaign sloganeering, Eisenhower's middlebrow messages, on the consequences of high inflation especially, connected with many lower-middle-class and upper-working-class voters in a way that Stevenson's high-flown oratory could not. So, too, did the amiable general's evident lack of strong partisanship, which opened the door for many centrist voters more accustomed to voting for Democrats to give him a try.[18]

Topping all that off was Eisenhower's evident readiness to handle the ever more demanding job of commander in chief during wartime. Voters turned out in the largest numbers since 1908 and handed the Eisenhower Republicans a landslide victory. So long were Ike's coattails on Election Day in November 1952 that they brought in GOP majorities in both houses of Congress as well. The long-awaited conservative revival had arrived, but not the one Hoover and Taft had wanted.[19]

The moderate sensibilities of the new administration were evident in the men who made up the president's cabinet, most of whom had made their names and reputations in fields other than government, such as business, corporate law, and, in Eisenhower's case, the military and higher education. These people came into their critical new positions with no restrictive allegiance to old-guard Republican ideology. For example, the new Treasury secretary, George Humphrey, a prominent Cleveland industrialist, sympathized with Hoover's and Taft's criticism of heavy federal spending. But Humphrey valued the practical over the theoretical or ideological and went along with leaving the overall size of the federal budget largely unchanged.[20]

The new secretary of state, New York corporate lawyer John Foster Dulles, came out of the Dewey camp and had even less interest in old-guard ideas about foreign policy. Neither did the new defense secretary, General Motors executive Charles E. Wilson, buy into the Hoover-Taft vision of a small national security establishment. He disagreed with the old guard, too, about the sensitive issue of labor unions. Obliged for years to bargain with the big and powerful United Automobile Workers union, Wilson tended to view the revival of a largely nonunion economy of the sort right-wing Republicans favored as both unrealistic and misguided, given what that would have meant for workers' wages and thus their ability to buy the kinds of cars GM made. Although liberal Democrats dismissed Eisenhower's cabinet as "eight millionaires and a plumber" (the latter a reference to the new labor secretary, plumbers' union head Martin Durkin), most ultimately served him well.[21]

Dwight Eisenhower soon became the most broadly appealing political figure of America's predominantly middle-class era, not just for who he was and how he performed as president, but also for what he stood for. Eisenhower-era conservatism, which he sometimes called "Modern Republicanism," had more intellectual substance than many of his liberal critics realized at the time, or later. In domestic policy, that conservatism emphasized doing things as privately, locally, and cheaply as possible, but would not rule out—as Hoover had during his ill-fated presidency—increasing the federal government's role substantially if that was the best option.[22]

Eisenhower Republicans believed in tempering the New Dealers' enthusiasm for bigger government in general and at the federal level in particular. Use and even increase the power of government when necessary, they argued, but rely on the localities and states as much as possible given the vastness of the country and its significant regional differences. Eisenhower Republicans also believed in using the power of government whenever possible to encourage private efforts to address social problems, because in a country such as the United States the private sector was so much bigger and stronger than the public one. Eisenhower Republicans saw mainstream religion as another piece of the puzzle—an institution outside the government that could help improve society by fostering constructive values and charitable endeavors. The administration was comfortable promoting that general idea while advancing no one faith in particular.[23]

Modern Republicans also thought it prudent to scale back the anger and the blame leveled at the wealthy and powerful. They believed that constantly provoking the elites would discourage them from participating in any reform efforts, further stoking social discord. Eisenhower's supporters thought it more constructive to simply promote a shared sense of social responsibility among all Americans. They also feared Democratic attacks on the business community and the wealthy undermined the investor-class confidence on which the prosperity of a market system partly depended. Understanding the harm caused by Truman-era inflationary government spending, the new breed of Republicans favored reducing the size and cost of the federal government, but only gradually, by increasing economic growth, rather than by the more simplistic, painful, and divisive budget-cutting favored by old-guard conservatives in Congress such as Bob Taft.[24]

In foreign policy, Eisenhower conservatives argued that the rise of the Soviet Union and the People's Republic of China necessitated a permanently big national security state, foreign alliances, and aid to allies of the sort Hoover and Taft had staunchly opposed. Yet the Modern Republicans cautioned against an overly broad and expensive containment policy of the sort the Truman administration had developed.[25]

They rejected, too, the calls from the more hawkish right, led by MacArthur, to use military force to roll back Communism in places where it had already taken hold, all too aware that such an aggressive strategy could lead to a catastrophic third world war. If applied cautiously, patiently, and firmly, their reasoning went, the containment policy would gradually weaken Communism, even if that meant some Communist regimes would remain in place for the long term. Moreover, Americans would need to work as closely as possible with allies, and through the United Nations, and be exceedingly careful about where and when to introduce US armed forces abroad. Eisenhower and his people carved out a middle ground concerning the challenge of Soviet and Chinese espionage on the home front, rejecting the Truman administration's inability, or unwillingness, to take the threat seriously, but also deeply unsettled by the opportunistic alarmism of Joseph McCarthy's anti-Communist crusade.[26]

In the view of these new, more centrist Republicans, domestic and foreign policy had become closely connected, given that the national security component of the federal government had become by far its biggest and costliest part. By the 1950s, as they saw it, the US role in the world had expanded so much that most major domestic problems had some national security aspect. For instance, the administration had taken an active role in promoting mainstream religion as part of American life, by doing such things as adding the words *under God* to the Pledge of Allegiance in 1954. Making that effort at home, in the face of the Communists' official atheism, could benefit the United States in the Cold War struggle around the world, especially in such potential East-West hot spots as the Middle East and Southeast Asia. Eisenhower Republicans also felt strongly that conservative Americans would be less resistant to new but necessary government action if they understood the increasingly close connection between matters domestic and foreign.

This penchant for avoiding extreme or polarizing positions, in favor of a commonsense middle ground, resonated strongly with many of those in the growing and ever more prosperous middle class. So pleased were they with Eisenhower's approach to governing that his approval rating in polls averaged 65 percent over his eight years in the White House. The term in vogue then to characterize that degree of support—*consensus*—somewhat overstated the appeal of Eisenhower-era Republicanism, but its broad popularity, with the middle class especially, signaled a sharp decline in the social divisions of the Roosevelt-Truman era. Most critics were to be found above and below economically, and further to the right and left philosophically, but during the middle 1950s those "wing people" became steadily less numerous and less noticeable.[27]

In more concrete terms, Eisenhower Republicanism during the mid-1950s addressed the most serious problems arising out of Truman's last few years as president, while continuing to fuel the growth of the middle class. Eisenhower's credentials as a military leader, Chinese fatigue with the Korean War effort, and, perhaps, fears that Eisenhower might opt to use nuclear weapons to break the stalemate, led to an armistice on July 27, 1953, that ended the fighting. The administration felt able to reduce military spending substantially thereafter, which helped bank the fires of wartime inflation. When the American economy lost steam in the fall of that year, Eisenhower and his aides pushed through Congress an economic stimulus package only slightly different from one the Truman administration had used to fight a recession in 1949–50. By early 1955, the economy was growing rapidly again, without much of a rise in prices, and the Modern Republicans seemed to have exorcised the ghost of Herbert Hoover's inept response to the advent of the Great Depression.[28]

The new Republican administration recognized the practicality of sticking with, and even reinforcing, those of Truman's domestic policies that seemed to be benefiting the nation, even if they ran counter to Republican orthodoxy. In 1954, Eisenhower got Congress to approve an expansion of Social Security that extended coverage to 10.5 million new workers, with an increase in monthly retirement benefits. Congress also went along with the Eisenhower administration's proposals to liberalize and extend unemployment insurance and worker compensation laws during the mid-1950s. Eisenhower supported a rise in the minimum hourly wage from seventy-five to ninety cents and, even though he worried that anything higher would prove inflationary, grudgingly went along when Congress opted to raise it to a dollar, in 1956. Eisenhower also overcame opposition in Congress to the creation of a seaway linking the Atlantic Ocean and the Great Lakes through the St. Lawrence River, something that Truman's administration had unsuccessfully sought. In 1959, Eisenhower helped dedicate the completed project, which lowered shipping costs from the upper Midwest to the Eastern Seaboard and beyond.[29]

Another, much bigger transportation-infrastructure initiative testified to the willingness to support Truman-era goals in key domestic-policy areas. The Federal Aid Highway Act of 1956 brought to fruition an idea Truman's administration had tried for years to move through Congress. The measure would provide 90 percent of the funds needed to construct a comprehensive interstate highway system, with localities expected to contribute the rest. Eisenhower wisely used a national security rationale to persuade Congress to approve the law and its funding, arguing that in the event of a war with the Soviet Union, such a transportation system would be vitally needed to move soldiers and supplies and evacuate targeted cities. Congress responded by appropriating $25 billion to launch this project, the largest sum yet for any primarily domestic program in the country's history. Here was a Modern Republican version of the kind of massive New Deal public works projects of the 1930s.

The resulting transformation in American society was virtually unprecedented. By linking all of the major metropolitan areas of the country and, no less important, city centers to the surrounding suburbs, the emerging highways accelerated the movement of middle-class families beyond city limits. Building the bulk of the new roadways, which totaled over forty thousand miles, would take the rest of the 1950s and all of the 1960s.[30]

The Eisenhower Interstate Highway System, as it eventually came to be known, created thousands of well-paid jobs across America for mostly young-adult male road builders, who, like WPA workers in the 1930s, spent that income in ways that stimulated the economy. Constructing the highway system also added substantially to the growth of the steel, auto, tire, glass, oil, trucking, and tourism industries. As the new highways took shape, they proved immensely popular, especially with the broad middle class, by making trips between city centers and suburbs faster and making vacation travel much easier and more affordable. While not without its problems, as would later become clear, the new Interstate Highway System literally broadened the horizons of postwar Americans, to their lasting satisfaction.[31]

Perhaps even more indicative of Eisenhower's middle path were his three appointments to the US Supreme Court during the mid-1950s. First he named California governor Earl Warren, one of the

140

most liberal-leaning Republicans in the country, as chief justice in the fall of 1953. Then came Associate Justices John Harlan in 1955 and William Brennan, a moderate Democrat, in 1956. John Harlan, although more conservative than either Warren or Brennan, still had no enthusiasm for right-wing activism on the Court of the sort that had provoked a political crisis during the mid-1930s. An apostle of judicial restraint in most areas, Harlan favored allowing the popularly elected branches of government to take the lead in making public policy, while many old-guard Republicans still considered the Court's primary role to be protecting private enterprise, property, and "rights" from government intrusion.[32]

The essentially centrist nature of the Eisenhower-era Court could also be seen in its most famous decision: the landmark school-desegregation case, *Brown v. the Board of Education of Topeka, Kansas*. In its first ruling in the case in May 1954, the Court found that its 1896 decision in *Plessy v. Ferguson*, which found "equal but separate" constitutionally permissible, to have been erroneous, at least as applied to public schools. The initial decision offered no guidance on just how the ruling might be implemented. In a second ruling a year later, known as *Brown II*, the Court found the Constitution did not require an immediate end to dual school systems based on race, but only that school districts move with "deliberate speed" toward that end. That legalistic term suggested an incremental approach to addressing social problems characteristic of Eisenhower and his primarily middle-class supporters.[33]

The lack of steady progress in school desegregation in most places until after 1968, though, illustrated the weakness of that approach on issues of race. So, too, did suburbia's continuing development as an almost entirely white phenomenon, which increased the number of children attending essentially all-white schools. Here was an area where America's ongoing transformation into a more middle-class nation seemed more exclusive than inclusive, with consequences that would affect generations to come.[34]

Coming as they did after years of simmering resentment, the two *Brown* rulings helped embolden the black community to mount a more forceful challenge to the institutionalized racism of the Jim Crow South. The most significant such effort began in Montgomery, Alabama, on December 1, 1955, when seamstress Rosa Parks refused to give up her seat near the front of a city bus to a white person and was arrested for violating the bus company's policy on racially segregated seating. Her protest helped spark the well-known Montgomery bus boycott, under the inspired leadership of the young Reverend Martin Luther King Jr. A year of protests backstopped by an ultimately successful legal challenge led to the end of Jim Crow rules on Montgomery's buses, but also to a lasting reduction in white ridership. That shift undermined broad public support in the city for mass transit, on which blacks depended more than whites. Thus, segregation proved so entrenched and polarizing that it remained stubbornly resistant to the moderate, incremental approach that Modern Republicans took on domestic policy.[35]

The Eisenhower administration's similarly centrist approach to foreign policy during the middle 1950s was somewhat more successful, but not entirely so. Eisenhower accepted a somewhat smaller army after the Korean War, which saved money, but he chose to compensate for that loss in conventional military strength by supporting an increase in the size of the country's nuclear arsenal. This entailed more H-bomb tests and the development of ever faster and more accurate bombers and missiles to deliver them. The premise was that Eisenhower's vast military experience and credibility as a national security strategist, along with more numerous and destructive weapons, would deter Communist aggression and keep the peace. That he did, and it was the single greatest achievement of his presidency.[36]

Other Eisenhower foreign-policy initiatives fell short. He didn't get far in his efforts to start arms-control negotiations with the Soviets. Such talks had become necessary, he felt, to head off a missile race that would prove enormously costly and ultimately imperil the entire planet. Eisenhower's decision to use the CIA as a kind of private presidential army to wage the Cold War also brought with it pluses and minuses. CIA-backed coups in Iran in 1953 and Guatemala in 1954 helped head off the possibility of Soviet infiltration, but installed pro-American regimes that would, in the years to come, alienate the populations of those countries.[37]

Eisenhower's policy in Indochina also produced mixed results, some of which would have disastrous long-term consequences. He decided against introducing American troops to rescue the French colonialists in Vietnam, but won aid from Congress to prop up the anti-Communist regime in South Vietnam while opposing elections that would likely have reunited the country under the rule of North Vietnam's Communist and nationalist leader Ho Chi Minh. The United States steered clear of Indochina for a while after that, but soon enough, a North Vietnamese–backed insurgency arose in the South, with the goal of reuniting the country by force.[38]

Eisenhower's attempts to turn down the heat of anti-Communist hysteria at home similarly brought about mixed results. The president could not abide Joseph McCarthy, the rabid anti-Communist crusader, but Eisenhower's efforts to bring the outspoken senator to heel represented something of a missed opportunity to stand up for democratic ideals. Eisenhower knew that McCarthy believed that any publicity was good publicity, so any public confrontation would only give McCarthy more time in the spotlight. Instead, Eisenhower and his aides worked behind the scenes to undermine McCarthy and in effect compelled the Senate to formally condemn him once his recklessness finally alienated the public in 1954. The strategy ultimately contributed to defanging McCarthy, but Eisenhower never gave a major speech about the dangers of irresponsible investigations of supposed political dissidents and how at odds with the American traditions of free speech and the rule of law McCarthy's tactics had been.[39]

Whatever blemishes were on Eisenhower's record in his first term as president paled in comparison with its successes, especially in the eyes of the broad middle class. When he came up for reelection in 1956, voters handed him an even bigger victory, once again over Adlai Stevenson. That second landslide was tinged with disappointment for some old-guard Republicans, who had expected "their" national ticket to usher in GOP congressional majorities as it had four years earlier. It seemed that voter contentment was a bit of a double-edged sword for Republicans. The Democrats had won narrow majorities in the House and the Senate in the midterm election two years earlier, a reaction to the post–Korean War recession. Voters were in such a good mood by the fall of 1956 that they chose to reward incumbents regardless of party affiliation. More incumbents seeking reelection to public office in the United States won that year than ever before in American history.[40]

The administration was buoyed by a recent economic upsurge, although critics complained, then and later, that the boom had mostly to do with military spending. They argued that money for the Pentagon had crowded out needed domestic spending, compelling America to live with puny social programs when compared with most western European countries, but that objection was too simplistic. America had put significant programs in place during the New Deal, such as Social Security and farm price supports, which continued to flourish during Eisenhower's administration. So, too, did other, less obviously public kinds of programs, such as housing and transportation.[41]

The biggest economic and social shift of the era—the emergence of mass suburbia—was driven by vast subsidies via the tax code, most significantly the tax deduction of home-mortgage interest payments. That tax break made possible unprecedented amounts of private home construction, rather than publicly funded apartment complexes of the sort favored in much of the rest of the developed world. The new Interstate Highway System—another cornerstone of suburban expansion—created a new kind of public transportation infrastructure, albeit one that depended on the private ownership of cars for its use, unlike the urban mass transit systems preferred in Europe. Even the funding for that massive system of roadways was less obviously "public" than those European systems because it depended so heavily on taxes on gasoline, tires, and trucks, which were paid by users, rather than on levies on the citizenry as a whole.[42]

The tax code also subsidized the baby boom by granting generous exemptions for parents raising children. Heavy government spending on new school construction for all of these new kids was another kind of government-assistance program, although most people didn't see it that way. The GI Bill, which assisted with the purchase of so many homes while providing educational and health-care subsidies, could be considered part of social spending, too, but of a more privatized form, given that veterans' access to these benefits depended on individual choices.[43]

The emerging American model of predominantly private medical insurance also depended far less on the national government than many of those in Europe and assumed that the majority of people were employed by some larger business entity that would provide that fringe benefit. The private citizen had to bear little, if anything, of the direct expense if he or she worked for an employer such as that. The government had played a decisive role in bringing about this privatized model of health insurance after World War II, throwing its support behind labor union demands for those kinds of benefits, and by offering subsidies to private insurers to help lower the cost of the health insurance they offered to employers and the public. But the system was of limited value to those Americans who worked outside the corporate structure or weren't part of organized labor or had incomes so low that they simply couldn't afford to pay for their own insurance.[44]

Critics who underestimated the size of the American welfare state of the 1950s failed to recognize the large number of Americans who participated in it indirectly, just as defenders sometimes missed how many were entirely excluded. The male-breadwinner model meant that most women and children gained access to the system as dependents, via husbands and fathers, rather than in their own right. In America, government programs supported families, which included a lot more people than just the men who headed them. On the other hand, champions of the American approach sometimes overlooked the big gaps in coverage, especially in the bottom fifth of the income distribution, where few of the jobs typically held by men provided any substantial benefits.

Again, geography and race were determining factors. The economies of the mostly nonunion South and Mountain West offered many fewer well-paid jobs with benefits to ordinary men. Relatively few of those kinds of jobs were available to people of color, no matter where they lived. And there were other gaps, too. As had been true since the 1930s, the expensive federally funded programs of the 1950s benefited middle-class families the most, rather than unmarried adults or orphaned children.

Through the fall of 1957, however, the fraction of all Americans living in middle-class families located in the heavily populated industrial states of the Northeast, Midwest, and West Coast steadily rose. Thus, a substantial majority of the population for the first time enjoyed heavy support from the uniquely designed American system of social insurance programs.[45]

145

• • •

As the middle class continued to expand, so did its influence over popular culture in all its various forms. By far the most consequential cultural development in the 1950s was the arrival of TV as the most powerful form of mass communication in history. Radio had emerged during the 1920s, when income inequality was growing, and almost half of the population was poor or nearly so. During the Depression, the poor and the almost poor made up a majority. But TV entered mainstream American life just as income equality peaked, proffering a healthy level of security and comfort to most of those in the middle three-fifths of the population. Consequently, TV became overwhelmingly middle class, child-and-family-centered in its formative years.[46]

In contrast to the European, statist model, in which a government agency produced broadcast programming and users paid fees for it, American television relied, as radio had, on private networks to produce programming, and on advertising to pay for it. With the number of middle-class families and incomes growing so fast, companies did whatever they could to tap into that expanding base of potential consumers. Accordingly, the commercial sponsors who paid for TV programming insisted upon shows that would attract that cohort of newly prosperous middle-class viewers. The Federal Communications Commission reinforced that demand by pressuring TV network executives to keep off the air anything (and anyone) that might seriously offend the new middle-class majority. The content restrictions developed by the TV networks in response closely resembled the film code. Beginning in December 1950, program content was further limited when an industry blacklist of suspected radicals went into effect.[47]

Thus, this new and improved medium, which its creators had long thought of as "radio with pictures," was mostly used to convey middlebrow messages of the sort that resonated with comfortably mainstream, middle-class people. The phenomenon prompted cultural critic Richard Schickel to observe that early television was "essentially the medium of the marginally affluent." As American households raced to acquire TV sets, the new medium quickly became more powerful and ubiquitous than radio, film, theater, magazines, or newspapers. By 1957, more than 80 percent of American families possessed at least one TV set, up from just 26 percent in 1950, and the standardized portrait of white, middle-class family life that was television's bread and butter had begun to insinuate itself into the nation's collective unconscious.[48]

One unexpected and remarkable aspect of fifties popular culture, and TV in particular, was the way performers and artists from well outside the mainstream could be transformed into avatars of middle-class normality. One need look no further than the most watched TV show of the 1950s, *I Love Lucy*. Its stars, Lucille Ball and Desi Arnaz, were hardly typical of Middle America. Even though she had grown up in Jamestown, New York, a place so far north and west in New York State as to be culturally part of the Midwest, Ball had migrated to Hollywood, where she lived with a radically leftist substitute father figure. She registered as a Communist in 1936 to please him near the end of his life. Ball married Arnaz, a Cuban musician and bandleader. He had grown up in a louche, upper-class Cuban world.[49]

The audience, however, didn't concern itself with their backgrounds. The couple's expressive faces, Lucille Ball's gift for slapstick comedy, and Desi Arnaz's charm helped catapult them to fame. In the show, they appeared as Lucy and Ricky Ricardo, the wholesome, youthful, and loving New York City couple whose misadventures— Lucy's especially—made millions of ordinary Americans laugh out loud, week after week, for six TV seasons from 1951 to 1957. Dwight and Mamie Eisenhower liked the show so much that they invited Lucy and Desi to dinner at the White House.[50]

Each week's episode followed the same basic premise: Lucy's search to escape the tedium of domesticity or to assert herself in some other way would land her in some kind of trouble, from which she would be rescued by Ricky, their friends Fred and Ethel Mertz (who lived upstairs), or some guest star. The messages of the show, so popular with middle-class male breadwinners of that era, and many of their wives, too, were that Lucy's various quests were misguided, and that women were emotional and impractical—and so needed the steadying influence of their husbands and friends to stay out of trouble.[51]

The reality for Lucy and Desi was different. Lucille Ball was a creative force, a keenly intelligent woman who served as the real producer and director of *I Love Lucy*, as well as the stabilizing figure in the Arnaz family. It was she who finally put an end to the show that had made her famous by divorcing Desi, whose alcoholism and infidelity had left both Lucy and their children damaged. Filming of the show's final episode literally ended in tears, in marked contrast to the lighthearted entertainment it had always offered. But the sadder side of *I Love Lucy* remained invisible to most viewers, during its heyday and after, when it became one of the most rerun series in TV history.[52]

Not all middle-class people then or later wanted to watch fictionalized versions of what they already knew, so not every 1950s show was set in a middle-class home. In its early years, TV experimented with a wide range of viewing options. War movies, westerns, sports, and police dramas, set in male-dominated milieus, were popular with middle-class males. Middle-class women were offered daytime soap operas that revolved around romantic and domestic challenges, as well as more serious fare such as *Matinee Theater*, which presented weekday dramas. Also on air were popular prime-time shows about unmarried professional women such as *Our Miss Brooks* and *My Little Margie*. Shows such as *Playhouse 90* presented plays that tried to bring the immediacy and intensity of the theater to the many millions who seldom, if ever, attended in person. For young children, some shows educated as they entertained, such as *Howdy Doody*; *Kukla, Fran and Ollie*; and *The Mickey Mouse Club*; as well as gentle comedies and dramas that were mostly about friendship, often involving lovable pets, such as *Lassie*. Boys in particular tended to like *Superman*, a domesticated version of the earlier comic strip and radio show, in which graphic violence was now minimized and the central character managed to fight crime while remaining mild mannered.[53]

And *for the whole family*, to use a popular fifties phrase, there were variety shows starring the likes of Jack Benny, Milton Berle, Sid Caesar and Imogene Coca, Ed Sullivan, and Lawrence Welk; religious-themed programs such as mainline Protestant Norman Vincent Peale and Ruth Peale's *What's Your Trouble?* and Catholic bishop Fulton J. Sheen's *Life Is Worth Living*; as well as situation comedies such as *The Adventures of Ozzie and Harriet*. Until the later 1950s, even the TV shows about family life were not primarily set in the suburbs. *The Honeymooners*, whose ratings in the mid-1950s were second only to *I Love Lucy*'s, was also set in an urban apartment building, and the popular *Lassie* on a farm.[54]

It's not that television producers and programmers were afraid to depict unusual characters or situations, or to address more complicated subjects. They knew they needed to keep viewers interested and not merely comforted. The problem was their inability to break out of their relentlessly white, middle-class, and middlebrow mindset. Viewers did see depictions of artists, intellectuals, the wealthy, the poor, and other kinds of people that Middle Americans tended to consider exceptional and even exotic, but mostly through the lens of white, middle-class perceptions. The more nonconformist—outside the new middle class—a character was, the more likely he or she would be presented as a stereotype or caricature. Thus, beatniks were depicted reciting gloomy poetry that did not rhyme, foreigners in the stereotypical dress of whatever country they were from, and the wealthy as country-club clichés.[55]

These presentations may have made for gentle comedy, but they were not harmless. The dominance of this middle-class perspective on television may have been most insidious when it came to black people. Contrary to what many think today, African Americans appeared regularly on TV during the 1950s (though seldom in commercials), usually in the kinds of lower-level service jobs in which the heavily white middle class were most used to seeing them. Whites and blacks living outside the South had little social interaction in that era, which always makes it easier for marginalization and stereotyping to take root. Pressure from sponsors didn't make the situation any better. They needed to reach as wide a national audience as possible, which meant accommodating the biases of southern segregationists in general and the southern affiliates of the major TV networks in particular. The short-lived appearance of NBC's *The Nat King Cole Show* in 1956–57 is a case in point. Some southern affiliates of the network refused to carry the program, which drove down ratings enough to curtail sponsorship, costing NBC $400,000 and forcing the show's cancellation after only one season. No matter that Cole, a popular and talented black performer, had studiously avoided anything controversial. Television stations and networks, and their sponsors, decided that America wasn't ready for a black TV star.[56]

Just as rare in those heady early days of TV were depictions of women outside of familial roles. Most middle-class people in the

1950s had little firsthand experience with highly educated or profes-
sionally successful women, and the resulting misconceptions were
mirrored in what few TV shows broadcast stories about these women.
Perry Mason's assistant, Della Street, played by Barbara Hale, was a
case in point. More a paralegal, the kind of job open to women trained
as lawyers then, Street was depicted essentially as a secretary because
that's how middle-class people imagined women in an office setting.[57]

None of this is meant to suggest that fifties TV, or popular culture
in general, was entirely lacking in nuance or sophistication. The culture of that period could be intelligent, sensitive, and entertaining,
but primarily in its depiction of unexceptional middle-class people and
their problems. The popular media understood those kinds of Americans best and sympathized with them the most. Take the memorable
drama *Marty*, which first appeared on television in 1953 and was then
remade as a major motion picture. The central character of the story,
by the playwright Paddy Chayefsky, is a bored and lonely butcher,
played in the TV version by Rod Steiger and on the big screen by
Ernest Borgnine. A good person but overweight and plain-looking,
Marty is still living at home with his overbearing mother, while dream-
ing of finding love and fulfillment elsewhere. He meets a woman at a
dance hall, played by Nancy Marchand on TV and Betsy Blair in the
film, and the two lonely outsiders come to understand each other. But
she is somewhat homely, and their budding romance is opposed by
Marty's mother and friends, which puts his core values to the test.[58]

Although sentimental in places, the film version presented those
problems, so familiar to average people, with such effectiveness and
grace as to win *Marty* four Academy Awards in 1955, including Best
Picture, Best Director, Best Actor, and Best Screenplay. So stunned
was the normally loquacious Chayefsky that his simple but moving
story about ordinary people had won such extraordinary acclaim that
he accepted his Oscar in silence. Here was a leading example of what
the creators of fifties popular culture did memorably and well.[59]

Print media reflected the same dominance of white, middle-class,
and middlebrow perspectives. In this era *Peanuts* cartoonist Charles
Schulz rose to fame. Although he had grown up in a middle-class Midwestern family, Schulz, like Lucille Ball, was hardly a typical product
of that environment. A depressed loner, he got little affection from his

parents. When Schulz appeared at his father Carl's barbershop immediately after returning from World War II, Carl did not come forward
to greet his son, preferring instead to keep cutting the customer's hair.
So glum was Charles that he told his bride, Joyce Halverson, at the
start of their honeymoon in April 1951, "I don't think I can ever be
happy." Her unspoken mental response reflected the determined optimism and intense commitment to marriage of the era: "Well, I'll just
make you happy."[60]

The driven and confident Schulz believed he could find national
success as a cartoonist. He first tried his hand at strips that featured
adults. When newspapers rejected that work as insufficiently original
and suggested he draw a strip with children as the central characters,
Schulz created his now-iconic *Peanuts* gang. In his words, "Kids finally
sold. So I just kept on drawing kids."[61] (All of them at first were white
and middle class.) United Feature Syndicate formally inaugurated the
strip on October 2, 1950, and as the baby boom exploded, so did the
potential audience. That fundamental demographic shift, when combined with Schulz's gifts as a graphic artist and his perceptive observa-
tions about middle class family life in postwar America—disguised as
the insights of the young—soon made the strip a hit. By 1957, *Peanuts*
was reaching countless millions of readers with its wry wisdom, and
Schulz was on his way to becoming the most commercially successful
and influential cartoonist in history.[62]

The popular vision of postwar America became increasingly con-
stricted, but continued to foster the kind of important literary and
artistic backlash that had begun with Mailer and others. In 1952,
the African American writer Ralph Ellison published *Invisible Man*.
Ellison took out his frustrations at the marginalization of African
Americans in a novel that became a bestseller and was immediately
recognized as a classic. Sophisticated readers were impressed, but
what Ellison had to say reached a far smaller audience than it might
have because it was presented in book form, rather than via TV. Even
so, the power of his message only grew as the onslaught of middlebrow
culture intensified, and as black artists, intellectuals, and writers were
consistently ignored and often persecuted. Internationally acclaimed
singer and actor Paul Robeson was one prominent example, and the
distinguished historian W. E. B. Du Bois another. Robeson found him-

self under more or less constant government surveillance for his anti–Cold War views and radically leftist associations. Du Bois, an avowed Marxist, experienced much the same treatment from the government. Both men were pushed to the margins of their respective professions during the heyday of McCarthy and the blacklist. Many African Americans still wanted to hear and see them, but not many members of the heavily white middle-class majority did.[63]

More mainstream black artists such as Louis Armstrong adapted to the times, but in so doing occasionally helped perpetuate racial stereotypes rather than undermine them. In the 1956 film *High Society*, a mediocre musical remake of *The Philadelphia Story*, Armstrong appears in the underdeveloped role of a musical Cupid. The part as written obliged Armstrong to behave at times like a grinning, eye-rolling black musician of the sort southern segregationists would have liked. Armstrong's genius as a musician came through loud and clear, but his character was a comic novelty that did not serve blacks well.[64]

Popular music more generally in the early-to-mid 1950s was dominated by ballad singers such as Tony Bennett, Nat King Cole, Perry Como, Rosemary Clooney, Doris Day, Ethel Merman, Mary Martin, Patti Page, and Frank Sinatra, who sang songs about love and life that were easy for middle-class people to enjoy. Fifties musicals also catered to the same audience with accessible lyrics and popular dance forms that everyone could appreciate. One memorably fine example of that phenomenon was the 1952 film *Singin' in the Rain,* in which stars Gene Kelly, Donald O'Connor, and Debbie Reynolds brilliantly combined a plot about Hollywood's transition from silent to talking pictures with song and tap dance. Musicals flourished on Broadway—success that depended less on costly sets and production values than on story lines and catchy tunes that could become popular hits beyond the stage and featured song-and-dance numbers of the sort popular with middle-class Americans. Financing relied not on smaller, upper-income audiences paying high ticket prices, but on bigger audiences of middle-class theatergoers buying less expensive tickets: a more affordable approach pervasive in fifties popular culture, whether on TV, in film, or onstage, leading to a wide viewership. The best of the resulting productions, such as *Guys and Dolls*, *The King and I*, and *The Pajama Game*, became staples of American musical theater.[65]

Even the mass culture produced by Hollywood and the pop-music industry had unexpected outliers. Three of those outliers—two actors from mid-America and a singer from the Deep South—proved to be revolutionaries, and their arrival caused an irreversible pivot in the nature of popular entertainment. Marlon Brando grew up in Omaha, Nebraska, the son of a conventional but overbearing father whose views and ambitions Brando rejected. He essentially played a motorcycle-riding version of himself in the 1953 film *The Wild One*. The movie offered up a raw, gut-level challenge to the servile conformity of the times, without offering any alternative. Brando's character sums that all up when someone asks him what he's rebelling against: "Whaddya got?"[66]

Indiana native James Dean endured the deeply traumatic death of his mother from uterine cancer when he was only nine years old, after which his father shipped him off to live with relatives. Like Brando, Dean could not relate to the celebration of middle-class family life so common in the 1950s. He made only three films, but in two of them indelibly portrayed youths alienated from mainstream fifties values even if they could not come up with a viable alternative. Dean's characters especially challenged the fifties emphasis on stability and security in roles he played with haunting power. His most memorable performance was in *Rebel Without a Cause*, which appeared in theaters in 1955 shortly after Dean's death from a car-racing accident. The title echoes Brando's line from *The Wild One*. In *Rebel*, Dean appeared as an adolescent who rejected the cult of middle-class domesticity represented by his father in a way that hit home with young people who resisted the notion that that was the one and best way to live.[67]

Elvis Presley grew up poor in the small town of Tupelo, Mississippi, and blended elements of the black music tradition of that region with country and gospel music into a unique blues-inspired rock-and-roll sound. Elvis performed with an earthiness and overt sexuality that shocked the older generations of middle-class Americans. Everything about him seemed to fly in the face of the heavy-handed and even repressive moral traditionalism that defined the era.[68]

All three performers represented an implicit critique of society's expectations of quiet, cautious conformity, which may have helped free many people from one set of problems but often did so at considerable cost to their individuality and personal freedom. Brando and Dean especially also questioned the simplistically positive view of middle-class family life that struck them as so foreign to their upbringings as to be essentially false.[69]

The Sindt and Perkins families in their own ways experienced the fallout from those trade-offs, as well as the disconnect between the ideal and the real in mid-1950s America. Beatrice couldn't understand her two daughters' resistance to her focus on getting them married early to high-status men who could guarantee their security. She was similarly frustrated by her kids' lack of enthusiasm for the mainstream religion that played such an important role in her own life. Beatrice had sent her daughter Carol to the local Episcopal high school as a day student, hoping that would help the girl get a fine education, entrée into the world of high-status people in the Davenport area, and a daily dose of mainline Protestant religious instruction. But Carol didn't go for the country-clubish young men her mother envisioned for her. They tended to like cocktails—Carol was a teetotaler—and they were too forward for her taste. Carol also found religious worship at school much too formal and intimidating. Although a rebel in her own way, she was so morally traditional that she saw little need to go to church to get that kind of message, or to watch Norman Vincent Peale or Fulton Sheen on TV, as her mother liked to do.

George Perkins also came up against the beginnings of what would eventually become known as the generation gap. His son, George Jr., whom everyone called Bud, had a reckless streak totally unlike anything in his father's personality. The Korean War broke out in the year Bud turned twenty, but rather than allow the draft to put such a daredevil in harm's way there, George Sr. persuaded him to enlist in the Rhode Island National Guard, whose units were generally sent to Europe. Even that sensible plan backfired when Bud volunteered to join a bomb-demolition team in Germany, for both the high pay and excitement. Although never seriously injured, Bud still got into trouble. He quarreled with his commanding officer and briefly went AWOL, before reluctantly giving in to heavy pressure from his father to return to duty and apologize. By the time Bud came home from Europe, he had lost interest in settling down in Providence and going to work for the state, as his father had wanted. Instead, Bud married his childhood sweetheart, and the two of them promptly decamped for Denver, where the GI Bill and his new bride helped put Bud through college.

As these glimpses into the lives of Beatrice and George show, a society and culture built around the prevailing middle-class model didn't leave a lot of room for people who thought outside the box. But up until the late 1950s, these situations rarely registered in the public consciousness. What changed toward the end of the decade was that these social and cultural anomalies came much more out in the open. The increased visibility of outliers and iconoclasts and all kinds of independent thinkers took most middle-class people by surprise, but also began to give traction to the idea that alternative choices were indeed possible.[70]

CHAPTER 7

Cracks in the Foundation

The faintest cracks started to appear in the new American system in the final years of the 1950s. Even as the cracks grew deeper and more threatening, they remained virtually imperceptible to the contented white, middle-class majority. No single crisis threatened the survival of the social order that had taken shape in America, but beginning in the fall of 1957, a series of unforeseen issues, both foreign and domestic but all closely related, were causing insidious fissures that would threaten America's complacency.[1]

The United States had entered a twilight zone between the heyday of Eisenhower's America and the coming turbulence of the 1960s. Periods of cultural transition can be both fascinating and challenging to live through, and that was certainly true of the late 1950s. New ideas were bubbling up to the surface, often finding expression from people who felt neither satisfied by, nor comfortable with, the middle-class model. A growing chorus of voices challenged the existing order to reform itself. Whether that was even possible was another question entirely, given the smug satisfaction with the status quo of the postwar moderate majority.[2]

Perhaps the most serious problems facing the United States in the late 1950s were in foreign policy. Chief among them was the arms race spawned by the Cold War. In the new world order virtually any conflict on any continent could reverberate in the greater ongoing hostility between the United States, its allies, and the Soviet bloc. As the 1950s came to a close, that arms race took a more dangerous turn, as both sides began to develop intercontinental ballistic missiles (ICBMs) to deliver nuclear warheads. Much faster than bombers and incapable of being recalled, ICBMs had greater potential to trigger an accidental nuclear exchange, given the limitations of radar tracking systems. If airplanes were the main means of delivering nuclear weapons, there was time to make certain the ominous images on radar were actually enemy attackers, and time for military and political leaders to decide how to respond. Once ICBMs came online, reaction times would drop to minutes, with terrifying consequences.

Making matters worse was the production of more hydrogen bombs, with roughly 750 times the explosive power of the atomic bombs dropped on Hiroshima and Nagasaki in 1945. By the late 1950s, the Cold War's two leading powers appeared to be on the verge of producing nuclear weapons in such numbers and with such destructive power—and with delivery mechanisms so fast and accurate—as to threaten humanity's survival.[3]

The first major sign of public concern with that situation appeared in April 1957, when a British publication called the *Sunday Graphic* published a story in four installments entitled "The Last Days on Earth." Its author, Nevil Shute, expanded the series into a novel published later that year called *On the Beach*. The book's title referred both to a Royal Navy phrase meaning "retired from service" and to a line about the end of days from a T. S. Eliot poem entitled "The Hollow Men." Shute wrote about the waning of what was left of human existence in the aftermath of a nuclear war, as radiation increasingly sickened and killed those still alive. *On the Beach* was set in Australia, driving home the book's message that no one and no place was safe from the consequences of a nuclear war between the United States and the USSR. The book struck a chord with informed readers around the world. That sense of danger helped inspire the creation of a new pacifist group, the Committee for a Sane Nuclear Policy (SANE), in 1957, and prompted Hollywood to make *On the Beach* into a major motion picture featuring bankable big-name stars Gregory Peck and Ava Gardner. The film flopped when it appeared in 1959 and lost $700,000, as the typical middle-class moviegoer of the time simply wanted no part of such a depressing story. While the alarm was being raised, it wasn't clear how many were hearing it or wanted to. The most fundamental problem about the intensifying arms race was how difficult it was to persuade large numbers of people that the danger it had created was real and demanded attention.[4]

What did get the attention of the American public was the launch of the first man-made satellite on October 4, 1957, because it was the handiwork of the Soviet Union. Roughly the size of a beach ball, *Sputnik* (Russian for "little moon") orbited the Earth every ninety-two minutes, emitting a beep that shortwave radios could pick up from Earth below. The Soviets' success in launching *Sputnik* spooked many Americans. It suggested that the USSR had moved ahead of the United States in rocketry, which had ominous implications for the emerging nuclear missile race, and in putting up spy satellites that could take pictures from above with high-powered cameras. Americans grew even more alarmed when a public test of the new American Vanguard rocket in December 1957 ended in a fiery failure that press critics labeled "Sputternik," "Flopnik," and "Stay-putnik." From that moment on, the American public was obsessed with catching up with the Soviets, increasing pressure on the Eisenhower administration to spend more money on missile and satellite development.[5]

Eisenhower, with his vast experience with military and national security issues, and access to secret intelligence on the state of the Soviet missile program, recognized that *Sputnik* was more of a propaganda ploy than a major technological breakthrough. But leading opposition Democrats such as Senators Henry Jackson of Washington, Lyndon Johnson of Texas, John Kennedy of Massachusetts, and Stuart Symington of Missouri argued the Soviet advances in rocket and satellite technology represented a genuine threat to America, a view supported by some military leaders such as Army Chief of Staff Maxwell Taylor, and some prominent Republicans, such as New York's Nelson Rockefeller. That alarmism spread to the general population, compelling Eisenhower to raise the number of ICBMs under development, though not the amount of overall military spending, and to establish the National Aeronautics and Space Administration (NASA). Rather than pushing for a slowdown in the terrifying arms race, Americans in the late 1950s seemed only to care about winning it. The generation that had come of age during the Munich conference of 1938 and World War II tended to think that the best way to promote peace was through military strength, which made less sense in the nuclear era than it might have fifteen years earlier. Most Americans, like their counterparts in the Soviet Union, simply couldn't get their heads around the idea that too much military strength could actually make the world more dangerous.[6]

Eisenhower and Soviet leader Nikita Khrushchev, much more aware of the potential cost and danger of a missile race, tried at times to head it off by promoting arms-control talks and by seeking a friendlier relationship between their respective nations. Their first agreement, in November 1958, was a voluntary halt to aboveground nuclear weapons testing. This nuclear testing moratorium could slow down the arms race significantly if it could be made permanent by a test-ban treaty; new weapons of such magnitude could not be deployed without testing. It promised to make the world safer in a different way, too, by limiting the radioactive material that the tests released into the atmosphere.[7]

When Khrushchev visited the United States in September 1959, satisfying a long-held desire to see the country while also hoping to establish a personal relationship with Eisenhower, it seemed that the Cold War was on the cusp of a genuine thaw. That sense of progress proved fleeting, however, when a superpower summit meeting in Paris eight months later ended prematurely with a Soviet walkout. Their righteous anger was perhaps not entirely unjustified. On the eve of the summit, the United States had sent a U-2 spy plane over the Soviet Union's most secret missile development areas with the goal of ascertaining how many ICBMs were operational there. The Soviets succeeded in shooting down the plane on May 1, 1960, and then caught Eisenhower in a lie about it thereafter. Under pressure from Soviet military leaders to distrust the Americans' sincerity regarding arms-control negotiation, Khrushchev abandoned his more conciliatory approach. So as 1960 came to a close, the two sides seemed further apart than ever and redoubled their efforts to develop more effective means of mass destruction.[8]

Of the many local or regional hot spots around the world with the potential to escalate into a much bigger confrontation, six in particular stood out: Berlin, Cuba, Indochina, Taiwan, the Middle East, and Africa. Berlin became a focal point of renewed tension because West Germany's economic recovery had by then encouraged an increasing number of East Germany's most ambitious, enterprising, and educated citizens to slip out of East Germany into West Berlin. Determined to put an end to that, Khrushchev issued an ultimatum in November

1958: unless the United States withdrew its forces from West Berlin by May 27, 1959, the Soviets would sign a treaty with East Germany authorizing it to deny American forces ground access to the city. When the Eisenhower administration refused, the deadline passed without Soviet action. Eisenhower had called Khrushchev's bluff, but concern grew that the often erratic Soviet leader might raise the issue again, returning both sides to a path that could lead to World War III.[9]

In Cuba, the overthrow on January 1, 1959, of the corrupt regime headed by dictator Fulgencio Batista greatly increased concern in official Washington over what would come next. Rebel leader Fidel Castro claimed that his new government would not be Communist, but Castro's brother Raúl, who played a key supporting role in the new regime, seemed to be an avowed Marxist committed to turning Cuba into a country more like the Soviet Union than the United States. Relations between the Castro government and the Eisenhower administration worsened once the Castros and their supporters confirmed the worst American fears and began confiscating the property of wealthy Cubans and American businesses. In short order, Fidel Castro signed trade agreements with the Soviet Union, criticized "Yankee imperialists," and established diplomatic relations with Mao's revolutionary government in China. The presence of an American military base on the island at Guantánamo Bay, and Cuba's proximity to Florida, heightened concern that the island could become the next major Cold War flash point.

Unable to turn the Castro brothers around, the Eisenhower administration responded by prohibiting the importation of Cuban sugar (which was central to the island's economy), banning American exports to Cuba, and cutting American economic aid. By 1960, Eisenhower and his aides had also begun to seriously consider an armed invasion to oust the new Cuban government, despite the likelihood that it would face the same kind of difficult challenge that Batista's regime had against Castro's sizable and battle-tested guerrilla forces on their mountainous home turf. If American military forces invaded Cuba and the Castros took the Soviets up on their promised military aid, the stage would be set for another localized confrontation that could escalate into global war. Even if that doomsday scenario could be avoided, an American-backed attempt to overthrow the Castro government could destabilize the Western Hemisphere, alienating other Latin American countries that would resent America throwing its weight around.[10]

In another part of the globe loomed the increasingly violent trajectory of Indochina, as the North Vietnamese–backed insurgency gained ground in South Vietnam. By the late 1950s, Ho Chi Minh's government in the North had begun moving men and supplies into South Vietnam via a route through neighboring Laos. Unless the so-called Ho Chi Minh Trail could be disrupted, Eisenhower and his aides believed, the growing insurgency would endanger South Vietnam's survival as a pro-Western "nation."[11]

The Soviets appeared to be trying to help Ho, making that situation even more urgent. But cutting that supply route would likely require the introduction of substantial numbers of US armed forces into Laos, which bordered not just Vietnam but also the People's Republic of China (PRC). US national security experts naturally feared that Mao might respond as he had in Korea, thereby precipitating a second US-China war. Even more worrisome, in some ways, was the progress of China's nuclear weapons development program. Mao could soon have such weapons at his disposal to use against American forces in Laos. If the United States did nothing, South Vietnam would likely collapse, which by 1960 led Eisenhower and his aides to consider pursuing a military intervention into Laos, no matter where that might ultimately lead.[12]

A continuing disagreement between Chinese and American leaders over the status of Taiwan likewise threatened to reignite armed conflict. Mao's regime saw Taiwan as essentially a renegade Chinese province where Nationalist leader Chiang Kai-Shek presided over a government that kept alive the possibility of overturning the Chinese Communist revolution. Determined to restore mainland China's authority over Taiwan and eliminate that threat, Mao had mixed verbal intimidation with occasional aggressive acts, such as bombarding the nearby islands of Quemoy and Matsu, which were controlled by Chiang's regime. When that shelling resumed in August 1958, the Eisenhower administration responded by ordering the US Seventh Fleet to escort Nationalist Chinese forces to the islands and installing American-made artillery capable of firing atomic shells. As neither the United States nor Communist China was willing to budge, and Chiang's government voiced support for a showdown, the possibility of a confrontation in the Taiwan Strait grew increasingly real.[13]

Another crisis arose in the Middle East, where the Arab nationalist regime in Egypt headed by Gamal Abdel Nasser opened diplomatic relations with the People's Republic of China, bought arms from Soviet-dominated Czechoslovakia, then nationalized the Suez Canal in 1956. When the canal's previous owners—in effect, the French and British governments—invaded Egypt to regain control over that vital shipping channel, they enlisted the help of the Israelis, thereby turning a property dispute into a much more explosive regional confrontation. The Eisenhower administration, which had been assured by the leaders of Britain and France that they would not use force to retake the canal, refused to support their invasion and successfully pressured them, and the Israelis, to abandon it. The Soviets saw an opportunity to turn the increasing tensions between Arab countries and Israel to their advantage. In response, Eisenhower tried to organize the nations of the region into an anti-Soviet bloc and signaled that the United States would intervene to prevent Soviet incursions. When those same tensions began to destabilize Lebanon, Eisenhower felt compelled in July 1958 to dispatch a contingent of US marines. They stayed only briefly and did no fighting, but the intervention demonstrated that the Middle East had emerged as yet another place where a regional confrontation might escalate into a much bigger Cold War clash.[14]

The trouble brewing in Africa largely arose out of the struggle against colonialism. In Algeria, which French leaders considered part of their nation, an increasingly violent and increasingly popular radical-leftist rebellion created a dilemma for the Eisenhower administration. To side with its ally France would align the United States with the resistance to ending colonialism in the third world, which could nudge more of those anti-colonialists toward Communism. To side with the rebels could create a major rift between the United States and France, disrupting the NATO alliance and endangering western Europe. The United States faced the same dilemma repeatedly as several sub-Saharan African nations such as the Congo, Ghana, and Guinea began winning their independence from European colonial powers. Political independence left these "emerging" nations of Africa free to chart their own courses, and to enlist the aid of the Soviets and the Chinese. Here was one more part of the world, indescribably remote to ordinary Americans, where local conflicts could degenerate into proxy wars between East and West, and perhaps even a global conflagration.[15]

As the number of such hot spots rapidly multiplied, a bigger foreign-policy dilemma started to come into focus: an overly ambitious containment policy was now becoming increasingly unmanageable. Despite Eisenhower's skillful efforts to scale back Truman's original and broad approach to containing Communism, some of the wisest critics within the conservative establishment couldn't help concluding that the US government was simply trying to do too much. George F. Kennan—the former State Department official who had by then moved to the faculty at Princeton—and the nationally syndicated columnist Walter Lippmann both argued persuasively that trying to contain the spread of Communism everywhere and mostly by military means had not just proved to be unworkable, but had become dangerous. Kennan and Lippmann favored a more considered approach, in which the United States would carefully weigh the potential costs and benefits of containment in a specific place, while remaining open to nonmilitary alternatives for achieving its goals.

Such arguments received elite media attention, but fell largely on deaf ears when it came to the middle class, in part because Eisenhower had succeeded in keeping the peace after the fighting in Korea ended. The likelihood that the next president, to be elected in November 1960, would never match Eisenhower's knowledge and experience in national security matters argued against that kind of complacency, but most middle-class voters didn't seem to understand clearly the danger in maintaining a hard-line, confrontational stance.[16]

Few middle-class Americans knew what to make of all these simmering conflicts in far-off corners of the globe, but perhaps more insidious was their general lack of understanding about the domestic problems quietly taking shape in the late 1950s. These developments were obvious to those left out of the great middle-class expansion, but not to those who benefited, who, focused on the positive consequences of that change, had trouble seeing the more negative ones. Among the economic issues were persistent price inflation, accelerating automation, and the revival of foreign competition, which together began to erode the prosperity in America's hugely important manufacturing sector. The fairly steady advance in worker wages and benefits since mass unionization in the mid-1930s and America's entry into World War II in 1941 had combined to make the American factory worker the best-compensated in the world by 1957. Even when the economy fell into a recession during 1958, wages in such core industries as automobiles and steel had actually risen, due to the protections built in to multiyear labor contracts. The lack of much foreign competition until then had likewise encouraged managers to reward themselves with ever-higher salaries.[17]

But as those high personnel costs squeezed profits, employers in basic manufacturing increasingly compensated by raising prices for their companies' products and by installing more machines to do the work. The resulting price inflation eroded real incomes, while increased mechanization reduced the number of secure, well-paid jobs. By the late 1950s, automation was enough on people's minds that it could serve as the central plot vehicle of a successful Broadway play *Desk Set*, and the subsequent 1957 film. In the Hollywood version, Spencer Tracy plays an efficiency expert bent on automating a television network's research department, headed by a librarian-type supervisor played by Katharine Hepburn. Although more a romantic comedy than a thoughtful discussion of automation and its consequences, *Desk Set*'s popularity testified to the issue's growing relevance to Americans.[18]

More seriously, growing foreign competition in basic manufacturing from western Europe and East Asia now chipped away at the foundations of American industry, though it had, at least in part, resulted from conditions the United States had encouraged and even helped to foster. The economic revival in those regions had improved quality of life, dampened radically leftist political movements, and strengthened America's allies in the broader Cold War struggle. But all that manufacturing output, powered by newly built and state-of-the-art factories filled with workers and managers who typically made a lot less than Americans, threatened to eat into the market share of American firms in industries such as automobiles and steel. But labor unions had become powerful in the US manufacturing sector, making it almost impossible to cut wages and benefits paid to those workers, which management tended to see as the only viable solution. Union leaders often chose to see foreign competition either as exaggerated ("management crying wolf") or as management's problem, especially because some firms had contributed to this dilemma by paying their managerial employees high salaries. Corporate profits had also been high during the 1940s and early-to-mid 1950s, which fed an understandable sense among union heads and workers alike that they were not primarily to blame.[19]

Rather than some kind of constructive compromise, however, what emerged in the late 1950s was a harsh new tug-of-war between labor and management. A business-backed campaign to weaken unions by passing state "right-to-work" laws, which would have allowed workers to opt out of union membership, met with intense resistance from workers and their representatives. Effective union-led political activism ensured widespread defeat for such measures during the 1958 election cycle. The right-to-work crusade worked against the longer-term interests of business leaders by dragging down to defeat many of the Republican state lawmakers associated with it. A new federal law to restrict union power, the Landrum-Griffin Act, did pass in 1959, due in part to a widely publicized congressional probe into union corruption that diminished labor's standing with the public. But that measure, which placed internal union affairs under more federal government supervision and restricted the ability of unions to conduct certain kinds of boycotts and picketing, seemed likely not to change much in the short term. Then, a massive, widely observed six-month steel strike in 1959—the biggest single strike in American history—ended in a defeat for management, seeming to confirm that direct confrontation with labor unions was not going to help solve any problems.[20]

Labor leaders wanted business owners and shareholders to accept a smaller share of profits in the years ahead and, if that were not enough, for the federal government to raise trade barriers to limit competition, but neither of those solutions seemed workable either. If profitability in basic manufacturing fell long-term, management there would be less able to raise the capital needed to innovate and keep up with foreign competitors that had more modern production facilities. That situation would likely push American business executives in basic manufacturing to begin diversifying into other, more lucrative lines of work in sectors and places where unions were weak or nonexistent. The market system in America would compel that kind of response, because neither the government nor the unions had the power to restrict the profitability of American business in general. Thus, even if managers had wanted to accept lower profits over the long run, banks and stockholders would have responded by putting their money into other businesses that promised higher returns. Bethlehem Steel comptroller Frank Brugler bluntly expressed that thought by saying publicly, "We're not in business to make steel. . . . We're in business to make money."

While raising trade barriers might ward off foreign competitors, that would also weaken their economies and lower the overall volume of trade between the USA and its friends abroad, which would undermine the anti-Communist alliance system and, perhaps, push western Europeans and East Asians toward the other side.[21]

In hindsight, it looks like something of a perfect storm of pressures converging on American manufacturing. American business and American labor unions had both boomed during a twenty-five-year period in which foreign competition was never a real problem. Heavy trade barriers during the 1930s, followed by massive wartime damage to foreign factories in the 1940s, meant that unions such as the United Automobile Workers and United Steelworkers of America could formulate wage and benefit demands without giving any thought to what workers in foreign nations were paid in the same industries. Management, likewise lulled into complacency by the absence of foreign competition, had gone along and paid themselves well, too, then preserved their companies' high profitability by passing rising labor costs along to their customers in higher prices for the goods and services they produced, which helped open the door to more foreign competition.[22]

The federal government had also unwittingly helped create the situation by encouraging management to grant steadily improving wages and benefits so as to promote the growth of the middle class. Had the new industrial unions emerged at a time when serious foreign competition existed, the deals struck in basic manufacturing would likely have been less generous and management salaries lower, but also more durable. At this point, though, there seemed to be no turning back, at least not in a way that would satisfy both management and labor. The longer American industry went without an effective response, the worse inflation, automation-induced unemployment, and foreign competition became. The result by the late 1950s was a sense of gridlock that endangered many of the jobs that had enabled the growth of the blue-collar part of the new middle-class majority.[23]

Eisenhower and his team tried to help by cutting federal spending and pushing the Federal Reserve System to raise interest rates, which helped bring down inflation. Fighting inflation took priority to protect not just household incomes but also to protect America's place at the center of the postwar international economic system. The US dollar had been designated at the Bretton Woods Conference of 1944 as the currency against which those of all other major market countries would be fixed. That had brought renewed stability to the West's economy and encouraged ever more international trade within "the Free World," but only as long as the value of the dollar remained stable. A continued decline would undermine the entire Bretton Woods system.[24]

But taking a strong stand against inflation had serious economic and political drawbacks. The new austerity measures pushed the economy into recession during 1958, driving unemployment up to the highest level since the end of the Great Depression and, as a direct result, paving the way that year for the election of many more northern, liberal Democrats to Congress, who would increase pressure to spend. Cutting federal spending and pushing for higher interest rates also proved less than ideal because while they reduced inflation, they did not eliminate it entirely. Even during the recession year of 1958, prices continued to rise. Economists began talking about a new economic phenomenon: a stagnant economy with persistent inflation, which eventually became known as stagflation.[25]

Eisenhower appointed Vice President Richard Nixon the head of a special cabinet committee to study that knotty problem, but identifying the causes of the problem didn't automatically lead to workable solutions. Even as the overall economy rebounded in 1959–60, factory towns across the highly industrialized—and unionized—states of the Northeast, Midwest, and West Coast continued to suffer from a slowdown in manufacturing employment. An economic sector that had lifted millions of once-poor people into the middle class appeared to be stalling, sparking unease and even anger in those communities.[26]

What was needed were new kinds of well-paid jobs in new industries that were not vulnerable to increasing foreign competition. Reviving that kind of entrepreneurialism proved hard, however, partly because of the high taxes of that era, which left the investor class less able to provide the capital needed to fund innovation and growth. The creation of new economic sectors was also stymied by long-standing barriers to immigration, which had earlier in American history brought in so many creative strivers and provided a hardworking and often low-paid labor force to bring new industries to life.[27]

In the mid-1950s, the average full-time workweek had fallen to about forty hours for the first time, as Monday through Friday, nine to five, finally became the norm. That kind of moderate work ethic had many positive implications. Workers generally remained healthier, and men especially had more time than before for family life. Fathers in the broad middle of the socioeconomic spectrum who held full-time jobs spent more time with sons outside work than ever before in modern American history, which usually made for more effective male child-rearing. But that more moderate work ethic could make workers complacent, and unwilling to make the more intense effort needed to bring whole new industries to life. Even if they were to do so, many would likely require more and different training, either in school or the workplace, which could prove highly expensive.[28]

In the South and in the Mountain West, whose upper classes had succeeded during the 1930s and 1940s in warding off much of the socioeconomic revolution of the New Deal, things were different. The low-wage and largely nonunion environment in the Sunbelt was proving by the late 1950s to be more resistant to foreign competition. If rapid economic growth could be encouraged there, it could narrow the economic inequality between regions of the country (though not within the Sunbelt if most of the rewards flowed to the top). But lighting an economic fire under the Sunbelt was much easier said than done. The region was generally so much poorer than the rest of America and had fewer top schools and universities to educate a competitive workforce. The area lacked high-quality medical care and the healthy diets that followed from higher incomes and better education that could keep workers fully productive over the long term. Much less of the modern transportation and communications infrastructure needed to help drive economic development was present. Most crucially missing from the Sunbelt were the large pools of investment capital required to translate entrepreneurial vision into economic reality.[29]

Despite those obstacles, the Sunbelt states began to make slow but steady economic progress in the late 1950s, primarily because some companies chose to relocate there, with corporate colossus General Electric (GE) taking the lead. It was something of a zero-sum game, however. The Sunbelt's gain meant a loss somewhere else, usually in the industrial Frostbelt states. Many of the people whose jobs went west or south either could not or would not follow them. Even if they did, what they typically found was a low-wage economy for ordinary workers, effectively turning back the clock on twenty-five years of middle-class advancement.[30]

Some American firms took GE's strategy a few steps further, moving their facilities overseas, to more impoverished countries with cheaper labor, to cut costs and improve profits. Like the shift to the US Sunbelt, this step promised to narrow the growing income and wealth gaps between the affluent northern countries and the global south, though not necessarily within them. And such relocations would invariably weaken the communities left behind. It was all but impossible for American workers to pick up and move to a comparatively impoverished country where they'd be paid less. Even if they wanted to give it a try, immigration laws and work-visa restrictions usually ruled it out. Like the shift of industry to the Sunbelt, the beginnings of what became known as off-shoring seemed likely to move the USA more backward than forward.[31]

Other unintended consequences of a quarter century of economic progress were also coming into view. The rapid economic growth, with fewer regulations than today, had also produced unprecedented amounts of environmental pollution. The nation's gross national product (GNP), after remaining essentially flat from the end of World War II to 1950, had doubled before the decade was complete. The manufacturing sector had driven the lion's share of that spectacular growth, leading to the emission of huge amounts of toxic waste into the ground, waterways, and atmosphere. With new suburbs and new highways spreading out across the landscape, the car had become the defining symbol of America, making air pollution so much worse. The first regular "smog alerts" began to be issued in cities such as Los Angeles, where the surrounding mountains tended to trap dirty air so that it would sit like a filthy brown blanket over the population.[32]

All those factories, all those cars, and all that suburban sprawl required the production of massive amounts of energy, which produced even more pollution, both from coal-fired power plants and from toxic chemicals produced as a by-product of oil extraction. But the form of pollution that ultimately caught the public's attention and raised an alarm was the greatly increased use of chemical fertilizers and massive spraying of commercial crops with pesticides, most notably DDT.[33]

The movement against pesticides began in the summer of 1957, when planes sprayed DDT on a nature sanctuary near the home of Olga Owens Huckins in eastern Massachusetts, resulting in the death of her beloved songbirds. Huckins was so incensed that she wrote a letter protesting the spraying to a Boston newspaper and in January 1958 sent a copy to her friend Rachel Carson, a nationally known marine biologist and science writer. Carson, like Huckins, appreciated the beauty of the natural environment and was disturbed by the thoughtlessness of the DDT spraying incident, in which the effort to rid the area of mosquitoes had such disastrous consequences for the local wildlife. Carson decided to investigate the use of that pesticide and others, comparing the optimistic claims of their producers and users with reports from naturalists regarding pesticides' effects. Carson quickly found herself questioning the views of a powerful industry, which contended that DDT and other pesticides like it produced no harmful effects, or at least none of concern to humans. The more Carson learned, the more serious the dangers of excessive pesticide use appeared to her. By the end of the 1950s she had begun working on a book about that issue, which would eventually change the public conversation about pesticides and environmental pollution more generally.[34]

Other factors posed mounting threats to public health as well. The rising tide of middle-class prosperity during the 1950s was beginning to produce a disturbing pattern of excessive eating, alcohol consumption, and smoking. The moderation mandated by the hard times of the Great Depression and the rationing of the war years was being forgotten. Americans with middle incomes, surrounded by unprecedented abundance, now had to actively manage their consumption. Some did, in part due to the habits they had developed earlier or inherent willpower. But others, encouraged by the constant onslaught of television commercials, used their growing incomes to buy and consume in ways that began to seriously harm their health: too much red meat and sugary snacks; too many trips to fast-food outlets such as McDonald's, which had been founded in 1955; and too many beers, mixed drinks, and cigarettes.[35]

It appeared that in its contentment, the middle class was letting itself get soft. During the 1930s and 1940s, the most common form of exercise for American adults was walking. But with the exodus from urban downtowns to car-based suburbs, simple walking seemed to be becoming a thing of the past. A quiet health crisis was taking shape, gradually and often imperceptibly, disguised by the continued rise of life expectancy, from about sixty-three years in 1940 to almost seventy by the end of the 1950s. Better medical care, new drugs (especially vaccines), and, for a time, anyway, an improving diet had contributed greatly to that longer life span. Americans, if they thought about it at all, simply assumed the upward trend would continue. It didn't occur to people that their health, and with it their quality of life, could take a downward turn even as longevity went up. More disconcerting still, signs appeared as early as the late 1950s that the trend toward greater longevity could eventually be reversed. Lung cancer was on the rise, as was heart disease, among men especially. But as with so many of the other challenges Americans faced by the late 1950s, no solution was obvious. The problem seemed too complex, and whatever sensible steps might have been taken required more self-sacrifice than most people were willing to contemplate.[36]

Another kind of zero-sum game was playing itself out in most major cities, giving rise to a new set of social problems. Middle-class suburbanization was draining urban centers of their white, middle-class population and tax base. This barely registered in the consciousness of the countless Americans who had moved out to the suburbs and so had much less exposure to downtown areas than in the past. Even official government statistics hid the problem, for a while. The 1960 census indicated that central cities' populations grew significantly during the 1950s. What that seemingly sunny news disguised was that the growth had come earlier in the decade and was mostly attributable to the baby boom. After 1957, as more middle-class white people—and the businesses that catered to them—departed for suburbia, the population of central cities, in the older Frostbelt especially, began to fall. A greater fraction of the population of central cities was now poor and black, while the tax base of such places began to decline. That growing gap between needs and resources posed a major challenge, especially with the growing demand for subsidized public housing in urban areas.[37]

The economic slowdown of the late 1950s compounded the problem by increasing the growing ranks of the unemployed in central cities. That most of these newly jobless were black made for even more social volatility. The first obvious red flag of this impending social crisis was a rise in central-city crime rates, which had been steadily declining since the early 1930s. That rise encouraged even more middle-class white people and the big companies they usually worked for to head for the suburbs. By 1960, the census reported, fully one-third of the nation's population of 179 million lived in suburbia, with the remaining two-thirds evenly divided between central cities and small towns/rural areas. That neat balance would not last. The ongoing shift of population into suburbia would increasingly erode the prosperity and stability of central cities.[38]

Small towns and rural areas felt the sting of these changes, too, nowhere more so than in Appalachia and on Indian reservations. Many central urban districts may have been in decline, but most of the economic growth of the late 1950s was in the metropolitan centers surrounding those cities. That represented opportunity, which led to a continued exodus out of rural America, especially of young people. Those left behind became, like the inner-city poor, increasingly invisible to the prosperous middle-class majority ensconced in suburbia. Cut off from the good life, residents of rural and semirural areas grew poorer on the later fifties, unless they were lucky enough to own a stable and successful farm. During the Eisenhower presidency, the emphasis on providing federal subsidies to farmers shifted even more toward big-budget farms, not the smaller ones. The larger, more heavily capitalized farms were perceived as more likely to survive long-term, but this favoritism hurried the decline of smaller farms, which went under as surpluses grew and prices fell. The result was a more rapid trend toward bigger and more mechanized farms employing ever fewer people in full-time, year-round jobs, which drove out much of the laboring population, except at harvesttime.[39]

Middle-class suburbanites, who were almost all white people at that time, rarely came into contact with the poorest Americans (urban or rural) in their daily lives and rarely, if ever, saw them on their TV sets, except occasionally on the nightly news broadcasts. TV and other mass media relied on advertisers who only cared about catering to people with money to spend. All the commercialized popular media did for poor people was to offer them a window into the affluent, suburban, middle-class world from which they were excluded. For middle-class suburbanites, the poor were almost invisible, even as their numbers began to rise amid the economic slowdown of the period. Male heads of middle-class households who commuted downtown at least had more of a reality check on urban poverty. But for the women and children of middle-class suburbia, the message that came through the TV set was that poverty had declined so much since the Depression as to have all but disappeared. In reality, by the end of 1957 slightly more than one-fifth of the population still lived below the official poverty line.[40]

Even if they had been paying attention, middle-class Americans may not have recognized the poor for what they were. The nature of poverty was changing. Many of the poor owned cars and televisions. Some faced hunger at times, but not usually starvation. What they lacked was meaningful access to quality education, housing, health care, and steady, well-paid jobs, making escape from poverty difficult. That the poor lived better in some important ways than they used to obscured to some degree both their very real problems and growing discontent, in cities especially. Even on paper, many Americans living in poverty looked better off than they really were: inflation had eaten into the real incomes of the working poor, even if their official hourly wages had increased.[41]

But the contented suburban middle class simply wasn't paying attention. Most of the poverty in metropolitan areas was confined

174

to people of color in the central cities, increasing the social distance between haves and have-nots. The South and parts of the Mountain West were disproportionately poor, and even though many of the poor people in those regions were white, they were just too remote from the major population centers of the much more affluent Northeast, Midwest, and West Coast. And neither group had any prominent presence in any popular media. All of these factors combined to produce a kind of amnesia about the problem of poverty in the late 1950s, and a paralysis in remedial action. As always, inaction only tended to increase the size of the problem.[42]

In the major population centers, and even in the wide-open spaces out West, people at the bottom of the economic scale were living in a separate society. In the South especially, racial segregation made that literally true. Jim Crow had flourished there as long as the South had remained a closed society, but by the later 1950s, the region was becoming more connected to the rest of the country. As black families dispersed during the Great Migration, they were exposed to the different racial rules elsewhere and sometimes let their relatives back in the South know about them. Military service also widened the horizons and increased the expectations among young black men from the South.[43]

Terrible things could happen when African Americans suddenly transitioned from life outside the South to life within it. In the most infamous of such incidents, a fourteen-year-old black boy from Chicago, Emmett Till, had been sent by his mother to spend the summer of 1955 with an elderly relative in the small town of Money, Mississippi. Unfamiliar with Jim Crow's rules, Till had an encounter in a store with a young white woman that offended her. She complained to her husband, who, with his half brother, abducted and brutally murdered the boy. Once Till's body was discovered, an effort was made to prosecute the murderer and his accomplice, but the trial ended in an acquittal. Pictures of the boy's mutilated body appeared in *Jet* magazine and shocked the black community nationally.[44]

This kind of tragedy and others like it helped weaken Jim Crow by exposing its most inhuman qualities. Meanwhile, the NAACP Legal Defense Fund and other groups had been working to make changes through the courts. They engineered major legal victories, none more significant than the famous *Brown* decision. Black people also wielded increasing economic leverage as their incomes rose, confirmed most famously by the success of the Montgomery bus boycott. The loss of so many bus fares put heavy pressure on the bus line operators to give in, reflecting financial resources that black residents of Montgomery had not possessed during the Great Depression. And Jim Crow came under global scrutiny as America settled into its new role as leader of the West in the struggle against Communism, and the focus of the Cold War shifted to developing nations. The Soviet and Chinese press delighted in writing about racial segregation and repression in America, factual stories that supported their anti-American propaganda campaigns. As colonies in sub-Saharan Africa began winning formal political independence in the late 1950s, a new kind of story began to show up in the Communist world press: the African diplomat denied service in a Washington, DC, restaurant that did not allow black people to eat there. Although black America was largely nonexistent on prime-time television, the rise of TV news did occasionally bring the struggle against Jim Crow to the attention of middle-class whites living outside the South who had little direct contact with either the region or African Americans.[45]

That struggle entered a new phase in the fall of 1957. Early in September, a few black students attempted to enroll in the previously all-white Central High School in Little Rock, Arkansas. Governor Orval Faubus had promised to keep the peace and then failed to do so, having no interest in desegregating the schools in his state, despite what the Supreme Court had decided. The ensuing violence was graphically reported in the national and international news media, eventually compelling the Eisenhower administration to respond. The delay in sending in soldiers to restore order and protect the black students infuriated many African Americans, including national celebrities such as Louis Armstrong and Jackie Robinson, who had never been particularly outspoken. Dispatching federal troops deeply offended many southern white people, who likened that to the government's attack on the southern way of life during the Civil War.[46]

The episode proved so stressful for Eisenhower that it contributed to a stroke that he suffered, while sitting at his desk in the Oval Office, on November 25. Although Eisenhower's mind was unaffected, he could not at first speak. In time, he regained his speech, but it was never quite the same. This seemingly hale and sturdy man was brought low, exposing the vulnerability and precariousness of his health, as if his condition was meant to somehow illustrate the fragile nature of the fifties system itself. In the last few years of the decade, the intractable defenders of Jim Crow staved off a series of challenges, but each new confrontation only intensified the frustration among black people and their white liberal allies. But as with the other major challenges facing America, no clear solution seemed in sight, especially given Dixiecrat dominance of Congress, which effectively neutered any federal civil rights laws it managed to pass.[47]

The insidiousness of racial prejudice infected every corner of the country, not just the South. The only slightly more subtle form of it prevalent up North was captured vividly in Lorraine Hansberry's play *A Raisin in the Sun*, which debuted on Broadway in the spring of 1959. It told the story of a black family in Chicago meeting strong resistance as it tries to move into a predominantly white neighborhood.[48]

Played with extraordinary effectiveness by its almost entirely African American cast, including memorable performances by the young Ruby Dee and Sidney Poitier, *Raisin* resonated not just with African American audiences but also with many white theatergoers. By addressing the mainstream aspirations and problems of the black family at the story's center, Hansberry grounded the play in basic 1950s ideals, making it appealing to a broad audience. The better-known film version predictably went a few steps further by deleting black slang, a scene with a black Muslim soapbox speaker, and all explicit references to African politics and racial discrimination. The film was sharply criticized for such compromises but nonetheless sparked a serious critical discussion about whether *Raisin* dealt with problems faced only by northern black people, or more universally by working-class people of any background. *Raisin* also reminded those who saw it of the potentially explosive consequences of confining the northern black population to decaying central cities and denying them entrée into mainstream, suburban America.[49]

Women, too, were growing more concerned about the way the fifties system treated them and, by voicing that concern, fostered an uneasy awareness among them that something was wrong. The origins of that

177

sense of grievance were varied, given how big and diverse that group was. It included college-educated, predominantly upper-middle-class or upper-class married women who aspired to professional jobs on equal terms as men in a system that heavily favored male breadwinners, and older married women of all social classes whose children no longer needed as much attention who, if they moved into the paid labor force, met blatantly unequal and demeaning treatment. And then there were married women who were more or less content with domesticity but found themselves increasingly pressed to take part-time jobs due to the economic slowdown of the late 1950s. These women were simply overburdened, expected to keep up with their domestic duties while also working for pay outside the home. Yet another group had played by the fifties rules and moved quickly into marriage and child-rearing only to be disappointed, either by the kind of man their husband turned out to be, or by the lack of personal fulfillment offered by domestic life, or both. Another cohort comprised unmarried women who wanted to lead lives of their own choosing, independent of men, but were frustrated both by societal pressure to conform, and by the difficulty of finding a job they believed worthy of their abilities and with a sufficient income to support them comfortably. And then there were poor women, who found themselves increasingly cut off from the rising middle class, and black women, regardless of income or social class, who faced discrimination daily. Collectively, these conditions produced yet another major challenge to the status quo.[50]

Those growing tensions found their way into a major study funded by the Ford Foundation, called *Womanpower*, which appeared in 1957. It endorsed more access to education and employment for women, but made little progress in changing public perceptions or attitudes, or in prompting a governmental response. The sense of unease grew as women fell ever further behind men in completing college. Another unintended by-product of the long-standing male-breadwinner model, reinforced in the postwar years by the GI Bill's educational benefits for veterans, this new, growing education gap could work against the best interests of marriage. A marriage that lasted usually depended on commonalities in the backgrounds of the husband and the wife, a key one often being shared levels of education. Although any organized women's movement was stuck in neutral in the late 1950s, the discontent simmering just below the surface would eventually get it moving.[51]

The end of the 1950s saw a domino effect in cultural rebellion. Each time another set of norms was called into question, each time some piece of accepted wisdom or long-standing custom was held up to the light, it seemed to open the door for a hard new look at some other institution. So perhaps inevitably this new questioning spirit came up against established religion and moral tradition. Interestingly, the challenges in these areas came from opposing ends of the cultural spectrum. First, the most secular Americans had finally had their fill of the arguably moderate but absolutely ubiquitous religiosity and middle-class-family orientation that percolated through political and cultural messages of the day. Even the sophisticated liberal version of religiosity exemplified by nationally prominent theologian Reinhold Niebuhr began to turn off secular people because the Niebuhrian emphasis on human sinfulness contributed to the national love affair with mainstream religion. Second, the most religiously observant and morally traditional citizens believed that modern mores were leaving the substance of specific religious traditions behind. They began to push for greater attention to theology in church and synagogue, for making religion central to people's everyday lives, and for even less deviation from old-fashioned propriety in popular culture. Thus, one saw by the later 1950s a growing polarization on the religion and morality fronts as "wing people" grew more numerous and visible, and the center began to stagnate. This polarization would take center stage in the "culture wars" a generation or two later.[52]

One early harbinger of the backlash against moderate moral traditionalism from the more permissive perspective was the appearance of Hugh Hefner's *Playboy* magazine. The first issue hit the newsstands in December 1953, but sold only fifty-three thousand copies, despite featuring a nude centerfold photo of Marilyn Monroe. Circulation climbed rapidly, however, in the late 1950s, as more and more men liked the vicarious rebellion against their family lives that the magazine represented. In 1960, *Playboy*'s monthly circulation topped a million for the first time, showing the growth of that trend.[53]

The magazine offered escapist images in words and pictures of a world where apparently single men were routinely out on the town, and having casual, commitment-free sex as often, and with as many women, as they liked. Those fantasies were accompanied, and funded, by ads for high-end liquor, clothes, and entertainment, which underscored *Playboy*'s emphasis on male gratification. *Playboy*'s commercial success hinted that an incipient rebellion was brewing among men, too. The well-publicized antics of older entertainers such as Frank Sinatra, Dean Martin, and Sammy Davis Jr., the so-called Rat Pack, whose idea of fun was drinking and carousing in Las Vegas, seemed to reinforce the male fantasies promulgated by Hefner's magazine.[54]

For younger Americans of both sexes, rebellion and escapism found the perfect vehicle in *rock and roll*, a slang term for sex that was applied to a new form of music. Such stars and groups as Bill Haley and the Comets and Buddy Holly and the Crickets led the way in songs aimed at the rising number of teenagers, with lyrics that tended to encourage their interest in sex, but also provided an outlet for all that teen energy. Rock and roll had so much more to it than that, but to those on the morally traditional side of the cultural divide, that was its most noticeable and disturbing aspect.[55]

At the other end of the religion-and-values spectrum were such prominent figures as the Reverend Billy Graham and pop singer Pat Boone, both masterful manipulators of mass media, especially TV. Graham was determined to make one's personal relationship with God a central focus of life for American Christians and led heavily publicized crusades, highlighted by televised revival meetings in major arenas. At once old and new, Graham's revivalism helped encourage the growth of what became known as evangelical Christianity, which began expanding from its base in his native South to much of the heartland and the Mountain West.

In the world of popular entertainment, Pat Boone exemplified the more morally traditional aspect of the rebellion against fifties moderation in values and behavior. His squeaky-clean image and songs about love and life encouraged the young especially to abstain from drinking and smoking *entirely*, and from experimenting with sex prior to marriage, even with one's fiancé(e).

To such ultra-squares, the much greater variety of sexual behavior that sex researcher Alfred Kinsey and his associates had conveyed in their landmark reports on male and female sexuality in 1948 and 1953, respectively, was to be resisted, not embraced. In particular, Kinsey's findings that a substantial fraction of American men and women had engaged in premarital and extramarital sex deeply disturbed the most morally traditional people, who were convinced those findings, if accurate, signaled a crisis.[56]

The 1950s were a uniquely interesting period of transition—at least in retrospect—for gays and lesbians. In the early part of the decade, when Senator Joe McCarthy and his imitators were digging up dirt on anyone who deviated much from the anti-Communist line, they sometimes publicly accused their targets of homosexuality. It was the first time that homosexuality was acknowledged and discussed in the American popular media in any significant way, which proved to be a double-edged sword. In the short term, at the height of McCarthy's monstrous power, being publicly labeled as a homosexual could destroy a person's life. From a longer-term perspective, however, that such behavior was even a topic for public discourse would make possible some gay and lesbian activism and resistance later in the decade.

The story of astronomer Frank Kameny is a case in point. When the US government fired him in 1957 because of his homosexuality—on the theory that it made him vulnerable to blackmail and thus a security risk—he did not go quietly, as so many homosexuals had earlier. Instead, he sued. Although Kameny lost in the courts, he didn't give up on gay rights activism. His efforts and those of other gays and lesbians demonstrated a growing resistance to the intense social pressure to remain closeted.

The fifties system had contributed to the growth of such resistance by creating an overall social climate so hostile to homosexuals as to compel those who could to cluster into a few major urban centers such as New York and San Francisco. In those communities arose a much stronger sense of gay and lesbian identity, although those groups remained, for the time being, very much under the radar of most middle-class heterosexuals. Those same urban centers also became gathering places for jazz musicians, artists, poets, and writers who wanted a comfortable creative, bohemian life in the company of like-minded people. From this cadre of artistic searchers were born the beats, a group of writers and musicians who challenged the repres-

sive conformity and materialism of Eisenhower's America. The beat
generation announced itself most emphatically with the publication in
September 1957 of beat icon Jack Kerouac's novel *On the Road*, which
turned the simple notion of wandering around in search of some other
way of life into a heroic quest.[57]

The imperceptible cracks in the seemingly solid American system
never got addressed in the late 1950s, nor was the system ready to
come apart. Change wouldn't come so easily. For one thing, the major
social institutions of the times—employers, unions, and government—
were simply too large and deeply entrenched. Social change would
have to come about at least partly via negotiation by leaders of organized interest groups, a system the Europeans called corporatism.
Whether "the establishment" could be pressured into making major
social changes seemed unclear. Big institutions bred passivity among
the general population, even among the young, and meaningful citizen activism had declined. Postwar affluence and mass popular culture, and especially the new craze for TV watching, had lulled much of
the younger generation into complacency, reluctant to engage in social
protest of any kind. Writer Thornton Wilder famously dubbed them
"the Silent Generation."

The majority of Americans, young parents especially, were preoccupied with their own lives. *The Man in the Gray Flannel Suit*, a novel
by Sloan Wilson that appeared in 1955 and was followed by a popular
movie version one year later, captured how the trend toward domesticity among middle-class people had reoriented many of them toward
security, materialism, and conformity and had also caused them to
question the wisdom of that shift, doubts that began to resonate more
strongly as the fifties came to an end. But the middle class, still growing in size and influence, tended not to think in terms of fundamental social change. They had seen the utopian visions associated with
fascism and Communism end in disappointment or in outright disaster. They also still hung on to a genuine respect for authority. The
apparent success of large American endeavors, since World War II
especially, bolstered the public's confidence in their leaders, whom
they believed ought not to be challenged. In addition, the cloud of
McCarthyism still hung over the United States, such that radicalism of
any kind seemed perilous. Even the most committed leftists remained

so wary of what political activism could cost that they often told their children "Don't sign anything," lest that land them on a blacklist. The Cold War helped muffle the Silent Generation in another way, too, by inhibiting criticism of the American system because that could, however unintentionally, contribute to the success of Soviet and Chinese propaganda. While true of other, similar countries in the late 1950s, this disengagement from political protest was more worrisome given US history, in which major social reform had always depended on citizen activism.[58]

Any protest tended to be muted, which could clearly be seen in how the issue of racial segregation played out in the lives of Beatrice and George. Beatrice had become firmly status-conscious, a by-product of the downturn her family had endured during the early years of the Depression. It had made her wary of close associations with black people. Beatrice's attitude offended her daughter, Carol, so much so that Carol spent a week at Howard University during her senior year of college at Bucknell in 1959–60, as part of an exchange program between the two schools. Carol never told her mother about that, fearing it would lead to an argument.

George Perkins, too, found a way to make his own private protest against Jim Crow. Outwardly, he looked by the late 1950s like a typical Eisenhower Republican, a mostly bald white man in late middle age who wore the kinds of suits and hats Ike tended to favor. However, George's work in the employment service, especially as head of its planning division, afforded him a clear sense of how automation was beginning to push black men and their families back down the economic ladder. So, too, did his dealings with officials from the Rhode Island Urban League, which was focused on trying to expand black people's access to middle-class jobs. George's growing awareness made him sympathetic to what in time would be called affirmative-action programs for young black men especially, to help them get into the kinds of well-paid middle-class jobs that white men had historically monopolized. But in the late 1950s, George's sympathy did not lead to any major public action. Like Carol Sindt, George Perkins's resistance to racial prejudice was mostly confined to the realm of private protest.

• • •

Even if the citizen-activist tradition could be revived, what kind of action to take was not clear. The approaching presidential election of 1960 would be a test not just of whether the activist spirit could be reengaged, but also, to what end. The conventional wisdom in the late 1950s was that the election probably wouldn't change much, especially because the most likely successor to President Eisenhower appeared to be his more partisan and less likable vice president, Richard Nixon. His rise seemed unlikely either to stir the people to action or to trigger any far-reaching reform. People naturally expected more of "the bland leading the bland," but that was not to be the case.[59]

CHAPTER 8

Trying to Cope

In the later 1950s, a young politician from Massachusetts brought a new way of thinking to American foreign policy, quickly becoming the closest thing the Democratic Party had to a national security star. In July 1957, John F. Kennedy was the first American political figure of note to endorse Algerian independence publicly, associating himself with the rising tide of anti-colonialism. By advocating for more US aid to India, whose leaders refused to align themselves during the Cold War either with the East or the West, Kennedy again indicated that he would not be bound by 1950s orthodoxy in dealing with non-aligned countries. He also called for more military spending after the *Sputnik* launch, demonstrating that he could balance sympathy for the emerging nations of Africa and Asia with toughness toward the Soviets. As the son of a former US ambassador to Britain and having lived and traveled widely abroad, Kennedy seemed a cosmopolitan figure who could work effectively with allies and through the United Nations, as Eisenhower had. The more America's foreign-policy challenges multiplied, the more opportunities Kennedy had to burnish a national reputation for expertise in that area.[1]

Kennedy also established himself as a defender of the domestic New Deal innovations that had helped the middle class grow and prosper, such as Social Security, labor unions, and the GI Bill. That he came from a wealthy family broadened his appeal in upper-class America. Like FDR, Kennedy championed the interests of the middle class out of a sense of social obligation. Thus, when Kennedy won reelection to the US Senate by a landslide in November 1958, he appeared to establish his stature as a viable presidential candidate.[2]

Kennedy, however, didn't see himself that way, at least not for the

1960 election. He thought that he was still too young, having turned forty-one in 1958, and that anti-Catholic feeling around the country was still too strong. Kennedy was persuaded to run by the compelling arguments of his larger-than-life father, Joseph P. Kennedy Sr. Rich, intensely ambitious for his children, and highly knowledgeable about business and politics, Kennedy Sr. felt at home among the country's power brokers. He firmly believed that conditions were more favorable than his son realized. Catholic Americans had come quite a long way since Al Smith's disastrous defeat in 1928, becoming more assimilated, more affluent, and, above all, more numerous. The creation of a middle-class nation had yielded the greatest demographic dividend in urban, industrial America, where most Catholic people lived. As the incomes there steadily rose, so, too, did the tendency to have larger families. As a result, Catholic voters by the mid-1950s comprised fully one-quarter of the national electorate. Joe pointed out to his son that a Kennedy candidacy in 1960 would likely create great excitement within the country's Catholic population, especially among younger Catholics who had not witnessed Al Smith's defeat. The strategic location of most Catholic voters in the major industrial states, which had by far the most electoral votes, would provide a crucial advantage to a Kennedy candidacy.[3]

Joe Kennedy was used to getting his way and prevailed upon his son John and so changed the course of American politics. JFK parlayed his vast financial resources, charismatic public persona, and appeal to Catholic voters into victories in all of the major contested primaries. The momentum carried him to a first-ballot victory at the convention. At that crucial moment, his father once again intervened decisively. Understanding his son's weakness with white southerners, without whose support no Democrat could hope to win, Kennedy Sr. urged his son to choose Senate majority leader Lyndon Johnson of Texas as his vice presidential running mate. Although the younger Kennedy disliked Johnson, whom he saw as an opportunistic wheeler-dealer, the logic behind choosing him for the number two spot proved irresistible. With that move, Kennedy succeeded in defusing the kind of intense Dixiecrat opposition that would have doomed his candidacy from the outset.[4]

Even so, the odds still seemed to favor the Republicans because their presidential ticket—Vice President Richard Nixon and US ambassador to the United Nations Henry Cabot Lodge Jr.—was so closely identified with the still popular Eisenhower administration. But the expected outcome, a narrow Nixon victory, was derailed by three unforeseen developments. First, Nixon unwisely decided to debate Kennedy on TV. Nixon was undone by his overconfidence; he had been a college debater, but he misunderstood the new medium of television and so failed to prepare properly.

Nixon came to the first debate in Chicago on September 26 looking pale and tired, and wearing a light gray suit that blended into the set's background. Kennedy, with a firmer grasp of the power of TV, arrived tanned, rested, and wearing a dark gray suit that looked as pleasing on camera as it was presidential. He had also carefully prepared. The unexpectedly large audience—between 65 and 70 million viewers—ensured that the debate would have a major impact on the election.[5]

Kennedy walked off with the debate and took a lead in the polls that he never surrendered. His performance unleashed an outpouring of enthusiasm in Catholic America of the sort his father had earlier predicted. The size of Kennedy's heavily Catholic crowds roughly doubled after the first televised debate and remained at that level for the remaining six weeks of the campaign. Television news saw a good story in that growing excitement and, by reporting on it, helped stoke the enthusiasm even further. Kennedy campaign volunteers, inspired by what they saw in the debates and at his public appearances, intensified their efforts, which increased the likelihood of a high turnout that favored their candidate.[6]

The second unforeseen development was an eleventh-hour shift in voting preferences among African Americans. Kennedy had been their least favorite choice in the Democratic primaries, in part because of the long-standing belief among black voters that Irish Catholic Democrats had little interest in their issues. Kennedy hadn't engaged much with civil rights and had chosen the Dixiecrat Johnson as his running mate, reinforcing that impression. Black voters had no reason to think that he would fight segregation any more than Eisenhower had. Moreover, many of them were Protestants who held strongly anti-Catholic views. That distrust among the roughly one-third of black Americans living in major urban areas outside the South—and thus able to vote—

seemed likely to sink Kennedy's chances in such key swing states as Illinois and Michigan.[7]

That situation suddenly changed when Martin Luther King Jr. was jailed in Georgia on October 19 for a civil rights protest. A judge there, irate that King had violated parole imposed for an earlier offense against segregation laws, ordered him sent to prison. King's wife, Coretta Scott King, feared that she would never see him alive again. Civil rights leaders associated with King appealed to both Kennedy and Nixon for help. Nixon, hoping to win several southern states and not wanting to offend the almost all-white electorate there, said nothing publicly. Kennedy, however, in response to prompting by aides, telephoned Mrs. King, pledged his assistance in getting her husband released, then let the national media know about the call, saying, "She is a friend of mine." Kennedy also instructed his brother and campaign manager, Bobby, to contact the judge and make the case that King's incarceration represented a potential danger to him from other inmates and guards. The judge relented and ordered King set free.[8]

Martin Luther King Jr.'s father, a prominent pastor in Atlanta who had already decided to vote for Nixon, announced at a mass meeting at Ebenezer Baptist Church that he was switching to Kennedy. At that meeting, which was reported in the national media, Daddy King, as he was called, observed that as a Baptist he had thought he could not bring himself to vote for a Catholic for president, but that Kennedy's decisive action in helping free his son had changed his mind. This candid endorsement was hugely important in persuading northern black voters to turn out for Kennedy. They ultimately went for him by a margin of about 70 percent to 30 percent, something no one had expected.[9]

The third improbable development was a similar late shift toward Kennedy among the Dixiecrats, triggered by a highly publicized confrontation in late October in the lobby of a Dallas hotel between Lyndon and Lady Bird Johnson and a crowd of affluent Nixon supporters. Stirred up by a right-wing Republican congressman named Bruce Alger, the "mink-coated mob," as the press dubbed them, verbally abused both Johnsons in a confrontation captured by TV cameras. The crowd's disgraceful behavior so offended Georgia senator Richard Russell, the unofficial leader of the congressional Dixiecrats, that he roused himself to campaign with Johnson during the week before the election. That action helped turn the tide in the South, giving the Kennedy-Johnson ticket a majority of the eleven states of the old Confederacy.[10]

The televised debates, the King jailing, and the Dallas confrontation combined to produce the highest turnout ever and a breathtakingly narrow victory for Kennedy in the national popular vote. His margin amounted to less than one-half of one vote per precinct nationwide. There were serious allegations of cheating in Illinois and Texas—the two states that gave Kennedy an electoral college majority—but no practical way to prove them. Against the odds, all of the key variables had gone Kennedy's way.[11]

What that outcome meant for the future of the middle class was less clear. The candidate more supportive of the policies that had made it a majority had prevailed, but only narrowly. And Kennedy was preoccupied with international affairs, in which he was so much less experienced than Eisenhower. The new president's lack of experience as an executive also seemed likely to lead to more turbulence, not less, at home and abroad, putting ever more strain on the mechanisms that had made the US a predominantly middle-class country.[12]

Under pressure from Kremlin hawks to put the untested new American president on the defensive, Nikita Khrushchev delivered a provocative address on January 6, 1961, that was publicly released just two days before Kennedy was inaugurated. Khrushchev explicitly pledged Soviet support for "wars of national liberation" in Africa, Asia, and Latin America. Correctly seeing the speech as a personal challenge, Kennedy responded in kind, by including in his inaugural address the sort of expansive Cold War rhetoric Truman had favored. Although the speech also expressed the new president's more peaceful aspirations, its indisputable message—an overreaction to Khrushchev's bellicose address—helped set the stage for increased US-Soviet tensions, especially in the Cold War hot spots of Cuba, Berlin, and Indochina.[13]

First came a clash in Cuba on April 17. The Soviet military buildup there, made in response to growing fears of an American-backed armed intervention to oust the Castro regime, provoked Kennedy to endorse an invasion plan. The poorly planned and even more poorly executed scheme used anti-Castro exiles, trained by Americans, as a proxy army in an attempt to overthrow the Cuban government. Pinned down on the landing beach surrounding the Bay of Pigs by Castro's battle-tested army, the exile fighting force was quickly defeated in what everyone agreed was a fiasco for the Americans. In hindsight, the ill-fated Bay of Pigs invasion produced the worst possible outcome: it escalated the tensions. The half-baked intervention failed to dislodge the Castro government and increased its fears of an eventual American military attack and its willingness to accept more Soviet military aid. Consequently, the situation in Cuba began building toward a frightening superpower confrontation.[14]

Neither the United States nor the USSR seemed able to back away from its provocative, confrontational stance. At a summit meeting between the two powers in Vienna in early June, Khrushchev renewed his earlier threat to sign a separate peace treaty with East Germany, allowing its government to halt the flow of refugees to West Berlin by force, unless Kennedy agreed to end the American presence there. Once again perceiving a personal challenge, JFK refused. As if the threat weren't enough, Khrushchev treated Kennedy rudely and dismissively, pointing out that he, Khrushchev, had a son Kennedy's age. Both leaders went home deeply discouraged about the prospects for world peace and, in response, sought major increases in military spending. Although that tended to stimulate the American economy, such spending meant less money for needed domestic reforms, such as the Medicare program that Kennedy had promised during the campaign.[15]

The Soviet leadership's decision to support building what became known as the Berlin Wall in August 1961 defused the immediate crisis there, but only at a considerable cost to the USSR's prestige. The spectacle of the East German government's incarceration of would-be refugees further tarnished Communism's benevolent image, especially in the countries just emerging from European colonial rule. The decision to wall off East and West Berliners from each other—family members included—contributed to a growing sense that behind the liberating rhetoric of world Communism lay the reality of repression. Understanding that his side had lost face by resolving the standoff in Berlin in that fashion, Khrushchev began seeking ways to restore the USSR's image of strength, as well as his own, which fueled even more confrontation with the West.[16]

For starters, the Soviet Union resumed atmospheric nuclear weapons testing in September 1961, ending the moratorium that had begun almost three years earlier. The American government responded in kind, resuming its tests seven months later. When Khrushchev and Eisenhower had worked to bring about the moratorium, they had thought it would lead the way to a nuclear-test-ban treaty, but by the spring of 1962, it had led nowhere.[17]

Even more provocative was Khrushchev's decision that summer to introduce nuclear weapons into Cuba secretly, including intermediate-range offensive missiles, which could travel up to eleven hundred miles and easily hit major metropolitan areas in the United States, as well as so-called battlefield missiles armed with nuclear warheads. The latter could travel up to thirty miles and could decimate an American invasion force. Nine of them were operational by the fall of 1962, and decisions about their use had been delegated to the Soviet commander on-site because of the difficulties of direct communication between the Kremlin and Cuba. The Soviets also decided to beef up their conventional military forces on the island. By mid-October, around forty-two thousand Soviet military personnel had been stationed in Cuba, which was roughly twice as many as the CIA had estimated. The covert Soviet military buildup had, by then, made Cuba into a major platform for the projection of Soviet power, which provoked the scariest East-West confrontation of the entire Cold War.[18]

On October 15, 1962, the CIA reported to the president that its U-2 reconnaissance flights had detected Soviet missiles in Cuba. Kennedy, grasping immediately the gravity of the situation, ordered the creation of a special task force, the so-called Executive Committee, or Excomm for short, composed of the administration's top national security experts, civilian and military. They were tasked with reviewing the intelligence gathered by the CIA and devising options for an American response. The hawkishness of most Excomm members tilted it from the outset toward an American military attack on Cuba to destroy the missiles and oust the Castro government. Kennedy himself was to blame for Excomm's aggressiveness. Considering himself a foreign-policy thinker who questioned the fifties orthodoxy, with its emphasis on resolving disputes through force rather than diplomacy, JFK had surrounded himself with national security advisers who reflected the conventional wisdom. That built-in balance made certain he would hear such views, even if he did not always share them. The result in this instance, as in others, was to place enormous pressure on him to favor a military rather than a diplomatic response.[19]

Kennedy's decision to let the entire world know about the missiles in Cuba via a TV broadcast a week later raised the stakes, as did his announcement that he had ordered the US Navy to form a blockade around Cuba to prevent any more Soviet supplies from arriving to aid the missile buildup. For the Soviets to back down now would cause a serious loss of face, which seemed, in the short run, to stiffen their resolve. In the terrifying week that followed, Soviet ships approached American ones, raising the possibility of an exchange of fire that could escalate into World War III. Meanwhile, the continued progress of the Soviet intermediate-range-missile installation in Cuba turned up the pressure on the Kennedy administration to resolve the crisis before those weapons became operational. Kennedy found himself facing an insistent demand from Excomm's hawkish majority to obtain an immediate Soviet commitment to abandon the missile program, or to allow American air strikes followed by a ground invasion of Cuba.[20]

The greater strength of American military forces, strong support from allies, and restraint on the part of both the American president and the Soviet premier ultimately saved the day, but only barely. Keenly aware of the larger American nuclear arsenal, Khrushchev bargained for two commitments: American withdrawal of nuclear missiles from sites near the Soviet border in Turkey, and a pledge not to attempt another invasion of Cuba to oust the Castro government. The first of these demands did not pose a real risk because the US missiles in Turkey had been rendered obsolete by submarine-based missiles. For Kennedy to accept the second demand was no easy matter, however, because making such a promise would mean that the Cuban regime would continue indefinitely, which his mostly hawkish advisers considered dangerous. To make a public no-invasion promise after Khrushchev's provocative step of putting missiles into Cuba could easily be interpreted as weakness and could encourage similarly reckless Russian and/or Chinese actions elsewhere. Kennedy insisted that the no-invasion pledge remain secret, which it did, for years. When Khrushchev agreed to accept on October 28, the immediate crisis was averted.[21]

In hindsight, however, the Cuban Missile Crisis continued to cast a grim shadow over the remainder of the 1960s and beyond. Its resolution strengthened the will of the Soviet Union's top leadership to pursue a vast expansion of its ICBM program. The imbalance in such armaments had left Khrushchev with no choice except to back down. Instead of an arms-control agreement in 1960 that prevented such a dangerous contest, an even more intense East-West arms race began in late 1962—exactly what Eisenhower had hoped to prevent. By the end of 1968 it would produce roughly equal US and Soviet stockpiles of strategic nuclear weapons, each numbering in the thousands. Coming so close to an atomic Armageddon did eventually scare the world into a new spirit of cooperation and negotiation, but also ended up driving both sides to continue arming in the meantime, which made the arms-control challenge that much greater.[22]

The support that Kennedy won for his handling of the crisis highlighted a painful dilemma created by the rise to dominance of the middle class. Usually more nationalist, hawkish, and patriotic than either richer or poorer Americans, middle-class voters rewarded Kennedy's seemingly adroit handling of the Cuban Missile Crisis by turning out in record numbers during the off-year elections that took place the following month and giving the Democrats an unexpected electoral triumph. Even more striking was the president's approval rating as measured by polls, which hovered around 80 percent in the immediate aftermath of the confrontation in Cuba.[23]

That kind of "rally round the flag" sentiment bolstered support in Congress for continuing and intensifying the Cold War, but it unnerved some of the most knowledgeable observers on both the left and the right. They had seen the world edge right up to the brink of nuclear war and feared that perpetuating the big national security establishment would surely land the world in the same predicament again. The high cost and inflationary consequences of that posture also aroused growing resistance, especially within the powerful American business community.[24]

A basic change in attitude regarding national security would, however, have threatened to undermine one of the important contributing factors to the growth and sustainability of the middle-class majority. Heavy military spending had helped propel the spectacular American economic growth of the previous twenty years; to reduce that river of public funds by spending less on conventional (nonnuclear) forces such as the army and the navy would likely lead to economic stagnation, unless the government opted to spend much more on civilians directly through social programs. The problem with that approach, however, was that conservatives had never shown much willingness to support heavy spending of that sort, or the high taxes required to pay for it. Only the national security emergencies of World War II and the Cold War had softened right-wing opposition to a big, expensive, and high-taxing national state, out of a belief that foreign aggression was best deterred by maintaining military strength.[25]

The massive national security state necessitated by World War II and the Cold War had also helped expand the middle class in another way, by providing crucial support for male breadwinning. Maintaining a strong military required a commitment to raising boys successfully so they could perform military service effectively. Military service had also made many young men more productive and had been the primary means of giving the mostly male veterans a legally sanctioned preference in employment, which helped young men obtain well-paid jobs. The draft had also encouraged the middle class to settle down and start families early because it tended to exempt married men with children from military service, during peacetime especially.[26]

The draft had also promoted the emergence of a middle-class majority in other, less visible ways. It offered men deferment or exemption from military service if they pursued higher education and then entered such moderate-paying fields as teaching and family medical practice, to give only two examples. Those kinds of incentives had improved the schools and the medical care available to middle-class families, which significantly increased their chances for success in life. If a majority of Americans came to believe that a big military establishment endangered the country rather than protected it, such a shift could lead to an end to the draft and all that it did to help form a more numerous, prosperous, and economically secure middle class.[27]

Yet, as 1963 opened, the sense grew in the United States, the USSR, and around the world that the frantic race to amass more nuclear weapons in the aftermath of the Cuban Missile Crisis had set the Cold War on an ever more dangerous course. Even as they each worked to make sure their arsenals were massive and intimidating, Kennedy and Khrushchev understood steps had to be taken to somehow reduce the threat level. To facilitate speedy communication during an emergency situation, something that had not been possible during the standoff over Cuba, a telephone link, the so-called hotline, was installed that summer, connecting the White House and the Kremlin directly. Even more important, the two governments resumed work on a treaty to ban atmospheric nuclear tests, as a first step toward meaningful arms control.[28]

Kennedy offered a resounding public endorsement of that process with a widely watched speech at American University on June 10, 1963. He rejected the search for a Free World victory in the Cold War imposed by force of arms, or merely a temporary truce. Instead of just "peace in our time," Kennedy instead spoke of a much more lasting superpower "peace for all time." In a pointed rejection of Woodrow Wilson's more parochial pledge to "make the world safe for democracy," he called for American and Soviet efforts to help "make the world safe for diversity." The tone and substance of the address delighted Khrushchev, who called it the best speech on US-Soviet relations by an American president since Franklin Roosevelt.[29]

Almost overnight, the push for a test-ban treaty acquired renewed momentum, culminating in the signing of an agreement by American, British, and Soviet representatives on July 25. To get it through the Senate, the Kennedy administration sought crucial support from former president Eisenhower, whose cautiously worded endorsement helped secure the needed votes. On September 24, 1963, the Senate voted 80–19 to ratify the test-ban treaty, the first successful arms-control agreement between the nuclear superpowers. Kennedy himself viewed it as the most important achievement of his administration.[30]

The signing of the treaty offered the first optimistic hint that a corner had been turned in the Cold War. The clearest sign of the change in the United States was the declining fraction of the nation's GDP devoted to military spending. The most meaningful indicator of America's commitment to a big national security establishment, that number fell below 10 percent in 1963 for the first time since the early 1950s. Although still a great deal of money given the enormous size of the US economy, it proved to be the start of a new, long-term pattern of reduced spending, as a fraction of GDP, on conventional military forces even as spending on less expensive nuclear weapons continued.[31]

This change would soon be overshadowed, however, by events in Indochina. The conflict there ultimately became the most challenging foreign-policy dilemma facing Kennedy and, later, President Johnson. Failure there would eventually help destabilize middle-class dominance in postwar America to an extent unimaginable in the early 1960s by turning many Americans against the Cold War–era military.

When Kennedy first assumed the presidency, the focus of the American national security establishment concerning Indochina was more on Laos than on South Vietnam. The two were closely related. Unless the movement of men and arms along the Ho Chi Minh Trail from Communist-dominated North Vietnam through eastern Laos could be stopped, the Diem government in South Vietnam seemed likely to collapse. When Kennedy met with Eisenhower during the presidential transition period, he was confused by the advice he got from the departing president. Eisenhower told Kennedy that introducing US troops into Laos to shut down the Ho Chi Minh Trail wasn't an attractive option because it might provoke the neighboring Chinese. Agreeing to an international plan for a neutralized Laos, which was the other choice in vogue, seemed even less appealing to Eisenhower, because neutralization would mean demilitarizing the Laotian government, thereby denying it the ability to halt the flow of men and supplies from North to South Vietnam. Eisenhower suggested instead that Kennedy find some way to bluff the North Vietnamese and their Communist allies into giving up on the Ho Chi Minh Trail, but JFK thought that unlikely to work. The Joint Chiefs favored introducing US troops into Laos, feeling confident that the Chinese government would not respond, but prepared to use battlefield nuclear weapons if they did.[32]

Kennedy soon decided that the military option wasn't worth the risk of another war with China. He opted for neutralizing Laos via international agreement, to the great chagrin of the Joint Chiefs. To America's senior military leaders, Kennedy's choice could only mean one of two things, both of which they found profoundly disturbing: either the new president didn't know what he was doing in Indochina, or he was prepared to give up on South Vietnam if, as seemed likely, its government crumbled under the pressure of the growing Communist insurgency. That would likely mean a major Communist-world break-through in Indochina during the 1960s, which could have adverse con-sequences across East Asia. Kennedy's inconsistent public remarks on Vietnam only increased the Joint Chiefs' concern about the likelihood of that outcome.[33]

Feeling the pressure from the Pentagon and from hawkish Repub-licans, Kennedy endorsed a major increase in the size of the American armed forces in South Vietnam, to help stiffen its resistance. During the almost three years of his presidency, total US military personnel there rose from about one thousand to almost seventeen thousand. The Kennedy administration also supported covert military operations in Laos aimed at deterring Communist guerrilla activity. But, just as his senior military leaders had expected, agreeing to the neutralization and demilitarization of the Laotian government created a power vac-uum in Laos, which allowed the Ho Chi Minh Trail to continue and enabled the destabilization of South Vietnam.[34]

Kennedy's motivations in Indochina have fueled debate and spec-ulation ever since. The most charitable, and perhaps most accurate, assessment is that JFK was trying to do everything he could to stem a major Communist advance there without provoking another war with China. That last possibility is what worried the leaders of Amer-ica's allies in Europe during the early 1960s, which may well have influenced Kennedy's thinking. But that explanation leaves one criti-cal open question: What was the backup plan? What would Kennedy have done if the assistance his administration provided failed to shore up the pro-US government in Saigon?[35]

As the Diem regime continued to lose support in 1963, Kennedy was persuaded to back a change in ruler, despite the lack of attractive alternatives. With his administration's tacit endorsement, a coup took place in South Vietnam on November 1, 1963. The South Vietnamese military figures who led the coup had Diem and his influential brother killed the next day to ensure they would never return to power. On top of being a flagrant violation of international law, the coup was simply wrongheaded. It did nothing to improve South Vietnam's ability to resist the Communist-backed insurrection. Diem had at least been a powerful political figure; no one of his stature ever held office in South Vietnam again.[36]

This senseless act of violence reflected the troubling tendency to favor force over diplomacy that had grown stronger as the numbers and influence of hawkish middle-class males had increased.[37]

TV, which was becoming a ubiquitous and dominant cultural force by the early 1960s, both reflected and reinforced those greater numbers and influence. The airwaves were filled with shows that were predicated on, and that reinforced, the centrality of middle-class white men to American life, including their customary fondness for dealing with "the bad guys" through force. The western series *Gunsmoke*, the most watched TV show in America from 1957 to 1961, glorified the heroic figure of 1870s Dodge City, Kansas, lawman Marshal Matt Dillon, played by James Arness. Every episode followed the same basic story line: a confrontation with one or more outlaws would lead to a shootout during which the villains usually got killed, not arrested. Each week *Gunsmoke* drew a huge number of middle-class male viewers, both fathers and their impressionable sons, but the show disturbed and perplexed critics. The African American writer James Baldwin neatly summarized his objections: "I am less appalled by the fact that *Gunsmoke* is produced than I am by the fact that so many people want to see it." So popular was the show that it grew from a half hour during its first six seasons to an hour starting in the fall of 1961. Even Lady Bird Johnson said it was her favorite TV show. By the time *Gunsmoke* went off the air in 1975, it had become the longest-running primetime TV show in history.[38]

The Kennedy administration did little to change the culture's emphasis on using force to resolve conflict and was focused instead on other domestic issues, most notably how best to limit the damage from the interconnected problems of inflation, automation, and foreign competition. Making that challenge its top domestic priority reflected the Kennedy administration's initial preoccupation with the problems of the heavily white middle class, and especially the employment prospects for its many children. A search was on for ways to preserve good jobs in manufacturing while also stimulating the emergence of new industries such as computing and information services that were less vulnerable to foreign competition, and that could employ the huge number of baby boomers who would begin entering the job market in the mid-1960s. The sense of urgency was heightened when the unemployment rate climbed to 6.8 percent shortly before Kennedy was inaugurated—the highest figure for the holiday season month of December since 1940. It signaled the arrival of an economic recession, which made the challenge of keeping the middle class prosperous and growing even more daunting.[39]

The two most influential figures in Kennedy's administration on those issues were Treasury Secretary Douglas Dillon and Labor Secretary Arthur Goldberg. Dillon, a prominent New York financier and registered Republican, had served as under secretary of state for economic affairs in the Eisenhower administration. He was appointed to Kennedy's cabinet to reassure foreign governments and American businessmen that the new president would work to maintain the value of the dollar and the system of fixed exchange rates among America's allies that had helped foster the post–World War II economic recovery.[40]

Kennedy's choice of Dillon also sent a clear message that the White House would not try to spend its way to greater prosperity, as FDR had done in the 1930s and many liberal Democratic economists and politicians would have liked. Thanks to his father's business background, Kennedy had a firm grasp of just how inflationary heavy government spending could be in the already prosperous 1960s, and thus its potentially self-defeating consequences. Persistent high inflation would likely shrink the real incomes of the middle class and, even more, the poor, reversing the trend since the 1930s of a narrowing gap between the most affluent and everyone else. With Dillon at the Treasury, the expectation was that the new administration would fight inflation in a moderate but firm fashion, as Eisenhower's usually had.[41]

Kennedy's appointment of Arthur Goldberg as labor secretary was intended to help keep excessive labor union demands in check. Goldberg was a nationally known labor lawyer based in Washington whose most important client was the powerful Steelworkers union. He, like Dillon, was respected by centrists in both political parties. Business leaders, most of whom were Republicans, tended to perceive Goldberg as an honest broker who understood the mounting economic problems the country faced. He envisioned developing broad support within labor, business, and government for practicing wage and price (of goods) restraint in manufacturing to preserve as many well-paid, middle-class jobs and incomes as possible. Such a course could not have stopped automation and foreign competition completely, Goldberg understood, but held the promise of minimizing it.[42]

Goldberg and Kennedy won labor support for their program by helping expand the union movement as a whole in the early 1960s. Prompted by his labor secretary, Kennedy issued an executive order that helped transform the federal workforce into a truly unionized one that could bargain effectively for higher wages and better benefits. State and local governments in the major industrial states tended to follow suit, which helped create more middle-class jobs in the public sector, which could not become vulnerable to foreign competition as private-sector jobs could. Unions of teachers, postal workers, and the like began adding what eventually became millions of new members. But if the new public-employee unions succeeded in driving up pay and benefits a great deal, that would substantially increase the cost of government, with higher taxes and/or more inflation as a result of bigger government budget deficits, as anti-union conservatives loudly pointed out.[43]

In the short run, however, the growing number of well-paid, middle-class jobs in the public sector helped offset somewhat the decline in those kinds of jobs in the private sector. This reinvigorated the making of a more middle-class country and culture. But these policies did not stimulate the kind of economic growth needed to employ the up-and-coming baby boom generation. To accomplish that, Kennedy and his closest advisers pushed for major changes in trade and tax policies.[44]

Dillon, at Treasury, believed that the high trade barriers in the early 1960s restricted growth at home and abroad and so negotiated new international agreements to lower them. So central was he to that complex bargaining process, which mostly took place in Geneva, that it became known in trade circles as "the Dillon Round" of the General Agreement on Tariffs and Trade (GATT). He also helped push changes through Congress in federal trade law, making renegotiation of those kinds of agreements easier for the executive branch. Those initiatives began driving up the volume of world trade, which by 1963 had helped spark a boom in western Europe and East Asia. Although that boom overseas could make US manufacturing more vulnerable to cheaper foreign imports, the hope and expectation was that Americans would ultimately gain more from expanding foreign trade than they lost.[45]

Kennedy and Dillon then devised a major tax cut of the sort that would later be characterized as supply-side economics. The idea was to reduce taxes substantially on business and the investor class to free up the investment capital needed to bring lots of new industries to life. Even more controversial than the changes in trade policy, the proposed tax cuts moved slowly through Congress. By the fall of 1963, though, passage of the tax bill had become assured. The logjam had been broken by an agreement to reduce taxes for everyone, but provided the largest reduction to the affluent. Although even that compromise struck many traditional New Deal liberals as unfair, the point of the measure was not to make the rich richer, but rather to give them more of the means needed to kick-start the kinds of businesses that could keep alive middle-class growth. If the investor class did its part, that renewed influx of capital could create many more good jobs in new areas of the economy as older sectors declined. Higher incomes for the affluent also had the potential to increase charitable giving and thus the size of the nonprofit sector, which could then do more to address social problems, especially ones in which the middle class seemed uninterested.[46]

The large federal tax reduction did arouse some grumbling on the right because the resulting loss of revenue seemed likely to increase the size of the federal budget deficit and fan the fires of inflation. The administration responded by emphasizing how much economic growth the tax cuts would likely stimulate. If the federal government could keep a lid on spending, the deficit would be modest at most because an expanding economic base would at least partly offset the reduced tax revenues. Even if the tax cut didn't literally pay for itself in that way, the size of the resulting budget deficit would not be great enough to bring a surge in inflation.[47]

The Kennedy-Dillon-Goldberg approach meant a continuation during the early 1960s of the kind of economic and social conditions middle-class people had known since the Korean War had ended in the summer of 1953. That helped sustain the baby boom and the related trend toward suburban homeownership among people with middle-class incomes. America in the early 1960s still appeared to be moving forward toward an ever more middle-class future. That so many white, middle-class Americans old enough to remember look back on the decade from 1953 to 1963 as the time when the American system worked best for them is no surprise.[48]

The centrist course that Kennedy, Dillon, and Goldberg were pursuing would not be easy to maintain. Signs of resistance began to appear within the nation's political system. GOP conservatives and their Dixiecrat allies had three main gripes: they were unhappy with greater government intervention into what was supposed to be the private-sector setting of wages and prices; they didn't like the emergence of unions in the public sector; and they feared rising federal budget deficits due to tax cuts.[49]

The left also found plenty of reasons to grumble. The Kennedy administration's promise to keep spending in check while cutting taxes had placated some on the right with regard to deficits, but had intensified left-wing concern about the prospects for new social programs such as aid to economically distressed areas and Medicare. If the tax reductions meant Congress would have less money to work with, how would pressing domestic problems be addressed in the 1960s? Many liberals, schooled in the era of the Great Depression and World War II, simply couldn't imagine private investment, philanthropy, and charity stepping in to create middle-class jobs and address major social problems while public spending remained restrained. Old-line liberals, with their acute awareness of the serious problems of the poor, could not envision the country navigating its way through its domestic challenges if the federal government didn't spend more generously.[50]

So, even as the heavily white middle class largely remained confident to the point of complacency in the early 1960s, the status quo was not without its challengers. Some of the most significant counternarratives were spelled out in books published about the domestic problems that first began to appear in the later 1950s.[51]

Among conservatives, the two most influential such works were Barry Goldwater's *The Conscience of a Conservative* (1960) and Milton Friedman's *Capitalism and Freedom* (1962). Goldwater was the strongly right-wing heir to a fortune stemming from a chain of department stores based in Phoenix, Arizona. He had first begun to attract national attention after winning a seat in the US Senate in 1952. In his first eight years in the Senate, Goldwater had assumed Robert Taft's informal leadership of the conservative Republicans. Goldwater shared with Taft, who died in 1953, a desire to reduce the size and cost of the federal government, and to cede more power back to the states and the private sector. Those positions, along with Goldwater's public dismissal of Eisenhower's Modern Republicanism as "a dime-store New Deal," also won the Arizona senator the respect of Herbert Hoover, who had never stopped searching for a candidate who could resurrect his conservative vision of America.[52]

Goldwater, however, parted ways with the old right of Hoover and Taft on foreign policy. Hoover, a Quaker pacifist, had objected to emphasizing military force in conducting US foreign policy. Taft, a Midwestern isolationist, had opposed NATO and the Roosevelt-Truman policy of building a large national security state to support that alliance system. Goldwater, in contrast, was a hawk who intended to win the Cold War. A believer in ensuring peace through military strength, Goldwater argued that the best way to address Cold War tensions was not through international cooperation, economic sanctions, arms control, and/or disarmament, but rather through more aggressive and effective prosecution of the fight against Communism worldwide. He enthusiastically embraced expanding US military capability to accomplish that, including heavy federal expenditures. Goldwater championed the development of advanced weaponry such as battlefield nuclear weapons (high in explosive power but low in radioactive fallout) and an antiballistic-missile system that could conceivably shoot down incoming Soviet ICBMs before they could be detonated. Goldwater envisioned an air force so big, and high-tech weapons so powerful, as to eliminate the need for a large army built by the draft, which entailed intrusions on personal freedom.[53]

If America's allies disagreed, Goldwater showed himself to be not so much an isolationist as a unilateralist, who wanted the US government to act more independently of allies and the United Nations. That was especially true, he believed, if other nations of the world resisted a more forceful approach to the threat of Soviet and Chinese expansionism in Africa, Asia, and Latin America.[54]

Goldwater's ideas reflected, to a degree, those of William F. Buckley Jr., the wealthy, witty right-wing pundit who had founded the magazine *National Review* in 1955 as a forum for criticizing Eisenhowerera Republicanism from the right. Buckley's brother-in-law, L. Brent Bozell, helped Goldwater write *The Conscience of a Conservative*, which had more of an impact on the voting public than Buckley's books ever did. For the first time, a New Right manifesto had come from a nationally prominent politician rather than an elitist eastern intellectual such as Buckley. Although dismissed by moderates in both parties as expressing extremist views, Goldwater's book began to win converts, especially among entrepreneurs living in the South and the Mountain West, the two parts of the country where the New Deal had done the least to change the class structure, and where income inequality remained high. More accustomed to that kind of situation than northerners were by the 1960s, affluent white Sunbelters were much less troubled by a vision of the future in which the country as a whole would become more like their parts of it.[55]

Goldwater's views gained some intellectual credence in 1962 when the University of Chicago economist Milton Friedman published his manifesto for a more modest national state. *Capitalism and Freedom* made the case, clearly and concisely, that the growth of the government in the 1930s and 1940s had contributed to the problems facing the country by the early 1960s. Friedman argued persuasively that high taxes and excessive government regulation had deterred entrepreneurship; that if labor unions went too far, they would undermine the middle class rather than support it; and that much of what the government did, from delivering mail to developing weapons, could be done more efficiently and at lower cost by the private sector. Friedman rejected, too, the notion that constant, heavy federal government spending was needed to keep the economy prosperous. His reading of what had gone wrong during the Great Depression stressed overly high interest rates rather than a lack of buying power among the general working population. Friedman advocated more intelligent application of what economists called monetary policy—the use of interest rates to encourage private investment—rather than Keynesian schemes that relied mainly on government spending to promote economic growth.[56]

Friedman's views, like Goldwater's, were generally dismissed as hopelessly outdated by the academic and political establishment. To the many moderates in high places, Friedman's book sounded like a call to undo elements of the New Deal that had become by then woven into the fabric of American life. Such an approach could conceivably increase overall economic growth, but it seemed unlikely to expand, or even preserve, the big middle class that New Deal–era reforms had helped produce. Centrists had a hard time imagining how the New Right could ever win enough support to put such ideas into action.[57]

What was most striking to conservatives of all kinds during the Kennedy presidency, though, was the renewed vitality infusing their movement, born out of opposition to Kennedy's efforts to sustain and expand the existing system through diplomacy abroad and activist government at home. The growing dynamism on the far right sometimes took extreme form, most notably in the rise of the John Birch Society (JBS). Named for an American Baptist missionary and army captain killed by Chinese Communists, the JBS tended to view centrist, Kennedy-era policies as the result of conspiracies rather than broad popular consensus. The Birchers and other, similar groups appealed to those on the right most alienated from the predominantly middle-class country the United States had become, seeing it as a place that did more to keep people where they were than to help the most talented and energetic achieve all they could. Although still not taken seriously by most Americans, especially in the big industrial states where the bulk of the country's population lived and the middle class was most influential, intense New Right organizing efforts were beginning to put pressure on more moderate conservatives to move away from Eisenhower-era Republicanism.[58]

At the same time a similar splintering was taking place on the left, also propelled in part by the publication of influential new books. Among them were *The Port Huron Statement*, a multiauthored tract primarily written by a student activist named Tom Hayden; Michael Harrington's *The Other America*; Rachel Carson's *Silent Spring*; Betty Friedan's *The Feminine Mystique*; and James Baldwin's *The Fire Next Time*.[59]

The first of those grew out of a conference held in June 1962 at a retreat in Port Huron, Michigan, owned by the United Automobile Workers union. There, fifty-nine members of the radically left-wing Students for a Democratic Society (SDS) wrote a manifesto that marked, as much as any single event did, the emergence of a New Left. Its goal was to replace the established left-wing orthodoxy, which had been closely identified with the American Communist Party and thoroughly discredited by Stalin's crimes. The New Left envisioned a political system based more on individual participation in governance than either the top-down Stalinist model or the current American system in which large, bureaucratic institutions played such powerful roles. The two main objectives articulated in the statement—besides what it called participatory democracy—were to move the United States from a policy of peace through military strength to one of disarmament, and to replace the southern system of racial segregation with one based on equality in law and life. Twenty thousand copies of the first edition of *The Port Huron Statement* were mimeographed in August 1962 and distributed to SDS chapters around the country, mostly on university campuses. Thus began the building of a cadre of left-wing student radicals who would pressure more centrist reform groups, most notably labor unions and the Democratic Party, to support SDS's agenda.[60]

A growing engagement with the plight of the poor also helped move many liberals further to the left. Social activist Michael Harrington played a big role in raising the public's awareness with his book *The Other America*. Rejecting the notion, so popular in the 1950s, that poverty was steadily declining and becoming less onerous, Harrington had gone out to see what life for America's poor was really like. His findings were published in a small book in March 1962 that began to draw a lot of attention after a respectful review appeared in the January 19, 1963, issue of *The New Yorker*. That President Kennedy himself appears to have read that essay, written by prominent New York intellectual Dwight Macdonald, also boosted the book's influence.[61] Harrington had found that poverty was not so much vanishing as becoming steadily less visible to the ever more comfortable middle-class majority, especially those who lived in suburbia. He estimated that 40–50 million Americans, over one-fifth of the country's population, lived in more dire need than most Americans knew. Harrington's grim but still sympathetic portraits of what life was like for those left out of American prosperity struck a nerve by illuminating the stark contrast between their way of life and that of the relatively affluent majority. Adding urgency was the continuing growth in the ranks of the working poor, beginning in the late 1950s, as automation began to eliminate well-paid jobs for unskilled and semiskilled laborers, thereby pushing people who had risen, financially speaking, in the 1940s and early 1950s, back down.[62]

The Other America also exposed how unevenly poverty was distributed *within* the country, with elderly, black, Latino, and Native American populations, as well as white people living in places such as Appalachia, far more at risk than other groups. Harrington's book was also a reminder that much of what had been done to create a predominantly middle-class nation had not reached many of the poorest citizens, including the introduction of Social Security, which required steady employment in specified job categories; legal protection for labor unions, most of whose members came from the upper half of the working class; military service, open mostly to healthy and physically fit young-adult males; and the GI Bill, whose generous benefits supported veterans and their families only. To the left, especially the younger generation, staying the course would mean continuing to exclude large groups of Americans from all those benefits. Harrington's book roused them to argue for more radically left-wing solutions, and to put pressure on their typically more moderate elders to support them.[63]

Rachel Carson's *Silent Spring* also benefited both from exposure in the *New Yorker* and President Kennedy's attention. The book, which she had begun in the late 1950s, was finally released in September 1962. It presented, in carefully documented detail, her findings about the harm that excessive pesticide use, of DDT especially, was doing to the American environment. Carson, a gifted nature writer as well as a scientist, crafted her book to appeal not just to readers' intellects, but also to their emotions, which drew the scorn of some in the scientific community. Having been trained as a marine biologist rather than a chemist, her expertise was also called into question. The sometimes forceful tone of *Silent Spring*, provoked in part by chemical-industry attacks on Carson's research prior to its publication, also generated a firestorm of criticism. The pesticide industry was naturally infuriated by her attack on their livelihood, but Carson was making a much more fundamental statement in the book: the existing balance of nature was a critical factor in humanity's survival, and excessive pesticide use was upsetting that balance in unforeseen and potentially disastrous ways. Her critics argued that human beings were already stepping in to take control of nature—not necessarily a bad thing in their eyes—so Carson's thesis didn't hold water for them.[64]

Silent Spring helped spark a renewal of public interest in the condition of the natural environment and the damage inflicted by rapid economic growth. President Kennedy's sympathetic comment about the book at a televised presidential press conference, and a favorable review from his science advisory committee, also helped overcome the intense criticism emanating from industry experts in a massive corporate public relations campaign to protect their interests. Carson's untimely death only a year and a half after the book's publication also made her something of a martyr. *Silent Spring's* defenders began to band together to put pressure on government and private industry to inform the public about the hazards of chemical pollutants and other toxins such as auto exhaust that were making the nation's air and water more dangerous to health. Among liberals in particular, the book served as a wake-up call that the economic growth that had been so important to the rise of the middle class could ultimately be harmful to them and everyone else.[65]

The appearance in February 1963 of Betty Friedan's *The Feminine Mystique* also helped push moderates further to the left. Friedan, a magazine writer and an affluent suburban homemaker with three children, seemed, at first glance, an unlikely firebrand. Just five and a half years earlier, Friedan's story in the middlebrow *Coronet* magazine about two patients with mental disorders who fell in love had won her its August 1957 "Mother of the Month" award. But Friedan kept hearing the same frustrations with the confining domestic life expressed by so many of her fellow alums from the Smith College class of 1942, feelings that echoed with her own regrets about abandoning graduate study in psychology to marry and start a family at a young age. Her life choice underscored in a personal way the pitfalls—for highly educated women especially—of the middle-class focus on early marriage and child-rearing. Undaunted by the resistance of mainstream magazine editors to publish an article with such controversial themes, Friedan chose to write a book.[66]

The educated and mostly well-off women with time on their hands about whom Friedan was writing also constituted a significant part of the book-buying public, so *The Feminine Mystique* attracted a lot of readers. (It became a bestseller.) The book's reassessment of early marriage and family made Friedan easily as controversial as Carson. Even her own husband harshly and publicly criticized his newly famous spouse and her work. She became an outcast in Rockland County, New York, where the family had lived since 1956, obliging them to move. Despite that kind of hostility, the book's success helped generate pressure on yet another tentpole of moderate middle-class dominance.[67]

The explosiveness of *The Feminine Mystique*'s message lay in its challenge to the male-breadwinner model, on which twenty years of growth in the middle class had been predicated. What helped Friedan's critique of that model reach well beyond her core constituency was the rising fraction of jobs that did not pay enough to support an entire family. As inflation, automation, and foreign competition began to erode the number of good, unionized jobs, more low-paying ones became available, especially in the burgeoning service sector. As inflation eroded the real incomes of middle-class men with more secure, white-collar jobs, the male-breadwinner model ran into even more trouble. The book's central message took on greater relevance, not just to more affluent women but also to women across the socioeconomic spectrum, more and more of whom found themselves pressured to take a paying job—a step husbands often resisted—or live with an inadequate household income.[68]

As the Sunbelt rose, so did a big-business model based on low wages paid to women workers. Thus was born Walmart in 1962, which eventually became the biggest single example of that phenomenon. By the early 1960s that employment model began to spread more widely in the central cities of the North and Far West, where the migration of employers to the suburbs and the Sunbelt helped shrink the number of male-breadwinner jobs downtown.[69]

All those factors combined to make sure that Friedan's critique of the status quo gained its greatest traction at first in the socioeconomic system's top and bottom, and in those parts of the country where the egalitarian changes wrought by the New Deal proved to be most limited and fleeting. As the Sunbelt model spread northward, however, the relevance of her message steadily expanded.[70]

The Kennedy administration responded first with an executive order creating the President's Commission on the Status of Women (PCSW). Headed by Eleanor Roosevelt, it was mandated to explore the issues and conditions facing women and recommend ways for improvement. Second, the PCSW supported passage of what became the Equal Pay Act of 1963. Although limited in scope, it marked the beginning of a greater emphasis in federal law on equal pay for equal work, regardless of gender.[71] How committed JFK was to greater equality for women in law and life is hard to know. With respect to gender he was a study in contradictions. He maintained a friendly and mutually respectful working relationship with professional women, such as Assistant Secretary of Labor Esther Peterson, who was the most influential person in the administration on the PCSW and Equal Pay Act initiatives. Kennedy and Peterson had known each other for years; as a former labor-movement lobbyist, she had dealt with him during his time in the Senate. But he was also a womanizer, so it's hard to imagine him being passionately supportive of a revived women's movement in the 1960s. The government's tepid response to the problems Friedan had identified, reflected by Kennedy's failure to appoint even a single woman to his cabinet or more women to high-ranking positions of the sort Esther Peterson held, seemed likely, sooner or later, to produce a social crisis.[72]

Of all the looming domestic challenges to the middle-class majority's hard-won gains, racial unrest proved the most powerful. It demanded and eventually got more of Kennedy's attention. His presidency began during the white-backlash phase of the civil rights movement. From 1958 to 1962 progress toward desegregation was glacial, fanning discontent in the black community everywhere. The heavy-handed, often violent repression visited upon typically peaceful protesters by southern sheriffs, police departments, and vigilante groups further stiffened the resolve of the rapidly growing movement to bring down Jim Crow.[73]

African American anger also grew in the poor urban neighborhoods of the North and the Far West, where much of the black population was stuck in low-wage jobs or not working at all. Black male unemployment in poor urban neighborhoods during the sixties was higher than it had ever been for the entire workforce since the Depression. The number of unemployed young males no longer in school steadily increased beginning in 1962, when the first baby boomers turned sixteen. Desperate to change the outcomes for the young men in their communities, black activists tried to exert pressure on government officials to desegregate workplaces and neighborhoods, but many working and lower-middle-class white people fiercely resisted. Although typically better off, such white people also had children coming of age in an economy with steadily fewer good jobs for those without specialized skills or higher education. As a result, white backlash in the cities up North also increased frustration within the black community.[74]

Inspired leadership grew out of the black community to help focus and channel that anger and give it voice. Martin Luther King Jr., who had come to some prominence for his role in the Montgomery bus boycott, and his associates—who generally adhered to Gandhian civil disobedience as the primary form of protest—had the greatest influence, especially in the South. African American labor leader A. Philip Randolph and National Urban League president Whitney Young, who were more focused on the urban employment issue and its far-reaching consequences, also gave direction and energy to black protest, as did Malcolm X in a more radical, separatist way. The writings of black intellectuals, most notably James Baldwin, also helped bring these issues more into the public discourse. His landmark essay, "A Letter from a Region in My Mind," appeared in the New Yorker in November 1962 and was then published in book form under the title The Fire Next Time. In those works, Baldwin detailed the challenges and inequities faced by African Americans and predicted their frustrations would soon produce a social explosion.[75]

The truth of Baldwin's vision first became clear in May 1963, when a protest against racial segregation in stores, restaurants, and other businesses in Birmingham, Alabama, spiraled out of control. Birmingham police commissioner Theophilus Eugene "Bull" Connor had used his officers to jail so many adult protesters that the failure of the protest seemed imminent. When Dr. King and his associates decided to allow children to participate directly, and when Connor used the same police dogs, water hoses, and police brutality against them that he had deployed against the adults, public outrage exploded. That phenomenon became national and even international as recently developed mobile TV news cameras vividly and immediately conveyed what Connor and the Birmingham police were doing.

The Kennedy administration's response to the Birmingham protests marked a major shift in its approach to segregation. The administration's main objective had been to keep civil rights protests contained, lest they divide the country and be exploited not only by the Communist propaganda machine, but also by the GOP against the Democratic Party. Events in Birmingham demanded more purposeful action. One month later, JFK delivered a televised address on civil rights—more extemporaneous than scripted—that was unlike any previous presidential remarks on the subject. Kennedy spoke eloquently and emotionally about the need for a new federal law to protect the basic civil rights of black Americans. He described the challenge before the nation as "a moral issue," something no president had ever before publicly said. The White House then submitted to Congress the first version of what would become the Civil Rights Act of 1964, delighting many African Americans and their white liberal allies. Kennedy's speech and proposed civil rights bill provided proof that their faith in him on Election Day in 1960 had not been misplaced.[76]

The speech also had a major impact on white moderates, Catholics especially, living in the urban North, as it expanded public support for civil rights legislation. Drawing on his deeply felt popularity in the major metropolitan areas of the North and his personal appeal and effectiveness as a communicator on TV, Kennedy used the speech to reorient their white inhabitants toward greater sympathy for African Americans' quest for equality.[77]

However, Kennedy's new proactive stance on civil rights was as polarizing among white southerners as the Birmingham protests had been. Within hours of Kennedy's speech to the nation, a white Mississippian deeply hostile to the idea of racial equality had gunned down the head of the state's NAACP chapter, Medgar Evers. The white backlash proved to be a more powerful force in the South than the liberal support Kennedy had been able to inspire elsewhere, and his overall approval rating in national polls dropped from the 70s into the 50s as many southern and border-state whites turned against his administration.[78]

Kennedy's new civil rights policy also helped fuel protest movements within both of the nation's two main political parties. Alabama governor George Wallace, a highly outspoken defender of Jim Crow, decided to enter the upcoming Democratic Party presidential primaries in 1964 as a pro-segregation candidate, convinced that some Democratic voters in all parts of the country would support him. Barry Goldwater's emerging bid for the Republican nomination also gained a boost from Kennedy's new stand on civil rights because the Arizonan strongly opposed expanding the power of the federal government to fight segregation. The proposed civil rights law also aroused intense opposition in Congress, mostly from conservative southern Democrats, who vowed to use their considerable leverage to block the bill.[79]

Even utterly peaceful advocacy for the bill and what it represented ignited controversy. The August 28, 1963, March on Washington, intended to send a dramatic public message of support for the passage of the civil rights measure, was carefully choreographed so as to appeal to the still vital center of the American electorate. In that context, the march was an unqualified success. However, by toning down the militancy of the younger members of the civil rights movement, the march's organizers felt stinging blowback from them and other, more radical African Americans for the generally conciliatory and uplifting tone of the event. Black Muslim leader Malcolm X gave voice to their disdain when he publicly labeled the event "the Farce on Washington." That extreme view failed to gain traction within the black community, but by then, the segregation issue had begun to divide the country deeply in far-reaching ways.[80]

Both the excessively militarized nature of American life in the early sixties and deepening divisions over gender and race in particular touched the lives of the Sindt and Perkins families directly in these years. Not every middle-class man favored force over diplomacy. Howard Sindt was a hawk, but George Perkins wasn't, having been chastened by his experience in the service. But even the more gen-

213

tle souls among middle-class American males found themselves bombarded by entertainment that carried messages of the acceptability of aggression. Howard's fourth and youngest child, Conrad, was a sensitive, brainy boy, fond of animals, who nonetheless learned how to hunt and owned a coonskin hat of the sort the *Davy Crockett* TV show had popularized. TV and the movies had the kind of power that could turn a huge new generation of impressionable boys into gun-toting men. Even if those boys fundamentally rejected violence, as Conrad did, they often found themselves pushed into environments where the use of force was glorified. That happened when Howard Sindt, concerned that his sometimes rebellious son was becoming a discipline problem, packed him off to a private military academy for high school.

The issue of gender-based discrimination likewise touched the Sindt family directly. Beatrice's daughter Carol had been an outstanding student both in high school and at Bucknell University, where she majored in political science. Carol moved to Denver after earning her bachelor's degree, worked in a department store, and met and married a liberal, intellectual New York City native who taught phys ed at a Catholic high school. In 1962, she became pregnant for the first time and confided this happy news to a coworker, who told the boss. He summoned Carol to his office and summarily discharged her, even though she felt able to keep working for a while longer. The painful memory of this patronizing and patriarchal act never left Carol. It also marked her exit from the realm of full-time paid work, which she never rejoined. At the time, she didn't see this episode as a form of injustice, as the feminist movement had yet to capture the attention of the middle class. But this life-changing event, some variation of which was repeated in the lives of countless women, strengthened the sense that something was fundamentally wrong with how the middle-class employment model of that era was working.

George Perkins had his consciousness raised as well, in his case with regard to racial injustice. George turned sixty-five in March 1962 and shifted to part-time consulting work for the employment service. That change freed him, he felt, to become public about his support for addressing the problem of black unemployment, albeit in his own low-key, mainstream way. Thus, when George heard about plans for what became the March on Washington to promote "jobs and justice," he, together with a professor friend from Brown, helped organize a delegation from Providence. Their fleet of buses made the run down to DC for the march, the memory of which George cherished for the rest of his life. He had always been drawn to lofty oratory, and he thought that Martin Luther King Jr.'s speech on that day was the best he'd ever heard. But no swift or significant response came to the problems highlighted by the march, and that meant steadily rising crime in urban areas, Providence included. Before the year was over, George and Emily would reluctantly leave the city for a suburban house in nearby Warwick, where they lived for the rest of their lives.

These seismic shifts in politics, economics, and society were mirrored by developments in popular culture in the early 1960s that were no less consequential. The shift was perhaps most apparent in the world of popular music. Teenage love and romance continued to dominate rock and roll, but a new strain of folk protest music emerged, led by such artists as Joan Baez, Bob Dylan, and Pete Seeger, who updated the Depression-era social-protest tradition associated with Woody Guthrie so that it could address the new social concerns of the 1960s.[81]

At first confined to the bohemian subculture of bars and coffeehouses in the biggest cities and college towns, the new folk music finally went mainstream in the spring and summer of 1963. In the years before America's massive intervention into Vietnam, protest music focused mostly on the existential threat of the Cold War and the burgeoning civil rights movement. The first song to break through into the mass consciousness was "Blowin' in the Wind," a Dylan ballad redone somewhat more harmoniously by the folk trio Peter, Paul and Mary. Their rendition began airing on the radio in May 1963, in the wake of the Birmingham protests. The single sold a staggering three hundred thousand copies within a month of its release. In August, the month of the March on Washington, "Blowin' in the Wind" reached number two on the pop charts, a first for any social-protest song. It had sold over a million copies and become world-famous. More such songs followed, and folk artists suddenly rose to the heights of fame and stardom, while themes of protest and social awareness found their way into rock and roll, gospel, and other music genres.[82]

A closely related trend was the growing prominence of African American musicians and singers, such as those associated with Detroit-based Motown Records, founded in 1959. Although rock and roll largely evolved from black musical styles, the most widely known rock and rollers in the 1950s had typically been young white men such as Elvis Presley, Bill Haley, and Buddy Holly. In the early 1960s, African American artists such as Diana Ross and the Supremes began breaking through to the mass market, eventually achieving unprecedented visibility for black artists. Certainly, TV had never before showcased so many black performers. The audiences for such performers also became more racially integrated. As the ranks of baby boomer teens expanded, so, too, did the market among young white people for tickets to concerts featuring black singers, and for their records. Suddenly, the young were posing a threat to Jim Crow that their elders had probably never contemplated. Though not an overtly political act, it still profoundly challenged the racial status quo.[83]

Hints of the impending revolution in the realm of race also surfaced in the world of jazz music, long dominated by black Americans. In the early 1960s, Louis Armstrong remained the best-known and most commercially successful jazz star, but tellingly, most of the fans who came to his performances were white. Many black jazz lovers were now drawn to the more introspective, blues-inflected music of Miles Davis, in part because, unlike Armstrong, Davis refused to present the exuberant exterior that middle-class white audiences preferred. Davis even often stood with his back to the audience as he blew his trumpet. As problems in the black community grew, the market for optimism in the world of popular culture declined, which Davis understood much better than Armstrong ever did.[84]

In hindsight, this missed opportunity to acknowledge the existence, contributions, and problems of the black population in the movies and especially on TV seems nothing less than perverse. *The Andy Griffith Show*, a highly popular situation comedy, was a case in point. Set in small-town North Carolina, the show first appeared on CBS in October 1960 and ran in prime time through the spring of 1968. *The Andy Griffith Show* owed much of its success to the considerable comedic gifts of the male leads, Andy Griffith, who played the town's sheriff, and Don Knotts, who portrayed his bumbling deputy. The show's creators avoided engagement with racial issues by setting the show in the mountainous, Appalachian part of North Carolina, which was overwhelmingly white. The unabashedly sympathetic portrayal of the kindly law officers was incongruous with the reality on the ground in the South, where many real-world southern sheriffs and deputies were using their considerable authority, often through violent means, to put down the growing black resistance to Jim Crow.[85]

The harmful results of this profoundly misleading depiction of American life were magnified by TV's steadily growing power and pervasiveness. Fifties TV had possessed more limited impact: fewer people owned TV sets, channels had been less numerous and broadcasting hours more limited, and the visual quality in this black-and-white era had been less vivid. In the 1960s, TV as a mass phenomenon really took hold, and broadcasting in the much more lively and exciting color became the norm. TV didn't tell people what to think as much as it told them what to think about. By leaving out black people, TV—and the broader popular-culture system in which TV stood at the center—alienated African Americans.

The growing rifts in American society over race and the Cold War converged in November 1963 to produce an untimely end to the Kennedy presidency. Kennedy was obliged to visit Dallas that month to smooth over differing views on civil rights and foreign policy between the liberal and Dixiecrat wings of the Texas Democratic Party, and thus boost his chances for carrying the state in 1964. Waiting for his motorcade on November 22, 1963, as it rolled toward Dealey Plaza was a twenty-four-year-old marine veteran and deranged Marxist named Lee Harvey Oswald. His anger over Kennedy's anti-Castro policy led him to kill JFK by firing on his motorcade with a high-powered rifle from a sixth-floor window. The sudden, violent death of such a youthful and popular president, a genuine symbol to many of America's bright future, shocked the nation. The loss of John Kennedy hit the middle class hard, especially the newly assimilated and prosperous middle-class white Americans who supported him most strongly.[86]

CHAPTER 9

Things Fall Apart

Over the next five years, Lyndon Johnson would take some steps that would further improve the lot of the middle class, such as pushing through landmark federal-aid-to-education bills that widened access to college for the baby boomers, and creating Medicare, the publicly funded system of health care for the elderly. He also pushed successfully for addressing some of the threats to continuing middle-class dominance, most notably in the area of civil rights. However, Johnson also made mistakes that slowed the trend toward an ever more middle-class country and culture, so much so that by Election Day in 1968 it had stopped.

Larger social forces were at work as well. Those above and below the middle class pushed for reforms such as racial desegregation and affirmative action, programs to assist the poorest, and funding to improve and expand the arts and humanities and to better protect the natural environment. Much of the middle class had resisted these kinds of reforms, which appealed more to those at the top and the bottom of the income scale. Landmark US Supreme Court rulings such as *Miranda v. Arizona* in 1966 that strengthened protections for criminal suspects and defendants likewise found more favor in upper and lower America than in between.

Johnson's economic-policy missteps, however, turned off middle-class people even more by spurring lasting high inflation that eroded their real incomes. His misguided Vietnam policy harmed them in another way, by undermining support for the draft, which had done so much to expand the middle class. Thus, despite Johnson's intentions to keep the middle class prosperous, growing, and supportive of his presidency, his administration in some ways contributed to just the opposite. To that often inspiring, frustrating, and sometimes tragic story we now turn.[1]

Kennedy had chosen Johnson as his running mate to increase his odds of winning, not because he liked Johnson or saw him as well qualified to serve as president. Once in the White House, Kennedy had effectively marginalized Johnson. Thus, when Johnson became president on November 22, 1963, he inherited problems and policies about which he knew too little. The circumstances of JFK's death in Dallas made Johnson's unexpected rise to the Oval Office even more awkward, given that Texas was Johnson's home state. (In some more unstable countries south of the Rio Grande, people commonly suspected a vice president had a hand in any untimely presidential death.) And if all that were not enough, Johnson had deeply felt insecurities, a product of his hardscrabble upbringing and southern identity in a party whose presidents since the Civil War had all been northerners. All of this made him thin-skinned, at best, in response to criticism. The stage was set for what would at times become a profoundly unhappy chapter in American presidential history.[2]

The first year in office was something of a honeymoon, with Johnson carefully avoiding anything too rash, and focusing instead on trying to complete what Kennedy had started. Using the skills honed during his six years as Senate majority leader from 1955 to 1960, Johnson pushed through Congress the 1964 Civil Rights Act as well as Kennedy's tax-cut legislation. Those signature domestic policies proved popular with voters, including the broad middle class, because they seemed likely to promote the related goals of calming social unrest and enabling greater prosperity. When the many centrist GOP presidential candidates all canceled one another out, allowing the sole New Right contender, Barry Goldwater, to win his party's nomination, Johnson found himself facing the weakest general-election opponent he could have hoped for. The thoroughly foreseeable result, an electoral landslide that expanded Democratic majorities in both houses of Congress, inclined Johnson to think he could become a successful president over the long run. Just as Harry Truman had mistakenly interpreted his unexpected reelection in 1948 over an unlikable opponent as a personal triumph that gave him a mandate for expanding the New Deal,

LBJ saw the electoral outcome in 1964 as a vote for more liberal social reform. And unlike Truman in 1949, Johnson in 1965 could rely on big Democratic majorities in Congress to help pass such legislation.[3]

Thus began the Great Society phase of the Johnson presidency. Using his legendary skills at moving legislation through Congress, Johnson won passage of many new laws aimed at remedying the major defects of American society. Among the most broadly popular was the program that became known as Medicare. Kennedy had promised such a program when he ran for president, and Johnson succeeded in delivering it in 1965. Some of the other measures Johnson pushed through Congress in the mid-1960s were ones that Kennedy had wanted, such as an aid program for the poorest and for federal aid to "distressed areas." But the size, scope, and cost of Johnson's reforms were much bigger than Kennedy had envisioned, which helped ignite the fires of inflation. Prices had risen at an annual rate of less than 2 percent in the first half of the 1960s, which the broad middle class could cope with through annual wage and salary increases. In the second half of the decade, however, the annual inflation rate shot up to over 4 percent, eroding the real incomes of many in the middle class. Unlike Kennedy, Johnson had little in-depth understanding of the risk of high inflation and so was comfortable pushing for far more spending on his domestic reform programs than Kennedy ever would have. And in the foreign-policy realm, Johnson's inclination to think big ignited a hugely expensive and ultimately unsuccessful effort to rescue South Vietnam from Communist North Vietnam's infiltration and overthrow, which made the likelihood of persistent, high inflation even greater. All this new federal spending, when combined with the loss of tax revenue stemming from the big 1964 tax cut (and LBJ's stubborn refusal to raise taxes until 1968), produced larger, recurring federal budget deficits, and the inflationary surge of the later 1960s. Higher prices then provoked unions to demand higher wages, which tended to make the trend toward more automation more pronounced, because demands for higher wages prompted employers to try even harder to replace workers with machines. Higher wages and prices also opened the door wider to imports, which could compete more effectively with higher-priced American-made goods. Heavy government spending and the expanding Vietnam-era draft calls (which drove down unemployment) did contribute to an economic boom, especially in sectors that serviced the military, but it wasn't sustainable.[4]

The inflationary surge of the later 1960s helped slow the thirty-year trend toward greater income equality in other ways. No move was made to raise taxes on the affluent during most of the economic boom that Great Society domestic and military spending had helped create, which caused interest rates to rise and the stock market to soar, while the real incomes of the middle class began to fall due to increasing inflation. The investor class had a lot more money to save and invest due to the 1964 tax cut, and all of a sudden could earn higher rates of return on it (as interest rates rose) than they had generally been able to since the Great Depression. Those conditions would soon cause the "class gap" between the top and the middle to start widening again, for the first time in decades. As that shift took hold, the rise of the middle class, economically speaking, hit a wall. As the number of well-paid jobs for American men without special skills or a lot of education fell, among urban black men especially, rioting in the central cities became a defining feature of American life.[5]

Johnson's Vietnam policy proved even more socially divisive and damaging to the middle class because massively escalating American military involvement in Vietnam turned increasing numbers of voters, even middle-class ones, against the draft. The war's vicious and perplexing nature undermined the appeal of military service to many young men (and their parents), weakening a mechanism that had aided the growth of the middle class in the previous generation. So, too, did the unfair way the Vietnam-era draft worked, by inadvertently but systematically targeting a less advantaged subset of the population. Fully aware of the war's unpopularity, Johnson resisted calling up the reserves or cutting back on college deferments even as enrollments there swelled. The army that resulted consisted of a much younger and poorer group of enlisted men than had served either in World War II or Korea. Their average age was just nineteen, as compared with twenty-seven in World War II and Korea. Roughly 80 percent grew up in poor or working-class households. With so many young-adult males in the mid-to-late 1960s due to the baby boom, just drafting such a subset of them yielded enough manpower for Vietnam. The profound inequity of this further eroded support for both the war and the draft.[6]

Johnson and his aides made matters worse by encouraging the American people to believe the war was going well, despite the weakness of the Saigon regime and its armed forces, and the inability to come up with a winning approach that would not provoke Chinese and/or Soviet escalation. Accidentally enlarging the war in Korea by provoking Chinese military intervention had fatally undermined Truman's presidency, something Johnson was determined to avoid in Vietnam. But fighting under the tight restrictions Johnson imposed as a result offered no real prospect of success. Confined to fighting in South Vietnam, the young American GIs quickly lost enthusiasm for a conflict so shockingly different from the sanitized version of World War II they had seen in countless movies and TV shows. Johnson took heat, as well, from the hawks on his political right, who urged him to take the war to the North—or bomb more heavily, even in civilian areas—all of which would only have escalated the conflict and increased the chances of China or the Soviet Union stepping in to support North Vietnam. The leaders of the Communist world saw Vietnam as another critical East-West flash point; the more the conflict grew, the more likely the Communist superpowers were to get more directly involved. Johnson thought the United States could wear down the North Vietnamese by sending in more troops and dropping more bombs, but the enemy showed remarkable staying power in the face of the increased military pressure. America found itself in a deepening mess. As the hollowness of the promises of military progress became clear, much of the broad middle class turned against not just Johnson's fruitless strategy, but also against the draft that had made it possible.[7]

LBJ's Texas-size mistakes with inflation and Vietnam especially caused a seismic shift in voter attitudes. In the off-year elections of November 1966, the GOP made major gains in Congress and in many of the state races. When combined with the blocs of Dixiecrats in the House and Senate, conservatives in Congress found themselves able to stifle much of the forward progress of Johnson's Great Society reform programs. One year later, pollsters reported that a majority of the electorate saw the Republicans as better able to handle the economy and foreign policy than the Democrats. This was the first time in a decade that the GOP had established a lead in these crucial areas, and it began a long-term trend. As the middle class found its sense of security shaken by inflation, urban riots, and stalemate on the battlefield, a new era in American politics dawned, one that would prove much less friendly to the middle class. The rise of the Democrats to majority-party status in the 1930s had greatly contributed to the emergence of a predominantly middle-class country. The popularity of Democratic policies and programs had also enabled greater influence for moderate Republicans within their own party. As Johnson's missteps eroded support for the Democratic Party nationally, the door was reopened for the kinds of policies (and politicians) that had been marginalized for the past generation.[8]

What made that hard to see at first was the growing fragmentation in American political life, as the number of mainstream centrists began to decline, and the ranks of those previously thought of as fringe types began to become much more numerous, vocal, and visible. By far the biggest such group was composed of strongly conservative people. Even though the New Right's first major champion had gone down to an ignominious defeat in November 1964, Goldwater's campaign had aroused intense enthusiasm in some parts of the country, especially the booming Sunbelt. Goldwater's victory at the GOP national convention was seen there as just the beginning of a new trend, not a dead end. Just two years later, Goldwater advocate Ronald Reagan came seemingly out of nowhere to win the California governorship by a margin of almost a million votes. That Reagan had trounced a fairly popular incumbent Democrat of the Great Society variety in the nation's most populous state clearly indicated to New Right true believers that the future would, sooner or later, be theirs.[9]

Many in that still relatively small conservative base felt hopeful that more of the electorate could be convinced of the wisdom of their approach. Reagan himself was a convert to the cause. Having started out in life as a fairly liberal Democrat, Reagan had moved steadily to the right since the late 1940s. He brought just the right persona and demeanor to the cause, as well. Unlike the edgy, upper-class Goldwater, Reagan had been born and raised in the Midwest and projected warmth, friendliness, and a genuine lack of pretension. He was also more attuned than Goldwater to the growing economic insecurity among the lower-middle class, having grown up in a family that constantly struggled to make ends meet.[10]

Reagan had also learned from Goldwater's mistakes in 1964, one of which was to allow ultra-right-wing groups such as the John Birch Society to associate themselves with his campaign. When Reagan ran for governor of California, he kept the kookier kinds of New Rightists at arm's length, which did much to reassure the broad middle of the electorate that he would be a practical New Right conservative.[11]

Reagan's Hollywood acting experience translated beautifully to television, which had by then become the politician's best tool for connecting with the public. His natural effectiveness on camera posed a stark and welcome contrast to Goldwater's. The Reagan revolution in California suggested to the New Right faithful that the problem in 1964 had been not so much the message as the messenger, something many of them saw for themselves at Goldwater rallies. Ronald Reagan had often performed as the warm-up speaker, doing so much better than the candidate as to confuse some observers about which one was the headliner. Thrown off by Reagan's age—he turned fifty-three that year and thus seemed too old to start a career in politics—otherwise astute reporters covering Reagan's performances as Goldwater's pitchman concluded that the actor had missed his true calling. The press sometimes saw Reagan up close, where the many lines etched in his face by the California sun made him look even older than he was, but the average voter seldom got that chance. With his show business background, Reagan had no problem concealing his true age and appearance by dyeing his hair and wearing heavy makeup on TV, which most American men at the time wouldn't have done.[12]

Demographic trends also contributed to the expansion of the New Right in the mid-1960s. The Sunbelt's predominantly low-wage, largely nonunion economy was growing rapidly, attracting more young-adult migrants from the North following the jobs moving out of high-wage states. As these newcomers arrived, some tended to rise economically and become more receptive to the strongly conservative ideas associated with Goldwater and Reagan and actively promoted by the business community and its partners in state and local governments. Those newcomers who fell down the economic ladder tended to fall out of the electorate in Sunbelt states, which usually lacked the kind of union-based political activism that boosted working-class turnout in Frostbelt states. As the upper-class demographic and institutions in the Sunbelt became more prosperous, more high school graduates in the Sunbelt made their way to those private colleges where New Right ideas were prominent. Evangelical Christian institutions of higher learning grew especially rapidly in the South, which expanded the New Right's next generation even more.[13]

The New Right, and others on the conservative fringe that had suddenly become numerous and acceptable to the mainstream, had their counterparts on the left. The New Left, the group whose manifesto had been *The Port Huron Statement*, and whose most important organization was Students for a Democratic Society (SDS), defined itself in opposition to top-down governance of all kinds, racial segregation, and the Cold War. For the New Left, democracy meant citizen participation in decision-making, and with it they believed would come an end to Jim Crow, the Vietnam War, and many other social ills. The New Left's core constituency—young adults attending public colleges and universities—also benefited from rapidly changing demographics. Their numbers swelled in those years as baby boomers came out of high school and found that most well-paid jobs open to them required higher education. In part that was due to decreased hiring in heavily unionized basic manufacturing, except for firms benefiting from the boom in Defense Department contracts as the war in Vietnam heated up. As factory jobs migrated to places where unions were scarce and wages for workers were low, the pressure to get more schooling intensified.[14]

A rapidly growing civilian public sector was fueled by more and bigger Great Society–style regulatory and administrative initiatives aimed at expanding educational and employment opportunities, fighting poverty, improving and expanding health care for the poor and the elderly especially, and protecting the environment. These initiatives increased the number of well-paid jobs in such professions as law, medicine, nursing, public administration, and teaching. Even in fields that hadn't before required a college degree for entry-level jobs, such as lower-level administration and journalism, employers increasingly wanted new hires to have one. A college deferment was also a good way for men to avoid getting shipped off to Vietnam. Thus, college enrollments suddenly reached unprecedented heights. Most of these impressionable young people were away from their parents' influence for the first time and were also frightened that the government might cut back on draft deferments, which generally made them receptive to the anti-authority messages of the New Left.[15]

Some young people became politicized by the civil rights movement or other social causes, but the overwhelming majority of crusaders of the New Left—largely middle- to upper-middle-class white students—came to it through their opposition to the Vietnam War. Once Johnson massively escalated American military involvement in 1965, the ranks of Students for a Democratic Society began to grow rapidly. Although the membership of this leading New Left organization was always a tiny fraction of all college and university students—as had been the case with the American Communist Party, the premier group of the old left in the 1930s—SDS's influence extended considerably beyond those who actually joined. As the war went on and became steadily less popular, young adults began questioning the views of the seemingly endless numbers of older authority figures who at least outwardly supported it. Questioning authority soon became a habit, if not a fashion, and a revolutionary one for those raised during the much more respectful fifties.[16]

The most recognizable manifestation of the growing revolt against authority were the hippies who flocked to San Francisco's Haight-Ashbury or New York's Greenwich Village to act out, at least for a while, a rebellion against the stifling caution and conformity of parents who had been scarred by Depression and war. Rejecting what they saw as the older generation's obsession with economic security, the "flower children" advocated living for the moment, a message many found refreshing and liberating. The media seemed captivated by the colorful and often flamboyant appearance of the hippies and their casual, uninhibited lifestyle, giving them more exposure than they ever dreamed of, or ever wanted. The impact was seismic and happened fast. So many young people were attracted by what looked like great romantic fun and adventure with little consequence. The new hippie generation was calling out the approaches, priorities, and values that had done so much to expand middle-class prosperity: settle down early, build a family and a household and a community, and focus on achieving long-run stability and security. The boomers lived free of the fears and uncertainties that drove their parents, and many couldn't see the need to follow their elders' example. The widening rift would become known as the generation gap.[17]

An even greater existential threat to that tidy middle-class model festered among the increasingly angry poor, in central cities especially, who by the mid-1960s were treated to endless daily depictions on TV of middle-class white prosperity, from which they were excluded. If those impoverished Americans also had dark skin, their resentment was even more acute, knowing that unless things changed radically in the country, they would never have access to the same opportunities and comfort simply because of how they looked. On the very night in July of 1964 that Barry Goldwater accepted the GOP presidential nomination with a provocatively conservative speech, a riot broke out in Harlem, long the center of New York's, if not the nation's, black community, the outrage and anger finding expression in crime and violence. The rioting spread to other cities, reaching its most destructive levels in the poor black neighborhoods of Los Angeles, Newark, and Detroit between 1965 and 1967.[18]

In so many American cities the growth of the urban underclass had created powder kegs that needed only the smallest spark to set one off. Johnson's administration tried to help by accommodating rising demands from the poor for welfare under the Social Security act. Unlike the New Dealers, who had strictly limited access to Aid to Families with Dependent Children (AFDC) in favor of work-relief programs, Great Society–era administrators relied more on welfare to deal with the immediate problems created by high urban unemployment. Allowing the welfare rolls to grow was faster and less difficult than trying to aid the poor in other ways via legislation, but many middle-class people preferred work-based relief programs, such as those the WPA had made famous in the 1930s, and found expanded welfare jarring. As objectionable as WPA "handouts" had been to some in the 1930s, expanded welfare appeared to be worse because it required no labor from its recipients and was more lasting than the temporary work-relief programs of the 1930s, which meant that welfare was even more likely to foster long-term dependency.[19]

Another source of resistance to expanded welfare, from white and black men, was that it was being done in a way utterly at odds with the male-breadwinner model that they had been told was the social norm. The reality in many households had always been different. That was especially true in African American families because their incomes were typically much lower than those of white households. Many married black women had been obliged to take paying jobs because those open to black men often paid poorly. But poor young men, especially in the mid-to-late 1960s, often resented the way the combination of higher unemployment for men and easier access to welfare for women altered the balance in gender relations.[20]

Growing support within the black community for radical protest and armed confrontation with the police, especially when white policemen brutalized black people and were not punished for it, led to another flash point. Though armed resistance was never anywhere near the norm, even among the poorest young black men, enough of them embraced what became known as the Black Power movement—which emphasized pressuring the white-dominated establishment through militant, direct action so as to address the plight of poor black people in the central cities—that it deeply frightened many middle-class white people still living there. Heavy media attention to that phenomenon increased the anxiety. As both the reality of increased crime and the fear of it rose, so did white flight to suburbia, which shrank city tax bases even more and made the underlying problem worse.[21]

Lyndon Johnson soon deeply resented rioters, believing that his policies, from extending and protecting the right to vote to spending a lot more federal money on urban problems, were making historic progress possible. He was stunned when the black neighborhood of Watts in Los Angeles went up in flames soon after he had spent much political capital to push through the Voting Rights Act of 1965. As the riots multiplied over the next few years, Johnson lost his appetite for the role of racial reformer. Martin Luther King Jr.'s public criticism in August 1965 of Johnson's Vietnam War policy soured Johnson even further. So, too, did the January 1966 decision of leading civil rights groups such as the Student Non-Violent Coordinating Committee (SNCC) and the Congress of Racial Equality (CORE) to oppose the war. That early and vocal opposition from influential black people, which grew louder in the years that followed, stemmed in part from the disproportionate impact of the draft on their community. In 1965, the first year of Johnson's massive escalation policy, almost a quarter of Americans killed in combat were black, although African Americans made up a much smaller percentage of the troops serving in Vietnam. That disturbing statistic reflected black soldiers' greater likelihood of drawing the most dangerous combat assignments. Johnson and his aides took steps to drive that number down to 16 percent in 1966 and 13 percent in 1968, but even those figures were still substantially higher than the percentage of African Americans in the US population. The racism inherent and institutionalized in the American system served to deepen the growing rift between the black community and the Johnson administration.[22]

Any improvements in the lives of African Americans that Johnson's policies made possible during the mid-1960s intensified resistance from many white people. The single most influential national leader of this latest phase of white backlash was Alabama governor George Wallace, who drew the overt support of a motley assortment of right-wing extremists and white populists, and the covert support of some lower-middle-class and working-class white citizens determined to preserve their racial privilege.

Wallace had burst onto the national scene in 1963 during the highly publicized confrontation at the University of Alabama over the admission of black students. First impressions are lasting, and for many, perhaps most, Americans, the indelible image of Wallace literally standing at the door of the University of Alabama trying to block the entry of black students permanently defined his public persona. While he was a die-hard segregationist during the Johnson years, there was more to Wallace than that. To many young white men whose economic prospects were poor because college seemed out of reach, he became a latter-day Huey Long, the Louisiana populist who, during the worst years of the Depression, had called for soaking the rich. Though reactionary on race, Wallace could sound positively left-wing on class, something that led the most popular New Right periodical, William F. Buckley Jr.'s *National Review*, to dismiss Wallace's program as "country and western Marxism."[23]

Wallace felt encouraged by the growing popular support for his message, enough so that he ran against Lyndon Johnson in the 1964

Democratic presidential primaries. Though Wallace lost all of the key contests, his potent message and extraordinarily effective public-speaking skills helped build a substantial following not just in the South but also in such places as Indiana, Maryland, and Wisconsin. Economically insecure middle-class white voters there could and often did cast a protest vote for Wallace without having to consider what a Wallace presidency would actually have been like, given the certainty that LBJ would ultimately prevail. As inflation began to eat away at voters' real incomes and rising crime eroded their sense of safety—two mainstays of middle-class life—the appeal of Wallace's white-supremacist protest message grew. Support seemed strong enough that Wallace even considered making a third-party bid for the presidency, once his challenge to Johnson's nomination fizzled. But leading Dixiecrats wanted to give Barry Goldwater, who had voted against the Civil Rights Act of 1964, a chance to beat Johnson in the South, so they persuaded Wallace not to run that fall. His merely flirting with the idea got Wallace's name on the ballot in sixteen states, which, coupled with his surprisingly strong showing in the primaries, threw a scare into the northern Democratic establishment.[24]

The intensity of support in the South and the border states for Wallace's pro–Jim Crow, racist stance also concerned Democrats deeply, as the Civil Rights Acts of 1964 and 1965 and a series of pro–civil rights Supreme Court decisions in the mid-1960s rapidly altered the outward appearance of the South. Business leaders in the southern and border states, determined to eliminate what many had come to see as a major obstacle to economic development, took down most of the notorious WHITES ONLY signs and other similar ones at public accommodations when the 1964 Civil Rights law went into effect that summer. Another swift change came in the nature of the southern electorate. By 1966 black people were voting in unprecedented numbers there. As significant as those reforms were in some respects, the region changed much more slowly in other ways. Many black people, accustomed to the Jim Crow facilities, often continued to use them rather than the newly desegregated ones, lest that lead to unpleasantness or worse from hostile whites. The deep-seated prejudice of many white people showed no sign of going away soon, something that white flight to suburbia and the growth of essentially all-white private schools signaled clearly. In the short run, any improvements in race relations in the South encouraged a backlash that boosted Wallace's movement.[25]

The southern (and national) political landscape did evolve as federal registrars began to enroll large numbers of black voters in the mid-1960s, but did so more slowly than many remembered later. The impact of that change was enhanced by a series of Supreme Court decisions in the early and middle 1960s that mandated the reapportionment of state legislative and congressional districts to comply more effectively with the principle of "one person, one vote." For decades previously, many states had failed to adjust the size of such districts after each census to reflect the growth of urban and suburban populations. Legislative bodies long dominated by rural- and small-town electorates were unwilling to see political power suddenly shift to major metro areas. State legislative and US House districts were often skewed, with some containing many more voters than others. The Supreme Court's reapportionment rulings required redrawing electoral maps after each census to create districts of equal population. In time, that new practice brought about a major reallocation of political power.[26]

Both the rebalancing of voter representation and its slowness were evident in Georgia during 1966, when the young Jimmy Carter, whose deeply held religious beliefs led him to reject racial prejudice and eventually Jim Crow, came close to winning the Democratic primary for governor. Many more black voters and equal-population districts would in time remake the southern Democratic Parties so as to bring out in the open the better angels of Carter's nature, and those of other southern Democrats like him. But not right away. The winner of the 1966 Georgia governor's race, Dixiecrat Lester Maddox, picked up the "segregation forever" refrain Wallace had so effectively used. In the short run, civil rights progress appeared to be expanding the ranks of the most outspoken bigots, rather than shrinking them. That phenomenon, combined with Johnson's inflationary spending, his unpopular war, and urban unrest, threatened the continued dominance of the Democratic Party nationally, in this instance by alienating the Solid South, which had formed one fundamental part of the Democrats' majority coalition.[27]

• • •

The feminist movement, which had gotten off the ground in the early sixties, started to gain enough momentum to come out of the fringes toward the middle of the decade and would pose another challenge to middle-class dominance. Like other movements of that era that arose to question the status quo, the response to feminism's resurgence was mixed and progress toward its goals slow. The President's Commission on the Status of Women (PCSW) issued a report in 1964 that was inherently contradictory. It called for reforms to ensure women's participation in education and the paid labor force on a more equitable basis, but also endorsed the primacy of women's domestic role. Most important, the PCSW helped jump-start a revived feminist movement, as similar commissions formed in forty-nine states and began working on issues of concern to feminists. Change at the federal level came at the behest of the National Organization for Women (NOW), founded in 1966 and led by *The Feminine Mystique* author Betty Friedan as its first president. NOW pushed for an executive order from Lyndon Johnson to prohibit sex discrimination in employment in the federal service and at firms holding federal government contracts, and for both to establish affirmative-action programs for women. Johnson issued the order in October 1967, which seemed to signal the start of far-reaching change.[28]

But on the ground, traditional gender roles and relations remained largely unchanged through the end of Johnson's presidency. Like Kennedy before him, Johnson failed to name even a single woman to his cabinet, although LBJ did appoint more women to lower-level positions than his predecessor had. However, the male-breadwinner model came under increasing stress as the fraction of well-paid jobs open to men without a college degree continued to fall, which put steadily increasing pressure on married women with school-age children to take paying jobs. Rising inflation put even more pressure on middle-class household budgets, sending yet more women into the workforce.[29]

The movement—and society's slow response to it—gradually focused the attention of more and more women on issues such as expanded education and employment. That women also met with second-class treatment when they did take paying jobs, and from the male leaders of groups supposedly dedicated to social reform, further galvanized support. As women's frustration mounted, so, too, did their opposition to a male-breadwinner approach that seemed increasingly unworkable. Men who resisted these inevitable changes generally failed to see how they were putting the middle-class lifestyle they so cherished in even greater peril. Their resistance only pointed up the need for change and radicalized many women.[30]

Progress in protecting the environment during the mid-to-late 1960s was also somewhat less than met the eye. The Wilderness Act of 1964, which set aside 9.1 million acres of federal forestland to be preserved from development, was the most notable of some significant environmental-protection measures. The Clean Air Act of 1963 and the Clean Water Act of 1965 made less of a difference because they lacked strictly enforced standards of air and water quality. The Endangered Species Preservation Act of 1966 led to the first official list of such species, but not much immediate progress in helping save them. The boom in basic manufacturing that Johnson's Vietnam policy produced, by greatly increasing orders for war goods, created more pollution and tended to make environmental problems worse. So, too, did the increasing number of cars on the roads and the still expanding system of interstate highways. As with other groups that had seemed marginal as recently as the early 1960s, environmental advocates grew in number and intensity, as did the public's engagement with the cause, all of which increased public opposition to the kinds of "smokestack industries" whose high, unionized wages had done so much to expand the middle class, and to the cheap, pollution-spewing cars they drove.[31]

The number of challenges to the middle-class status quo continued to multiply. As the Sunbelt and the coasts (where the bulk of the most affluent were concentrated) rose, economically and politically, and the Midwest declined, the nation's social and cultural life became more polarized, too. That pattern emerged clearly with religion. The rise of the Sunbelt increased the numbers and influence of strongly religious people associated with Southern Baptists and other evangelical Christian denominations native to that region. As the coasts, home to the largest concentrations of much more secular Americans, also became more visible and influential, the other kind of wing people in the realm of religion, the most secular, also gained ground. The middle years of the 1960s saw a decline in the moderate, middle-class religiosity so prevalent in the Midwest among mainline Protestant and Catholic people. That world seemed increasingly out of step with ongoing social change, giving rise to a new term of identification, *Middle America*, first coined in 1968 by syndicated columnist Joseph Kraft. As Americans became more varied in so many ways, mainstream Midwesterners would no longer be seen as representative of American society and culture as a whole, in the realm of religion or anything else, but rather as just one fading part of it.[32]

Changing attitudes toward health also reflected a departure—in both directions—from the moderate middle in social-cultural matters. On college campuses, especially in the coastal population centers, the later 1960s brought much more experimentation with illegal drugs, especially LSD and marijuana. At the same time, the growing number of moral traditionalists in the Sunbelt recast even moderate smoking and drinking as questionable behavior. When the surgeon general issued a public warning in 1964 about the dangers of cigarette smoking, the federal government launched its campaign not just to limit smoking but to end the practice altogether. Antidrinking messages likewise proliferated. Both of these crusades led eventually to the end of ads for cigarettes and hard liquor on TV. The juxtaposition of exploding illegal drug use among young adults, and intensifying campaigns against smoking and drinking, spoke volumes about the polarization in public attitudes about health and lifestyle.[33]

Perhaps the single most significant cultural shift was in popular music, which more explicitly gave voice to the rebellious spirit of the moment. On the day Kennedy went to Dallas, hardly anyone in America had ever heard of the Beatles. Five years later, their music had become a permanent fixture of the cultural landscape. Like the hippies of Haight-Ashbury, the Beatles and other pop and rock groups founded in the sixties—from the Rolling Stones to the Who—challenged the stodgy, risk-averse life choices of so many grown-ups shaped by the Depression and World War II. Although most such music was not overtly political, it encouraged the young to be spontaneous and to experiment, which their more cautious parents usually discouraged.[34]

Changing income demographics influenced that willingness—perhaps even eagerness—to break with conformity. Real income was growing at the top end from tax cuts, higher interest rates, and a boom-ing stock market. Expanded welfare, food stamps, and medical assis-tance for the poor, while not income in the conventional sense, gave them more access to goods and services in the modern market econ-omy. Suddenly, these two distinct sectors of the population acquired more influence on tastes, which had been dominated for decades by those of the vast middle. Some aspects of this change were profoundly positive, as groups toward the top and the bottom that had been mar-ginalized and stereotyped over the past three decades began to see more (and more accurate) images of themselves in the mass media. They also found more things for sale that were aimed at them, whether at expanding fancier department-store chains such as Saks and Neiman Marcus for the affluent or at new discount retailers such as Kmart and Walmart that were popular with those who had the least.[35]

Greater attention to the needs and outlooks of those above and below typically inspired less enthusiasm among members of the mid-dle class, older ones especially. Upscale stores typically offered little in merchandise or employment to them. The discount retailers achieved their low prices by operating with low-paid, nonunion workforces, something the heavily unionized blue-collar part of the new middle class disliked. That the poor had more to spend thanks to expanded public assistance also alienated some middle-class people, such as the city worker who complained, "I go shopping with my wife and I see them with their forty dollars of food stamps in the supermar-ket, living and eating better than me. . . . Let them tighten their belts like we do." Stability- and security-minded, both the blue-collar and white-collar members of the middle class tended to live cautiously, to follow society's rules, and to stay focused on protecting their future well-being. Those habits had long been characteristic of the econom-ically insecure middle ranks of society, patterns the Depression had intensified. Upper-income Americans tended to be greater risk-takers, the young among them especially, knowing that they could fall back on family resources if something went wrong. The poor lacked that kind of cushion, but their incomes in many cases were so low that they didn't concern themselves with the middle-class mantra of gradual upward mobility and greater economic security through settling down early and incrementally accumulating savings and a nest egg in owning a house. The poor also had less of a sense of connection to labor unions, from whose ranks they were mostly excluded.[36]

With a pop-culture machine so heavily driven by ticket sales and advertising, more money flowing to the top and the bottom and less in the middle reshaped the audiences that filmmakers and the commercial sponsors who funded TV were trying to reach. In the movies especially, which were popular with teens and young adults, messages less friendly to the middle class, such as experimenting with sex outside marriage, drinking, drugs, and the like began to appear in the later 1960s. Supreme Court decisions weakening censorship of various kinds also helped enable this cultural trend. The motion-picture production code in place for thirty years began to collapse, gradually leading to more graphic sex and violence on-screen, and the use of more profanity. The 1967 film *Bonnie and Clyde*, featuring Warren Beatty and Faye Dunaway as the infamous outlaws Clyde Barrow and Bonnie Parker, was one of the first and most memorable examples of those changes. Considered by critics and scholars to be one of the first films of the "New Hollywood" era because it broke so many previous taboos, *Bonnie and Clyde* featured one of the bloodiest death scenes in Hollywood history. A spate of new films followed that were no longer aimed at moderately morally traditional, family-oriented middle-class audiences, as code-era films had been. As middle-class incomes began to stagnate and upper-class ones rose, making films that resisted the middle-class, code-era norms began to be more profitable than making movies that conformed with them.[37]

TV programming, with a much wider viewership than ever before, changed, too. The three major TV networks began to feature shows that paid less attention to lower-middle-class white people in particular, to depict them in less sympathetic ways, and to set more dramas and comedies in the realm of upper America. The pattern was not so much to create whole new genres as to revise them. Thus, the situation comedy with a supposedly typical suburban family began to be set in more affluent surroundings. In an indirect nod to the reality of divorce, which middle-class influence had helped keep off the air during the 1950s, single-parent families became more common on TV, although invariably ones in which the single parent was a widower or widow.[38]

My Three Sons, starring Fred MacMurray, premiered in 1960 and was a pioneering and highly influential example of this kind of transitional TV show. MacMurray played an amiable upper-middle-class widower raising his three boys with help from an elderly male relative, Grandpa "Bub," played by William Frawley, who was replaced by a character named Uncle Charley, played by William Demarest, when Frawley's health declined. The show's 380 episodes shown over twelve seasons made it second only to *Ozzie and Harriet* in the category of long-running, live-action TV sitcoms. In contrast to that fifties favorite, *My Three Sons* was set in a big suburban house, with a father explicitly identified as a professional. Those markers of social class were often communicated subtly—dad wore a suit and tie to work, carried a briefcase, had a secretary, and occasionally went out of town on business trips—but they were there, week after week. The idea was not so much to ignore people of more middling social status as to make them more marginal to the various story lines. Thus, in *My Three Sons*, the elderly relative comes across as a more average person in class background, but was seldom at the center of things.[39]

The same trends carried over to other tried-and-true programming genres. *The Big Valley*, a western that premiered on ABC in September 1965 and ran for four seasons, boasted Barbara Stanwyck as the widowed mother of an upper-class California ranching family, in which the bad guys were almost all working- or lower-middle-class white men. The show weekly endorsed the view that socially responsible rich people could and should do more to solve community problems, especially racial prejudice. This new kind of western was distinctly different from the still popular *Gunsmoke*.[40]

Police dramas, too, reflected new economic and political realities. *The Fugitive*, which ran for four seasons starting in the fall of 1963, starred David Janssen as Dr. Richard Kimble, a man on the run, having been wrongly convicted of murdering his wife. The show was controversial with law enforcement officials because in many episodes someone helped Dr. Kimble elude police capture as he searched for the real murderer. That kind of assistance could be considered aiding and abetting a fugitive from justice, which was a felony. The show also depicted the police through the eyes of someone who saw law enforcement as the enemy, a radical departure from earlier police dramas on

TV, which tended to be more reverent toward law and authority. As in the new westerns, most of the bad guys depicted in *The Fugitive* were lower-middle-class or working-class white people, including the real murderer. The series' finale, in which Dr. Kimble finally catches up with him, garnered the largest audience up to that time for a TV episode. When it was broadcast in 1967, fully 72 percent of all households watching TV tuned in to see the good doctor finally confront and reluctantly kill (in self-defense) the evil blue-collar villain, then walk off into the distance, a free man at last.[41]

One can see these changes as needed correctives to themes, story lines, and characters that for twenty years had been overly influenced by middle-class white experiences, perspectives, and tastes—and many people did, especially younger viewers, who tended to be more open to change. One of the most positive developments was the gradual expansion in the nature of roles open to African Americans, but even that was typically less than ideal. The 1967 film *Guess Who's Coming to Dinner*, starring Sidney Poitier, Spencer Tracy, and Katharine Hepburn, offered a sympathetic depiction of a mixed-race couple. The film broke new ground, but its approach to the challenges posed by such a pairing was simplistic. The decision to make all of the leading characters affluent professionals made the plot all the more remote from the lives of most mixed-race couples. Poitier in particular came under criticism for making a series of films in the mid-1960s that made white audiences feel good about themselves, but denied the reality of intense racial prejudice against black people.[42]

In the television show *I Spy*, the young Bill Cosby portrayed a professional tennis player who, with his white partner (Robert Culp), toured the world, playing professional tennis while working undercover as CIA agents out to stop Communist intrigue. While the mixed-race friendship at the center of the story was revolutionary, most of the plots were terrible, making it somewhat harder to take the show seriously. Comic strip–type villains were invariably thwarted, week by week, over the show's three seasons on NBC from 1965 to 1968.[43]

The original *Star Trek* TV series, which premiered on NBC in the fall of 1966, was also a mixed bag. To his credit, the show's creator, Gene Roddenberry, insisted on a black character who was an officer stationed on the bridge of the USS *Enterprise*, despite resistance from station managers at some of NBC's southern affiliates. (He convinced them by pointing out that *Star Trek* was set so far in the future as to be unrelated to contemporary racial issues.) Played by gifted stage actress Nichelle Nichols, Lieutenant Uhura (from the Swahili word *uhuru*, for "freedom") was an inspiration to many younger black females accustomed to seeing black women mostly playing maids on TV shows. But the overall depiction of gender roles and gender relations on the original *Star Trek* was decidedly reactionary. The distant future was still a man's world, in which Captain Kirk's roving eye and amatory designs led to countless romantic conquests.[44]

Not all TV shows in the mid-1960s depicted women that way, though the vast majority continued to emphasize domestic roles for them. One landmark program that both embraced that idea and changed it was Julia Child's how-to-cook show, *The French Chef*. It premiered on Boston's public television station in February 1963 and ran for almost ten years. Convinced that the turn against "flavor satisfaction" in American cooking had gone too far, Child was determined to change minds by showing how middle-class French cooks did their work. Child was a populist whose cookbooks and TV shows featured only those ingredients one could find in the standard American supermarket. She was a refreshing and appealing media personality, much in the same way Kate Smith had been a generation earlier. Tall and gangly, with an unintentionally comic way of speaking and more than willing to let things go wrong on her show, she had little in common with the generic prim television stars of the day and easily connected with her audience of average home cooks bored with middle-American food and looking to improve. Unpretentious and boisterous, Child helped launch a revolution in American cuisine.

Around the same time, some of her French-trained colleagues, chefs Pierre Franey and Jacques Pépin, went to work for the popular Howard Johnson's motel chain to improve the food sold by its restaurants. Their vision, like Child's, was of a new-and-improved middle-class cuisine, a step or two up from the bland fare of midcentury America, but still not overly refined or out of reach. Even that middle-ground approach would prove hard to sustain as the retreat from middle-class perspectives, tastes, and needs accelerated over the Johnson years.[45]

The success of *The French Chef* reflected in part the waning of the baby boom, which officially came to a close in 1964, though sooner on the coasts than in the heartland. During the boom's heyday from 1946 to 1964, all of those young mouths to feed had discouraged inventive cooking in favor of a lowest-common-denominator approach of producing familiar fare that everyone was certain to eat. As the birthrate began to fall sharply in the mid-1960s, that obstacle to culinary experimentation began to fade.

The end of the baby boom reflected in part stagnating middle-class incomes and the advent of the oral contraceptive soon known simply as the pill, which together made having several kids early in adulthood less affordable and more avoidable. Expanding access to higher education also slowed down early family formation. Another major factor driving that change was the growing backlash against early marriage and childbearing among the young, who had seen up close the toll it had sometimes taken on their parents. All of these factors began to mean more twentysomethings without kids and more forty- and fiftysomethings whose kids had grown, which together helped drive the revolution in home cooking.[46]

As middle-class people began to have fewer children, the fraction of overall population growth resulting from immigration slowly began to rise. Pressures mounted in the middle 1960s to allow more immigrants in, to contribute to a revival of the kind of entrepreneurialism that had helped create whole new industries earlier in the nation's past. As the need to do that again became clearer, the arguments in favor of easier immigration gained ground, something that was accomplished with the passage of a new immigration law in 1965. The number of immigrants entering illegally began to rise as well. At first the numbers were not large, but those changes posed yet another long-term challenge to the native-born middle class because immigrants typically worked longer and harder for less. Although one could see this change, as with so many others, as a needed correction given the economic challenges facing Americans, it could and eventually would undermine the more moderate, Monday-through-Friday, nine-to-five work ethic so popular among native-born middle-class families.[47]

So much of American life had been configured since the later 1940s to work well for middle-class families that when social trends veered off in other directions in the mid-to-late 1960s, change came seemingly everywhere in the social-cultural realm. Popular print publications had to grapple with the new circumstances that faced films and TV. The business model for such leading middlebrow magazines as *Life* and *Look* became unsustainable, as advertisers increasingly lost interest in a middle-class readership that remained large but had less money to spend. The same was true for the middlebrow books that had commanded such influence over the previous twenty years. By the late 1960s, publishers of periodicals and books had begun to chase a smaller but more affluent demographic.[48]

The old, middle-class-dominated status quo reached something of a breaking point in 1968. The country experienced one unexpected shock after another that year, starting with the North Vietnamese–led Tet Offensive, which began on January 30. Unlike the North's previous military incursions into the South, this one targeted cities. Although ultimately unsuccessful in the narrowest sense, given that the US military and its South Vietnamese allies defeated the effort to stir revolutionary uprisings there, the offensive laid bare the falseness of the Johnson administration's official stance that the war was moving toward a satisfactory conclusion. The urban nature of the fighting enabled TV news crews to film it much more easily than they could the war in outlying areas, and that coverage found its way into millions of American living rooms. An attack on the US embassy in Saigon in particular, though quickly repulsed, made for riveting television. The images on the nightly TV news left the overwhelming impression that no end to the fighting was in sight. That fundamental shift in public perception completely upended American politics.[49]

On the Democratic side, it meant the decline and fall of Lyndon Johnson's bid for another term as president. The discouraging news about Vietnam eviscerated LBJ's support and breathed life into the antiwar candidacy of Senator Eugene McCarthy from Minnesota. On March 12, McCarthy won 42 percent of the vote in the first presidential primary of the year, held in New Hampshire, a startlingly strong showing for a little-known, single-issue candidate. That unexpected event soon led to another: the entry of New York senator Robert Kennedy into the race. A much better-financed candidate than McCarthy ever would be, Kennedy had star quality and so posed a much more serious challenge to Johnson's renomination. When even most of LBJ's own top foreign-policy advisers, the so-called Wise Men, opposed sending more troops to South Vietnam, Johnson finally grasped the futility of trying to use increased (but still limited) military force to achieve victory. Rather than try to hang on to power, he abruptly decided to abandon his bid for reelection, delivering that shocking news at the end of a televised address on Vietnam on March 31.[50]

Although many in the media interpreted these unlikely events to mean the public increasingly favored US military withdrawal from Vietnam, the truth was more complicated. Antiwar sentiment did grow, but much of it had to do with the strategy Johnson had pursued. At least as many, and perhaps more, voters who watched the Tet Offensive unfold on their TV screens concluded that the solution was to expand the war by abandoning the kinds of restrictions on US fighting in Vietnam that Johnson had imposed from the start. What declined was support for Johnson's middle course, which had rejected both abandoning South Vietnam entirely and waging the war more aggressively and thereby risking Chinese and/or Soviet escalation in response. As a result, the unwelcome news from Indochina didn't just energize McCarthy's and Kennedy's campaigns, it also brought momentum to the leading hawkish candidates: Richard Nixon, who won a spectacular victory in the GOP's New Hampshire primary; and George Wallace, who opted to run that year as an independent candidate for president. To muddy matters further, Vice President Hubert Humphrey joined the race as Johnson's anointed successor, but too late to enter any of the primaries. Humphrey's public stance on the war seemed to be the same as Johnson's, and the president's influence over party leaders, who chose a large majority of the convention delegates, made a Humphrey nomination likely, regardless of the outcome of the Democratic primaries.[51]

Rather than cool down, the political situation continued to heat up—but the nation's attention was turned away in a single instant by the assassination of Martin Luther King Jr. on April 4 in Memphis. The killing prompted a wave of riots in poor black urban neighborhoods across the country, including in Washington, DC. Forty-three people died in what became 126 major urban disturbances, and approximately 21,000 black people were arrested and charged with riot-related crimes. King's murder dealt a heavy blow to the strategy of nonviolence within the civil rights movement. As racial tension reached a breaking point, it became harder to find Americans willing to tolerate a more measured, moderate path toward social reform.[52]

On the day of King's murder, Bobby Kennedy was in Indianapolis on a campaign stop. He announced the death to a mostly black crowd there and, in an impromptu speech, acknowledged the pain and outrage he knew they were feeling, recalling the killing of his own brother JFK. But Kennedy also made a moving and compelling plea for wisdom and restraint and nonviolence as the only reasonable way to move forward. It's difficult to gauge the impact of that speech, but to many observers it was Bobby Kennedy's finest hour and might have changed the outcome of the upcoming election had other circumstances not intervened.

King's untimely death reflected the changing times, as he was in so many ways emblematic of the middle-class era. King's life span corresponded exactly with it. Born in 1929 into a minister's family, he was never rich and never poor. King had married young, fathered four children, and typically wore the rather formal attire so typical of educated middle-class people of his generation. Even his mainstream religiosity fit perfectly within the social-cultural preferences of that time. No radical (or reactionary) in lifestyle, King had an overarching social goal that many middle-class people, black and white, could relate to: to include African Americans fully and equally within the kind of middle-class life that flourished after World War II. What made that message even more typical of that era was King's unswerving optimism that what he sought would one day come to pass. By 1968, King was after not just an end to segregation laws but also wanted affirmative efforts to open more pathways to the middle class for black people. King made clear his faith that this would happen in what became a haunting farewell message delivered the night before his death, when he said:

"I just want to do God's will. And He's allowed me to go to the mountain. And I've looked over. And I've seen the promised land. I may not get there with you. But I want you to know tonight that we as a people will get to the promised land."[53]

Two months later, the nation lost the most electrifying white champion of that message when Robert Kennedy was killed shortly after winning the widely watched Democratic presidential primary in California. His shocking death cleared the path for Humphrey's nomination, thereby denying general-election voters an antiwar option. They would have to choose from three contenders—Humphrey, Nixon, and Wallace—who were publicly on record as intending to carry on in Vietnam. The sense of alienation on the left became profound. What energy was still left in that resistance to the war and to the status quo was expressed in street protest, most famously during the Democratic National Convention in Chicago in late August.[54]

The more that the leftover middle-class establishment—men such as AFL-CIO president George Meany, for example—voiced their support for the war, the more disillusioned became the antiwar liberals and leftists around the country. FBI director J. Edgar Hoover had his agency conduct intensive surveillance of the overlapping worlds of civil rights and antiwar activists and concluded they were part of the international Communist conspiracy. These two men exemplified the people and the institutions that had contributed to social progress during the rise of the middle class, but were now seemingly on the wrong side of history.[55]

Even some establishment figures who had doubted or disagreed early on with Johnson's escalation policy were usually reluctant to express their views publicly, lest that encourage the nation's military adversaries during wartime. Johnson skillfully manipulated that kind of patriotic reflex, which had grown out of the experiences of World War II, Korea, and the Cold War. As a consequence, the perception grew that just about all makers of the middle-class era were misguided hawks.[56]

Within business circles, the reaction against reflexive support for the war could be seen in the changing response to former Federal Reserve chairman Marriner Eccles's opposition to it. His resistance had first surfaced at a White House dinner for business and labor leaders in July 1965 that Johnson had organized to solicit support for his escalation policy. Eccles had listened as seven other men delivered ringing endorsements of what LBJ had done, before rising to denounce it. Looking directly at Johnson, Eccles had informed his host that he could not "subscribe in any sense" to that decision, saying it was based on "fatal errors," prophetically labeling it "a course of action that is bound to be ruinous." Eccles's dissent was met by a thunderous silence in the room, but two years later, the response was different. When he spoke to a group of three thousand businessmen in September 1967 from much the same perspective, Eccles was interrupted fourteen times by applause, capped by an enthusiastic standing ovation.[57]

Johnson's UN ambassador, the nationally known union lawyer and former labor secretary Arthur Goldberg, had much the same experience, albeit more privately. He sent LBJ a letter in May 1966, telling him that the escalation policy was a mistake. After Goldberg repeated that view in a meeting with Johnson later that same month, Johnson froze him out of most high-level discussions of Vietnam policy. But when the new defense secretary, Clark Clifford, invited Goldberg to attend a meeting of the foreign-policy experts known as the Wise Men in late March 1968, the ambassador's penetrating questions helped demolish the administration's case for putting even more men into Vietnam and won the support of most of the advisers in the room. But the public never learned about Goldberg's dissent, or those of the other in-house critics such as diplomat George Ball, because they were not publicly aired.[58]

Even sadder, in some respects, were the ways leading figures in the world of popular culture became unwitting public defenders of the status quo during the mid-to-late 1960s. Louis Armstrong, for instance, scored a major hit in 1967 with his unabashedly optimistic "What a Wonderful World" at a time when many black people were becoming deeply disillusioned with systematic racism and lack of opportunity. And Bob Hope, that iconic entertainer of the middle-class era, found himself increasingly identified with support for the war because he carried on his tradition of entertaining the troops serving in the field. Hope had done so much good in earlier conflicts—most notably World War II when he courageously toured combat zones—and was now doing the same thing in a more morally ambiguous war. Hope's popularity and celebrity status, whatever his intentions, tended to be viewed as adding support for Johnson's Vietnam policy. Like so many other entertainers of his age, Hope seemed hopelessly dated and out of touch to the generation he was trying to support.[59]

• • •

The sense of a generation losing its leadership role was also felt in smaller, more personal ways, by people who weren't famous. In March 1967, the still healthy and vigorous George Perkins turned seventy and fully retired from working for the employment service. He was feted at a dinner that month, where the most memorable testimonial came from the head of the Rhode Island Urban League. Impressed by what Perkins had done to expand employment opportunities for black people—and by his participation in the March on Washington— that official explained that because the state legislature was that very night considering legislation of importance to the Urban League, he should have been elsewhere, but his high opinion of George Perkins compelled attendance. With that memorably positive conclusion to his professional life, Perkins, by then a grandfather, redirected his ener- gies into home and family life, something he kept doing until his death thirty years later.

The arc of Beatrice Sindt's life in the mid-to-late sixties was similar. The last of her four children left the nest and she became a grand- mother. Liberated from heavy domestic responsibilities, she invested much of her energy into civic and community groups, the local Unitar- ian Church, and socializing with her women friends. Seeing the nice new appliances in their homes, she became frustrated that Howard would not agree to pay for upgrading theirs. Taking a page from the emerging women's movement, Beatrice covertly obtained her certi- fication as a substitute teacher and began making money from that, until Howard found out and put a stop to it. By then she had bought the new things she wanted (which is what had alerted Howard to what was going on), so her rebellion was brief yet productive. Beatrice also enjoyed spending time at their second home in Yuma, Arizona, where the lack of a local Unitarian church led her to dabble in New Age reli- gion. She also evolved on racial issues, becoming much more openly supportive of the civil rights movement and black equality than she had been during the conformist fifties. Still capable of growth, Bea- trice nonetheless, like much of her generation, found the new choices of the next one sometimes troubling. Nothing they or anyone else did ever deterred her from sticking with the values of stability and security that had defined her life before, even as she lived, like George Perkins, to one hundred. Both of them, and many others of their distinctive generation, remained very much a part of the social landscape after 1968, but now they were more in the background.

As people such as George and Beatrice and other, much better-known figures increasingly relinquished the leading roles at home and beyond, people who had stood at the margins of American life began to come to the fore. Nowhere was that clearer than in the presidential election held in the fall of 1968, when Richard Nixon completed an unprecedented comeback. Just six years earlier Nixon's career in politics seemed to be over, after he lost a race for California governor and compounded that setback by angrily telling reporters, "You don't have Nixon to kick around any more because, gentlemen, this is my last press conference."

But like Goldwater and Reagan, Nixon, a native of greater Los Angeles, found a future in politics as the Sunbelt milieu in which he had thrived boomed in the mid-to-late 1960s. As that shift lifted Sunbelt politicians, Nixon skillfully rode the wave. His effective campaigning in 1966 for GOP candidates across the country had made him once again a leading contender for his party's nomination. The lack of broadly appealing and well-qualified alternatives helped propel him to a narrow victory at the 1968 Republican National Convention, as did his pledge to southern conservatives that he would follow their lead on race-relations issues in the South. Although never broadly popular with the overall electorate, Nixon benefited from the rupture in the national Democratic Party that year. Facing two lifelong Democrats that fall, northerner Hubert Humphrey and southerner George Wallace, Nixon eked out a narrow victory. He became the first GOP presidential candidate with strong ties to his party's right wing, with its essentially pre–New Deal vision for America, to win the White House since the 1920s. Here was the single clearest sign that the trend toward an ever more middle-class country and culture had come to an end.[60]

CHAPTER 10

The Era in Retrospect

When Richard Nixon became president in January 1969, the middle class had stopped growing, but it had not yet begun a precipitous decline. During Nixon's first two years as president, the middle class more or less treaded water, in part because Nixon was slow to make any major breaks with the past. Having won with only 43 percent of the vote in a three-way race in which the Democrats had kept control of Congress, he did not come into office with the security of a convincing mandate. For the first two years he moved cautiously, acting more like an Eisenhower-era Republican than a New Right conservative.[1]

It wasn't in Nixon's character or background to make any sudden departures from the status quo. Unlike Goldwater or Reagan, the other major conservative players in his party, he had entered politics more as a careerist than as an ideologue, perhaps more interested in holding on to his office than in promoting a deeply felt set of ideas. He had no personal fortune, as both Goldwater and Reagan did when they first ran for public office, and would not risk losing his job in four years without much else to fall back on. Nixon's cagey approach to politics had helped him outmaneuver the more likable but less experienced Reagan and other, less remembered rivals for the 1968 Republican presidential nomination, and then to edge past the polarizing general-election alternatives of Humphrey and Wallace. Nixon was not about to suddenly throw caution to the wind when he entered the White House. By then, his tendency to try to appeal to both wings of his party, and to disgruntled independents, had become firmly ingrained.[2]

Despite his chameleonlike qualities, Nixon did have a vision for the future, shaped by his formative years in the Los Angeles metropolitan area. Southern California had long had much greater income and wealth inequality than the Northeast or Midwest. In LA, government was small, taxes were low, unions scarce, and the middle class less numerous than in most major cities of the Frostbelt. The appeal of the LA model grew during the middle 1960s, however, as the old way of doing things in the industrial North began to founder. Southern California's economy was growing because its workers typically cost so much less to employ than workers in such places as New York and Ohio in such sectors as construction and manufacturing.[3]

The Sunbelt economy also provided much greater rewards to those at the top of the employment ladder—in such fields as aerospace engineering and the entertainment industry—than could usually be found in the Frostbelt. Those factors attracted more economic development to LA, which meant more jobs, at both the low end and the high end, and more and more people relocating from other parts of the country to fill them. The New Right envisioned greater prosperity amid greater inequality, which followed from lower taxes, smaller government, and greater rewards for entrepreneurs and the investor class. Nixon understood that vision much better than Frostbelt politicians because it had taken concrete form in Los Angeles during his lifetime, just as it had in Barry Goldwater's Phoenix. After 1970, that model began spreading rapidly throughout the country as a whole, with increasing support from the Nixon administration, which eventually became anti-union.[4]

History remembers 1968 as the year in which American society changed forever, not only in political or economic terms, but as a shared culture. The greater economic instability for most people in Los Angeles, as in other Sunbelt cities, and a smaller, weaker public sector, had helped rearrange the social order in some ways. LA was, for example, one of the most lightly policed major cities in the country, in stark contrast with New York and Chicago. That led to a greater sense of individual freedom that made LA in some respects an easier place to be a nonconformist. However, a conservative backlash from morally traditional people also had room to grow. As the two cultural extremes flourished unchecked, Los Angeles became known as much for its bars, swingers, and drug users as for its big churches, evangelical faith, and teetotalers.[5]

Other factors contributed to the huge diversity of lifestyles and cultural movements associated with Los Angeles in the later 1960s. As the center of the entertainment industry, especially film and television, and increasingly pop music, the city attracted all manner of creative, independent, ambitious, and often unusual people. Meanwhile, the lack of many well-paid jobs for men without special skills or a lot of formal education made the economy less tied to the male-breadwinner model, which contributed to a much higher divorce rate. So, too, did the unusually large number of affluent families, for whom divorce was more of a workable option than for middle-class couples. Proximity to Mexico had helped give Southern California a more ethnically and culturally varied population than was true for the nation's heartland during the middle-class heyday. The region's climate had also helped Angelenos adopt a novel physical appearance and social posture, much more informal in dress and attitude than most of Middle America. Even during the reign of fifties squares, LA had lots of little old ladies wearing tennis shoes. After 1970, those trademarks of life in Southern California spread east to the rest of the country.[6]

Most Americans took a while to grasp that the shift toward the Sunbelt lifestyle signaled an end to the middle-class model that had dominated the country for so long. Perceiving this was particularly hard for Frostbelters, many of whom had never given much thought to any alternatives to their way of life and, if they had, could easily have seen those alternatives as "un-American." With the passing of the next five decades, however, that change—and its enormous consequences—became starkly apparent to all. Now that we know for sure that we live in a different kind of country, how can we best understand the middle-class era that flourished before?

The growth, and eventual primacy, of the American middle class in the middle decades of the twentieth century surely stands as one of modern American history's more astonishing and far-reaching social developments. No single policy or program or leader or historical event can be pointed out as the driving force behind this phenomenon. We can't even look to one particular political attitude or philosophy as having pointed the way. Not only did many forces converge over decades to forge the middle class, but those forces were championed by both liberals and conservatives, albeit ones located nearer the center of the political spectrum rather than its ends. While many policies that fueled the middle-class rise originated on the political left, they could not have succeeded as they did without a boost from programs and policies more identified with the right.

A strong and active federal government got the ball rolling during the Depression era, as pervasive economic insecurity made Americans more willing to accept such things as federally funded social programs financed largely through deficit spending, powerful labor unions, and government regulation of business and finance, which together helped establish both the floor and the ceiling that secured the middle class. When World War II and then the Cold War arrived, pervasive insecurity of another kind, which was fear of foreign military aggression, helped reorient Americans toward massive government spending on national defense, much of it paid for by heavy, redistributive taxation. Helping make the overall arrangement work, especially the higher wages for workers and higher taxes for the investor class, were restrictive trade and immigration policies that helped keep competition in check, both for jobs and for production. It's also important to remember that the middle-class dominance during the last century partly depended on a broad political coalition that combined the interests of workers in such heavily unionized sectors as construction, manufacturing, mining, and transportation with lower-middle-class white-collar workers across the northern tier of the country and those of the agricultural South.

That political unity also helped bring together disparate cultural forces. If the South was traditionally the dominion of a small minority of old-line affluent Americans, the industrial Frostbelt became, over time, the region of the country most welcoming of more recent waves of immigration. People who wax nostalgic about the heyday of the middle class too often forget the Americans who never had the opportunity to share equally in that prosperity. Blacks and other ethnic groups experienced the rise of the middle class very differently from the white majority. While not totally excluded, they were often made to feel as though they were on the outside looking in. Women were arguably included, but not on equal terms with men. Rather, the programs, policies, and institutions that underpinned the growth of the middle class depended on women remaining in support of their breadwinner husbands.

The nostalgia for that bygone middle-class America—and the willingness of politicians to exploit it—reveals a fundamental truth: being middle class was as much a state of mind as an economic or demographic reality. Being middle class meant more than having a secure job and retirement, knowing that your children would eat well, get an education, and likely do better than their parents had. It meant sharing a national pride and purpose, even while one remained comfortably within one's ethnic and/or socioeconomic enclave. At the heart of that unanimity was the shared national experience of two unprecedented traumas: the Great Depression, which produced widespread, lasting economic insecurity; and chronic, serious national security challenges. If not for the deep-seated insecurities created by the Great Depression, World War II, and the Cold War, none of the initiatives—governmental, social, economic, or cultural—that drove the growth of the middle class would ever have become big enough or lasted long enough to produce the overall changes that they did. But millions of the poorest Americans who experienced those cataclysms along with the rest of the nation never got the chance to share much in the benefits of all those initiatives. Instead, the rise of the middle class left them even further behind.

When things started to unravel for the middle class in the 1970s, the decline stemmed not just from economic and political shifts but also from fractures in that state of mind. Group after group of marginalized Americans—from the urban poor, whose employment prospects steadily worsened as suburbanization accelerated; to the middle-class white housewife, whose husband's income, eroded by inflation, increasingly failed to support the family comfortably; to her more affluent and educated sisters, for whom domesticity alone was not enough; to the fringe religionists and secularists bothered by middle-of-the-road theology and morality; to the urban Bohemians and political radicals, infuriated by the draft, the expanding war in Vietnam, and the stultifying, stale middlebrow lifestyle—all began to stand up and strike back at the system that no longer seemed to be working so well for anyone.

Because things ended so badly, this era tends to be seen as a mistake, but it should not be written off so hastily. The era that came before it ended even more disastrously with the arrival of the Great Depression, but not everything about the Progressive Era or the 1920s deserves to be dismissed. Like that time, the middle-class era of the mid-twentieth century brought with it some valuable and lasting innovations. How many of us would want to abandon federal insurance for bank deposits, or Social Security? If an overall lesson is to be learned from the rise of the middle class, it's that one can take the trend toward expanding the middle class too far, which tends to create new problems, and to make some older ones even worse. High taxes on the truly affluent narrowed the gap between them and everyone else, but so much so that money for new business growth and charitable giving shrank so much as to eventually cause serious problems. High barriers to trade and immigration helped foster greater income and wealth equality within the United States, but also widened the gaps in those areas between the United States and its neighbors to the South. A heavy emphasis on promoting economic growth helped bring greater prosperity to the middle class, but also more environmental pollution that increasingly menaced their well-being (and everyone else's). Bigger, stronger unions helped raise wages and benefits and improve working conditions, but also helped make entire sectors of the economy, most notably manufacturing, more vulnerable to growing competition from places where labor costs were a lot lower. Higher middle-class incomes reduced hunger in America but led to overeating, overdrinking, and oversmoking, which undermined public health in serious ways. Higher middle-class incomes also led to the creation of more and better popular culture aimed at the majority, but middlebrow eventually became so dominant as to marginalize other groups' perspectives, which bred ever more alienation from those left out. The military draft helped promote the rise of the middle class, but also a more militarized male population, which eventually contributed to more war, not less. The male-breadwinner model helped the middle class expand, but created a new set of problems for women and men. The advent of mass suburbia improved the quality of middle-class housing, but in the long run weakened central cities and increased racial segregation, with profoundly harmful effects. Other examples could be offered to make the same basic point, which is that the rise of the middle class, and the growth of the mechanisms that powered it, eventually undermined the stability of that achievement in many different ways.

Or, to express that thought in a somewhat different way, this story teaches us that one needs to keep in mind that not everything that seemingly works well at first for mainstream, middle-class people does so over the long term, or for the rest of the population, at home or abroad, and their situation matters, too, not just to them but to us all.

Acknowledgments

This book grew out of the research and writing that I first began doing in a serious way while in graduate school at Columbia University in the 1980s. One of the nice things about a project that builds on everything I have done since then is the chance it affords to thank the many people who helped along the way. Joe Mitchell's wise advice to choose Columbia helped me get there. At Columbia the most important contributors were the late Eric McKitrick, who advised my MA thesis and smoothed my way in the grad program more generally; Eric Foner, a historian as brilliant as he is busy, who agreed to work with me even though I didn't intend to focus on his field of specialization; and Joshua Freeman, who opened my eyes to the latest scholarship in modern US labor history and was very generous with his time. Among his most helpful interventions was to introduce me to Nelson Lichtenstein, whose work mine has been in dialogue with ever since. And then there was the late Alan Brinkley, who agreed to serve as an outside reader of my dissertation and was endlessly helpful to my work and me.

Columbia had a great group of graduate students in American history during the 1980s, and working with them also sharpened my analysis in all kinds of ways. The two who aided me the most from that group were Tyler Anbinder and Pat Williams, who helped me navigate generals, tolerated my preoccupation with the middle third of the twentieth century, and provided the kind of friendship and support that can make grad school not just educational but also fun. Nick Spiliotes also helped me get the most out my grad school experience with his wise words of advice on many subjects.

Ev Dennis, the director of what was then the Gannett Center for Media Studies at Columbia, taught me a great deal about the role of

ACKNOWLEDGMENTS

the media, as did the distinguished scholars in residence there, and the guests who gave such informative presentations to the weekly fellows' seminars.

At Yale, where I taught as a lecturer for two years after finishing my PhD, I met David Bell, who was very interesting to talk to and from whom I learned a lot. David was kind enough to read a draft version of *Promised Land* even though his own field is the French Revolution. Predictably, his comments were insightful and gently expressed. At Yale I also had the chance to meet and teach some very fine grad students such as David Koistinen and Ted Liazos, and their comments inside and outside class also informed my work. I also got to know Steve Gillon, a prolific historian of modern America, who has given me more than a little good advice over the years. Will Hitchcock and Mark Shulman helped me to better understand foreign-policy issues, then and afterward.

At Ohio State, where I have taught since leaving Yale in 1993, a trio of senior colleagues (Manse Blackford, Susan Hartmann, and Austin Kerr) taught me a lot about the history of modern America and how to teach it well, among other highly useful things. So, too, in more recent years, did other colleagues in American history such as Paula Baker, Kevin Boyle, John Brooke, Clay Howard, Hasan Jeffries, Katherine Marino, Dan Rivers, and David Steigerwald. The military historians (a field in which Ohio State is internationally distinguished) also taught me a lot, none more so than Allan Millett and the other members of the Force and Policy Group (of OSU's Mershon Center), which Allan chaired for many years. Also very informative were discussions with David Brakke, Alice Conklin, Chris Otter, Chris Reed, and Birgitte Søland, among others. I have taught a great many grad students at OSU, and that is a form of education as well. Frank Blazich, Nate Citino, Russ Coil, Pippa Holloway, Ethan Kim, Sarah Siff, Greyson Teague, and many others helped me to understand things that made this book better than it would have been otherwise. At OSU's Moritz College of Law, where I also teach, there were several faculty and staff members I learned a great deal from. Among the most helpful were (and still are) Terri Enns, Ned Foley, Steve Huefner, Daphne Meimaridis, Dan Tokaji, and the other members of the Election Law Group; and Nancy Rogers, who took an early interest in having me join the law faculty and somehow made that happen. OSU also has very distinguished political scientists and very strong graduate students in that field, from whom I have learned a good deal. The member of that faculty who has helped the most is Paul Beck, whose encyclopedic knowledge of American government and politics sheds light in all directions. Thanks to Paul, too, for taking time to read and comment on an early draft of this book. Special thanks go to my friend Mike Flamm, with whom I discussed many of the ideas contained in this book.

The wider world of the historical profession has also been a great help in formulating the ideas expressed in this book. Volker Berghahn, Andy Gordon, Charles Maier, Nicole Jordan, and Irwin Wall joined me on a panel (the first time I ever gave a paper) that looked at the middle-class era internationally, giving me a kind of big-picture perspective from the start. Two specialized groups, the Business History Conference (BHC) and the Policy History Conference (PHC), have been very good places for me to present papers and to learn from others. Thanks go to such BHC stalwarts as Bill Becker, Bill Childs, Lou Galambos, Richard John, Ken Lipartito, Phil Scranton, and Mary Yeager, among others, who helped me think about American political economy in broad ways; and to such PHC regulars as Mike Bowen, Vince Cannato, Don Critchlow, Geoff Kabaservice, Bill Rorabaugh, Tim Thurber, Mark Wilson, and others too numerous to name individually, who taught many insightful lessons on the connections between politics and public policy. I also owe a debt to colleagues in the United Kingdom who work from their own, somewhat different, vantage point on modern America, especially Nigel Bowles, Barry Langford, Robert Mason, and Iwan Morgan. Thanks go to Robert also for reading and commenting on an early draft of this book. Ellie Shermer's invitations to present my work at the Newberry Library's History of Capitalism Seminar in Chicago involved me in sessions there as informative as they have been pleasant. Conversations with Brian Balogh, David Chappell, Bill Cronon, Roy Domenico, Mo Fiorina, Gary Gerstle, Michael Kazin, Alex Keyssar, Jim Kloppenberg, Maria Mitchell, Tim Naftali, Charles Stewart, and John Witt about various aspects of American history have been very helpful, too. None of these scholars, nor anyone else listed above or below, will likely agree with all of *Promised Land's* arguments and conclusions; they are mine alone.

ACKNOWLEDGMENTS

And then there are the people who were part of the process of turning a draft manuscript into a published book. Special thanks are due to Joyce Pfister, an early and hugely helpful mentor who persuaded me to approach commercial publishers with my manuscript; to Elizabeth Manus, who carefully and critically reviewed the draft manuscript; and to Gerry Howard, who both grasped the importance of this topic and helped guide me to the right literary agent, the endlessly impressive and fun Jill Kneerim. Kudos to her and her colleagues at Kneerim & Williams. Jill helped steer me to Kathy Belden at Scribner, who has done for the manuscript exactly what I expected she would, which was to gently and patiently (yet firmly) edit out things that were unnecessary and/or positively wrongheaded, improve the organization and writing, and generally provide the kind of support an author needs to get a book like this done. Jill also connected me with David Sobel, who made many helpful changes in form and substance to my draft so as to improve its overall readability, and was a real pleasure to work with. Thanks also go to Nan Graham, senior vice president and publisher at Scribner, who firmly believed in the need for a book on this subject; Sally Howe; Jason Chappell; and others there and elsewhere at Simon & Schuster, without whose assistance this book would never have been published.

Much closer to home, my spouse, Karen Simonian, patiently read and marked up multiple drafts, asked endless good questions, and made the result better in countless ways. Our son, Ben, helped, too, by not distracting me too much when I was writing, and by humoring me when I talked too much about an earlier era. Thanks, too, to our various friends and relatives who expressed interest and enthusiasm in the topic, including Ann Goebel, Carol Simonian, and Conrad Sindt, experts on Beatrice Bauch Sindt, who makes occasional appearances on the pages of *Promised Land*.

David Stebenne
Columbus, Ohio
December 2019

Notes

Introduction

1   For one of the most influential examples of a work of history that argued mass prosperity and a great big middle class were defining features throughout American history, see David M. Potter, *People of Plenty: Economic Abundance and the American Character* (Chicago: University of Chicago Press, 1954).

2   Michael Barone, *Our Country: The Shaping of America from Roosevelt to Reagan* (New York: Free Press, 1990), 16–453; David M. Kennedy, *Freedom from Fear: The American People in Depression and War, 1929–1945* (New York: Oxford University Press, 1999); James T. Patterson, *Grand Expectations, the United States, 1945–74* (New York: Oxford University Press, 1996), 3–709; and David Goldfield, *The Gifted Generation: When Government Was Good* (New York: Bloomsbury, 2017).

3   Barone, *Our Country*, 16–25; Warren Sloat, *1929: America before the Crash* (New York: Cooper Square Press, 2004), especially at 11–83, 151–253; and Kennedy, *Freedom from Fear*, 12–29.

4   Barone, *Our Country*, 20–25; Kennedy, *Freedom from Fear*, 13–16; and Sloat, *1929*, 97–100, 103–8.

5   Hugh Brogan, *Penguin History of the USA*, 2nd ed. (London: Penguin, 1999), 496–97; Kennedy, *Freedom from Fear*, 14–15; and D. W. Meinig, *The Shaping of America: A Geographical Perspective on 500 Years of History*, vol. 4, *Global America: 1915–2000* (New Haven: Yale University Press, 2004), 121–34.

6   Barone, *Our Country*, 23; Kennedy, *Freedom from Fear*, 18–19; Sloat, *1929*, 325; Meinig, *Global America*, 117–18; and "Jazz: Our Language," PBS video.

7   Barone, *Our Country*, 37–38; Kennedy, *Freedom from Fear*, 31–32; Joan Hoff Wilson, *Herbert Hoover: Forgotten Progressive* (Prospect Heights, IL: Waveland Press, 1975), 3–30, 79–133; Brogan, *History of the USA*, 504; and William E. Leuchtenburg, *The Perils of Prosperity, 1914–32*, 2nd ed. (Chicago: University of Chicago Press, 1993), 229–40.

8   Kennedy, *Freedom from Fear*, 18–19; Nell Irvin Painter, *Creating Black Americans: African-American History and Its Meanings, 1619 to the Present* (New York: Oxford University Press, 2007), 148–50, 178–79, 193; and David Burner, *The Politics of Provincialism: The Democratic Party in Transition, 1918–1932* (New York: Norton, 1975), 237–39, 240–42.

9 Barone, *Our Country*, 23; Kennedy, *Freedom from Fear*, 18–19; "Jazz: Our Language"; Terry Teachout, *Pops: A Life of Louis Armstrong* (Boston: Houghton Mifflin, 2009), 25–140; and Wikipedia entry for Louis Armstrong.

10 Meinig, *Global America*, 3–172; Barone, *Our Country*, 16–24; and Kennedy, *Freedom from Fear*, 13–23.

11 Meinig, *Global America*, 3–172; and Sloat, *1929*, 39–43, 93–94.

12 Meinig, *Global America*, 43–55; Sloat, *1929*, 183–84, 309–18; Robert S. Lynd and Helen Merrell Lynd, *Middletown: A Study in Modern American Culture* (Orlando, FL: Harcourt, Brace, Jovanovich, 1957), 98, 171–74, 269–71; Paul Starr, *The Creation of the Media: Political Origins of Modern Communications* (New York: Basic Books, 2004), 328–61; "Empires of the Air," PBS video; and Marina Moskowitz, *Standard of Living: The Measure of the Middle Class in Modern America* (Baltimore: Johns Hopkins University Press, 2004), especially at 220–38.

13 Leuchtenburg, *Perils of Prosperity*, 193; Meinig, *Global America*, 114–21; Kennedy, *Freedom from Fear*, 15, 16–18, 22–23, 27; Lynd and Lynd, *Middletown*, 21–109; and Moskowitz, *Standard of Living*, 220–38.

14 Meinig, *Global America*, 3–109; Kennedy, *Freedom from Fear*, 12–42; Barone, *Our Country*, 16–24; Lynd and Lynd, *Middletown*, 3–222; and Moskowitz, *Standard of Living*.

15 Lynd and Lynd, *Middletown*, especially 21–180, 315–495; and Alice Kessler Harris, *In Pursuit of Equity: Women, Men, and the Quest for Economic Citizenship in 20th Century America* (New York: Oxford University Press, 2001), 19–63.

1. A Dream Deferred

1 Kennedy, *Freedom from Fear*, 10, 16, 48; Brogan, *History of the USA*, 504–5; Sloat, *1929*, 222–24; and Barone, *Our Country*, 37–38.

2 Leuchtenburg, *Perils of Prosperity*, 48, 52, 56, 241–55; and Kennedy, *Freedom from Fear*, 70–73.

3 Leuchtenburg, *Perils of Prosperity*, 48, 52, 56, 241–55; Kennedy, *Freedom from Fear*, 70–73; and Robert Skidelsky, *John Maynard Keynes: Hopes Betrayed, 1883–1920* (New York: Penguin, 1994), 357–402.

4 Skidelsky, *Hopes Betrayed*, 357–402; and John Stevenson, *British Society: 1914–1945* (New York: Penguin, 1984), 105–7.

5 Kennedy, *Freedom from Fear*, 72–73; Leuchtenburg, *Perils of Prosperity*, 12; and Sloat, *1929*, 22–27, 68–69.

6 Leuchtenburg, *Perils of Prosperity*, 108–12.

7 Leuchtenburg, 108–12; and David M. Kennedy, *Over Here: The First World War and American Society* (New York: Oxford, 1980), 296–347.

8 Leuchtenburg, *Perils of Prosperity*, 244–46; and Meinig, *Global America*, 3–18, 35–43.

9 Sloat, *1929*, 33–35, 37–38, 41, 62; Brogan, *History of the USA*, 493–95, 505; and Mark Wayne Nelson, *Jumping the Abyss: Marriner S. Eccles and the New Deal, 1933–1940* (Salt Lake City: University of Utah Press, 2017), 34–45.

NOTES

10 Leuchtenburg, *Perils of Prosperity*, 241–46; Brogan, *History of the USA*, 505–10; Kennedy, *Freedom from Fear*, 37, 51–59; and Nelson, *Jumping the Abyss*, 43.

11 Leuchtenburg, *Perils of Prosperity*, 244–46; Kennedy, *Freedom from Fear*, 58–59; and Brogan, *History of the USA*, 505–6, 509–10.

12 Leuchtenburg, *Perils of Prosperity*, 98–103, 178–202, 241–46; Kennedy, *Freedom from Fear*, 54–58; and Brogan, *History of the USA*, 492–506.

13 Leuchtenburg, *Perils of Prosperity*, 246; Kennedy, *Freedom from Fear*, 65–80, 131–32; and Brogan, *History of the USA*, 517–18.

14 Brogan, 514.

15 Kennedy, *Freedom from Fear*, 85–87; Leuchtenburg, *Perils of Prosperity*, 247–53; Brogan, *History of the USA*, 514–15; Robert S. McElvaine, *The Great Depression: America, 1929–1941* (New York: Times Books, 1984), 72–82; and T. H. Watkins, *The Hungry Years: A Narrative History of the Great Depression in America* (New York: Henry Holt, 1999), 37–103.

16 Watkins, *Hungry Years*, 54–103; and McElvaine, *Great Depression*, 91–92.

17 Leuchtenburg, *Perils of Prosperity*, 250–53; Kennedy, *Freedom from Fear*, 90; Watkins, *Hungry Years*, 54–103; McElvaine, *Great Depression*, 79–81; and "The Great Depression: The Road to Rock Bottom," PBS video.

18 Nancy Woloch, *Women and the American Experience* (New York: Knopf, 1984), 440–52; and Alan Brinkley, *The Unfinished Nation: A Concise History of the American People*, 6th ed. (New York: McGraw-Hill, 2009), 608–13.

19 Leuchtenburg, *Perils of Prosperity*, 247; and Barone, *Our Country*, 43–44.

20 Wayne J. Urban and Jennings L. Wagoner Jr., *American Education: A History*, 4th ed. (New York: Routledge, 2009), 271–318; Wikipedia entry "Education in the United States"; and William E. Leuchtenburg, *Franklin D. Roosevelt and the New Deal, 1932–1940* (New York: Harper & Row, 1963), 21n9.

21 Barone, *Our Country*, 31; Kennedy, *Freedom from Fear*, 61–62; Leuchtenburg, *Perils of Prosperity*, 217; David E. Kyvig, *Repealing National Prohibition* (Chicago: University of Chicago Press, 1979), especially at 138–40, 154–57, 170–75, 178–82, 199, 200; and Burner, *Politics of Provincialism*, 98–102, 248.

22 Burner, *Politics of Provincialism*, 98–102, 248; Kyvig, *Repealing National Prohibition*, 64, 147, 165; and Wikipedia entry for Albert Ritchie.

23 Starr, *Creation of the Media*, 348–61.

24 "Empires of the Air." See, too, Leuchtenburg, *Perils of Prosperity*, 196; and Starr, *Creation of the Media*, 348–58.

25 Leuchtenburg, *Perils of Prosperity*, 249; and Starr, *Creation of the Media*, 295–323.

26 Hoff Wilson, *Herbert Hoover*, 79–231; Kennedy, *Freedom from Fear*, 44–48, 70–85; and "Road to Rock Bottom."

27 Hoff Wilson, *Herbert Hoover*, 133–67; Kennedy, *Freedom from Fear*, 70–79; and "Road to Rock Bottom."

28 Sloat, *1929*, 218–24; Kennedy, *Freedom from Fear*, 49–51, 70–94; Hoff Wilson, *Herbert Hoover*, 121–208; Barone, *Our Country*, 45–49; Leuchtenburg, *Perils of Prosperity*, 250–61; and Nelson, *Jumping the Abyss*, 62–64.

NOTES

29 Hoff Wilson, *Herbert Hoover*, 164–67; Kennedy, *Freedom from Fear*, 62, 91–94; Leuchtenburg, *Roosevelt and the New Deal*, 13–17; and Barone, *Our Country*, 45.

30 Brinkley, *Unfinished Nation*, 613–14; Kennedy, *Freedom from Fear*, 89–90; and Watkins, *Hungry Years*, 54–80, 93–103.

31 Stebenne and Simonian family history; and Barone, *Our Country*, 44–45.

32 Hoff Wilson, *Herbert Hoover*, 163–67; and Barone, *Our Country*, 43–45.

33 Arthur M. Schlesinger Jr., *The Crisis of the Old Order, 1919–1933* (Boston: Houghton Mifflin, 1957), 317–439; and J. William T. Youngs, *Eleanor Roosevelt: A Personal and Public Life,* 3rd ed. (New York: Pearson, 2006), 66, 81–86.

34 Kennedy, *Freedom from Fear*, 95–101; and Sloat, *1929*, 300–305.

35 Quoted in Barone, *Our Country*, 52.

36 Barone, 54.

37 Franklin D. Roosevelt address to the Democratic National Convention, July 2, 1932, American Presidency Project, document 131, www.presidency.ucsb .edu, p. 3.

38 Holly Allen, *Forgotten Men and Fallen Women: The Cultural Politics of New Deal Narratives* (Ithaca, NY: Cornell University Press, 2015), 11–67.

39 Hoff Wilson, *Herbert Hoover*, 163–67; Leuchtenburg, *Roosevelt and the New Deal*, 3–17; and Barone, *Our Country*, 43–57.

2. Roosevelt to the Rescue

1 Schlesinger, *Crisis of the Old Order*, 317–25, 327–410; and Kennedy, *Freedom from Fear*, 115–19, 131, 244–48.

2 Leuchtenburg, *Roosevelt and the New Deal*, 41–94, 148–49; Kennedy, *Freedom from Fear*, 131–59; Brogan, *History of the USA*, 524–44; and Barone, *Our Country*, 62–78.

3 Kennedy, *Freedom from Fear*, 131–37, 377; Barone, *Our Country*, 62–63; Brogan, *History of the USA*, 524; and Leuchtenburg, *Roosevelt and the New Deal*, 43–45, 60–62.

4 Barone, *Our Country*, 64; Leuchtenburg, *Roosevelt and the New Deal*, 20, 58–60; Wikipedia entry for Ferdinand Pecora; and Brogan, *History of the USA*, 527.

5 Leuchtenburg, *Roosevelt and the New Deal*, 90–91; Kennedy, *Freedom from Fear*, 366–68; and David Burner, *John F. Kennedy and a New Generation*, 2nd ed. (New York: Pearson, 2005), 9–10, 13–14.

6 Barone, *Our Country*, 65–66; Leuchtenburg, *Roosevelt and the New Deal*, 50–51; and Kennedy, *Freedom from Fear*, 154–57.

7 Barone, *Our Country*, 65–66; Leuchtenburg, *Roosevelt and the New Deal*, 79–82; and Kennedy, *Freedom from Fear*, 197–99.

8 Kennedy, *Freedom from Fear*, 144–47, 170–76; Wikipedia entry for Gifford Pinchot; Barone, *Our Country*, 64; Brogan, *History of the USA*, 526; and Leuchtenburg, *Roosevelt and the New Deal*, 52–53, 120–21.

9 Kennedy, *Freedom from Fear*, 144–45; Arthur M. Schlesinger Jr., *Coming of*

NOTES

the New Deal (Boston: Houghton Mifflin, 1958), 335–41; Barone, *Our Country*, 64; and Allen, *Forgotten Men*, 68–95.

10 Kennedy, *Freedom from Fear*, 175–77; Leuchtenburg, *Roosevelt and the New Deal*, 121–23; and Barone, *Our Country*, 76.

11 Barone, *Our Country*, 64–65; Kennedy, *Freedom from Fear*, 147–49; Leuchtenburg, *Roosevelt and the New Deal*, 54–55; and Brogan, *History of the USA*, 526, 617–18.

12 Kennedy, *Freedom from Fear*, 147–49; Leuchtenburg, *Roosevelt and the New Deal*, 54–55, 87, 157, 165, 174, 312; and Wikipedia entry for Wendell Willkie.

13 Kennedy, *Freedom from Fear*, 147–49; and Leuchtenburg, *Roosevelt and the New Deal*, 54–55, 87, 157, 165, 174.

14 Leuchtenburg, *Roosevelt and the New Deal*, 48–50, 72–78; Kennedy, *Freedom from Fear*, 140–43, 190–96, 199–213; Anthony J. Badger, *The New Deal: The Depression Years, 1933–1940* (Chicago: Ivan R. Dee, 1989), 147–89; and Barone, *Our Country*, 64.

15 Leuchtenburg, *Roosevelt and the New Deal*, 48–52, 72–78; Kennedy, *Freedom from Fear*, 140–43, 190–96, 199–213; Wikipedia entry for Henry Wallace; Badger, *New Deal*, 147–89; and Barone, *Our Country*, 64.

16 Kennedy, *Freedom from Fear*, 206–13; Leuchtenburg, *Roosevelt and the New Deal*, 74–78; Brogan, *History of the USA*, 538–39; Badger, *New Deal*, 163–89; and Jack Temple Kirby, *Rural Worlds Lost: The American South, 1920–1960* (Baton Rouge: Louisiana State University Press, 1987), 50–79.

17 Ira Katznelson, *Fear Itself: The New Deal and the Origins of Our Time* (New York: Liveright, 2013), 133–51.

18 David L. Stebenne, "Thomas J. Watson and the Business-Government Relationship, 1933–1956," *Enterprise and Society* 6 (March 2005): 45–75, at 54.

19 Stebenne, 54–75; and David L. Stebenne, "IBM's 'New Deal': Employment Policies of the International Business Machines Corporation, 1933–1956," *Journal of the Historical Society* 5 (Winter 2005): 47–77.

20 Kennedy, *Freedom from Fear*, 177–86; and Leuchtenburg, *Roosevelt and the New Deal*, 64–71, 88.

21 Kennedy, *Freedom from Fear*, 186–89; and Leuchtenburg, *Roosevelt and the New Deal*, 64–71, 145–46, 185.

22 Kennedy, *Freedom from Fear*, 186–89; Leuchtenburg, *Roosevelt and the New Deal*, 64–71, 145–46, 185; and Steven Horwitz, "That's Not Kosher: How Four Jewish Butchers Brought Down the First New Deal," Foundation for Economic Education, May 30, 2012.

23 Leuchtenburg, *Roosevelt and the New Deal*, 53.

24 Leuchtenburg, 53; and Kenneth T. Jackson, *Crabgrass Frontier: The Suburbanization of the United States* (New York: Oxford University Press, 1985), 190–203.

25 Kennedy, *Freedom from Fear*, 153, 199; Schlesinger, *Coming of the New Deal*, 45; and Alonzo Hamby, *For the Survival of Democracy: Franklin Roosevelt and the World Crisis of the 1930s* (New York: Free Press, 2004), 128.

26 Kennedy, *Freedom from Fear*, 138; and Barone, *Our Country*, 63.

27 Jane Ziegelman and Andrew Coe, *A Square Meal: A Culinary History of the Great Depression* (New York: Harper, 2016), 145–56, 188–203.

NOTES

28 Ziegelman and Coe, 122–44, 188–279.
29 Ziegelman and Coe, 150. See, too, at 11–254.
30 Ziegelman and Coe, 54–121, 188–279; Kennedy, *Freedom from Fear*, 168–75; "Road to Rock Bottom"; and Leuchtenburg, *Roosevelt and the New Deal*, 22–24.
31 Ziegelman and Coe, *Square Meal*, 128–44, 229–79; Ruth Milkman, "Women's Work and the Economic Crisis," in *A Heritage of Her Own*, ed. Nancy F. Cott and Elizabeth H. Pleck (New York: ACLS History E-Book Project, 2006), 507–41; and MaryAnn Moore, "The Joy of Cooking," in *Essence of Emmet, Part III: 1918–1960* (Emmet County, MI: Historical Organizations of Emmet County, 2016), 70–71.
32 Kennedy, *Freedom from Fear*, 160–89; Erich Rauchway, *The Great Depression & the New Deal: A Very Short Introduction* (New York: Oxford University Press, 2008), 38–49; and Milkman, "Women's Work," 507–41.
33 Kennedy, *Freedom from Fear*, 160–89; Rauchway, *Great Depression*, 38–49; and Milkman, "Women's Work," 507–41.
34 Richard Gid Powers, *Secrecy and Power: The Life of J. Edgar Hoover* (New York: Free Press, 1987), 181–96; Leuchtenburg, *Roosevelt and the New Deal*, 334–35; and Robert C. Wadman and William Thomas Allison, *To Protect and Serve: A History of Policing in America* (New York: Pearson, 2003), 83, 101.
35 Wadman and Allison, *To Protect and Serve*, 101; Leuchtenburg, *Roosevelt and the New Deal*, 90; and Wikipedia entry for Richard Whitney.
36 Thomas Doherty, *Hollywood's Censor: Joseph I. Breen and the Production Code Administration* (New York: Columbia University Press, 2007), 31–76; and Laura Wittern-Keller, *Freedom of the Screen: Legal Challenges to State Film Censorship, 1915–1981* (Lexington: University of Kentucky Press, 2008), 17–64.
37 Doherty, *Hollywood's Censor*, 7–48, 77–96; Wittern-Keller, *Freedom of the Screen*, 54–56; and William D. Romanowski, *Reforming Hollywood: How American Protestants Fought for Freedom at the Movies* (New York: Oxford University Press, 2012).
38 Doherty, *Hollywood's Censor*, 77–120.
39 Doherty, 77–120; and Wikipedia entries for *It Happened One Night* and *Mutiny on the Bounty*.
40 Doherty, *Hollywood's Censor*, 77–120; and Ellen C. Scott, *Cinema Civil Rights: Regulation, Repression, and Race in the Classical Hollywood Era* (New Brunswick, NJ: Rutgers University Press, 2015).
41 Doherty, *Hollywood's Censor*, 31–120; and Leuchtenburg, *Perils of Prosperity*, 157–77, 241, 265.
42 Leuchtenburg, *Roosevelt and the New Deal*, 199–203; Kennedy, *Freedom from Fear*, 155–59; Brogan, *History of the USA*, 528–29; and the Wikipedia entry for "The Star-Spangled Banner."
43 Leuchtenburg, *Roosevelt and the New Deal*, 199–203; Kennedy, *Freedom from Fear*, 155–59; and Brogan, *History of the USA*, 528–29.
44 Leuchtenburg, *Roosevelt and the New Deal*, 199, 203–5; and Kennedy, *Freedom from Fear*, 389–90.

266

NOTES

45 Leuchtenburg, *Roosevelt and the New Deal*, 207–9; and Kennedy, *Freedom from Fear*, 390–92.

46 Leuchtenburg, *Roosevelt and the New Deal*, 63–117; Kennedy, *Freedom from Fear*, 190–217; and Barone, *Our Country*, 71–78.

47 Leuchtenburg, *Roosevelt and the New Deal*, 116–17; Kennedy, *Freedom from Fear*, 215–17; and Barone, *Our Country*, 72–77.

48 Leuchtenburg, *Roosevelt and the New Deal*, 95–117; and Kennedy, *Freedom from Fear*, 214–17.

3. Hour of Discontent

1 Leuchtenburg, *Roosevelt and the New Deal*, 143–96; Kennedy, *Freedom from Fear*, 249–380; Barone, *Our Country*, 79–131; and Ronald Steel, *Walter Lippmann and the American Century* (Boston: Little, Brown, 1980), 291–92.

2 Leuchtenburg, *Roosevelt and the New Deal*, 91–142; Kennedy, *Freedom from Fear*, 252–57, 288–322; Roger G. Kennedy, *When Art Worked: The New Deal, Art and Democracy* (New York: Rizzoli, 2009); Sharon Ann Musher, *Democratic Art: The New Deal's Influence on American Culture* (Chicago: University of Chicago Press, 2015); and Victoria Grieve, *The Federal Art Project and the Creation of Middlebrow Culture* (Urbana: University of Illinois Press, 2009).

3 Leuchtenburg, *Roosevelt and the New Deal*, 218–30, 275–86; Kennedy, *Freedom from Fear*, 381–419; and Hamby, *For the Survival of Democracy*, 176–255, 371–406.

4 Barone, *Our Country*, 83–84, 95; Leuchtenburg, *Roosevelt and the New Deal*, 124–25, 130; and Kennedy, *Freedom from Fear*, 249–52.

5 Leuchtenburg, *Roosevelt and the New Deal*, 125–29, 193–95; Kennedy, *Freedom from Fear*, 252–57; and Hamby, *For the Survival of Democracy*, 276–280.

6 Leuchtenburg, *Roosevelt and the New Deal*, 125–29, 193–95; Kennedy, *Freedom from Fear*, 252–57; and Hamby, *For the Survival of Democracy*, 276–80.

7 Leuchtenburg, *Roosevelt and the New Deal*, 125–30; Kennedy, *Freedom from Fear*, 253–54; Hamby, *For the Survival of Democracy*, 277–80; and Rauchway, *Great Depression*, 67–69.

8 Leuchtenburg, *Roosevelt and the New Deal*, 70, 133–34, 257; Kennedy, *Freedom from Fear*, 151–52, 178–79, 251–52; Hamby, *For the Survival of Democracy*, 275–78; and PBS video for *American Experience*, "New Deal, New York."

9 Leuchtenburg, *Roosevelt and the New Deal*, 126–28; and Kennedy, *Freedom from Fear*, 254–57.

10 Leuchtenburg, *Roosevelt and the New Deal*, 126–28; Kennedy, *Freedom from Fear*, 254–57; Kennedy, *When Art Worked*; Musher, *Democratic Art*; and Grieve, *Federal Art Project*.

11 Alan Brinkley, *The Publisher: Henry Luce and His American Century* (New

NOTES

York: Vintage, 2010), 108–44, 202–39; and Frank Luther Mott, *American Journalism: A History, 1690–1960*, 3rd ed. (New York: Macmillan, 1962), 672–73.

12 Brinkley, *Unfinished Nation*, 642–43; and Wikipedia entries for the Book of the Month Club and *Reader's Digest*.

13 Wikipedia entries for the Hardy Boys, Nancy Drew, and Superman.

14 "Empires of the Air"; and Wikipedia entry for the NBC Symphony Orchestra.

15 Ross Firestone, *Swing, Swing, Swing: The Life and Times of Benny Goodman* (New York: Norton, 1993), 17–49; Wikipedia entry for Benny Goodman; and "Jazz: Our Language."

16 Quoted in the Wikipedia entry for Benny Goodman. See, too, Firestone, *Swing, Swing, Swing*, 50–218.

17 Firestone, 105–218; and Teachout, *Pops*, 205–31.

18 Grieve, *Federal Art Project*, 135–62.

19 Wikipedia entries for Ernest Hemingway, John Steinbeck, Richard Wright, Zora Neale Hurston, Bessie Smith, and Woody Guthrie; Kennedy, *Freedom from Fear*, 364; and Watkins, *Hungry Years*.

20 Leuchtenburg, *Roosevelt and the New Deal*, 130–32; Barone, *Our Country*, 84–85; Kennedy, *Freedom from Fear*, 257–71; and David L. Stebenne, *Modern Republican: Arthur Larson and the Eisenhower Years* (Bloomington: Indiana University Press, 2006), 144.

21 Leuchtenburg, *Roosevelt and the New Deal*, 130–32; Barone, *Our Country*, 84–85; and Kennedy, *Freedom from Fear*, 224–25, 260–72.

22 Leuchtenburg, *Roosevelt and the New Deal*, 132; Kennedy, *Freedom from Fear*, 260–70; Katznelson, *Fear Itself*, 259–60; and Linda Gordon, *Pitied but Not Entitled: Single Mothers and the History of Welfare* (New York: Free Press, 1994), 183–306.

23 Leuchtenburg, *Roosevelt and the New Deal*, 132; and Kennedy, *Freedom from Fear*, 261–65.

24 Leuchtenburg, *Roosevelt and the New Deal*, 131; Kennedy, *Freedom from Fear*, 263–65, 281–82; and Kim Phillips-Fein, *Invisible Hands: The Making of the Conservative Movement from the New Deal to Reagan* (New York: Norton, 2009), 3–25.

25 Leuchtenburg, *Roosevelt and the New Deal*, 131; Kennedy, *Freedom from Fear*, 263–65, 281–82; and Phillips-Fein, *Invisible Hands*, 3–25.

26 Stebenne, "IBM's 'New Deal,'" 47–77, at 57–58.

27 Stebenne, 57–58.

28 Leuchtenburg, *Roosevelt and the New Deal*, 131–33; Kennedy, *Freedom from Fear*, 270–73; and Arthur M. Schlesinger Jr., *The Politics of Upheaval* (Boston: Houghton Mifflin, 1960), 270–72.

29 Barone, *Our Country*, 88–89.

30 Barone, 88–90; and Henry Pelling, *American Labor* (Chicago: University of Chicago Press, 1960), 79–154.

31 Barone, *Our Country*, 90–91.

32 Barone, 90–92; and Leuchtenburg, *Roosevelt and the New Deal*, 150–52.

33 Leuchtenburg, *Roosevelt and the New Deal*, 106–14; Robert Zieger, *The CIO, 1935–1955* (Chapel Hill: University of North Carolina Press, 1995),

NOTES

22–89; Kennedy, *Freedom from Fear*, 288–322; Barone, *Our Country*, 98–100; and Steven Fraser, *Labor Will Rule: Sidney Hillman and the Rise of American Labor* (Ithaca, NY: Cornell University Press, 1991), 259–348.

34 Leuchtenburg, *Roosevelt and the New Deal*, 106–14; Zieger, *CIO*, 22–89; Kennedy, *Freedom from Fear*, 288–322; and Barone, *Our Country*, 98–100.

35 Leuchtenburg, *Roosevelt and the New Deal*, 150, 154–57.

36 Leuchtenburg, 157–58; and Meinig, *Global America*, 45–51, 141–44.

37 Leuchtenburg, *Roosevelt and the New Deal*, 152–54; and Kennedy, *Freedom from Fear*, 275–77.

38 Leuchtenburg, *Roosevelt and the New Deal*, 158–61; Kennedy, *Freedom from Fear*, 273–74; and Nelson, *Jumping the Abyss*, 123, 140, 179, 198, 202–28, 232, 233, 236, 242, 272, 324, 327.

39 Leuchtenburg, *Roosevelt and the New Deal*, 143–46, 170–72, 175–95; and Kennedy, *Freedom from Fear*, 273, 278–84.

40 Sarah E. Igo, *The Averaged American: Surveys, Citizens and the Making of a Mass Public* (Cambridge: Harvard University Press, 2007), 103–37.

41 Igo, 103–37; and Barone, *Our Country*, 103, 105–7.

42 Kennedy, *Freedom from Fear*, 285–86; Leuchtenburg, *Roosevelt and the New Deal*, 193–95; and Barone, *Our Country*, 103, 105–7.

43 Leuchtenburg, *Roosevelt and the New Deal*, 188–89; Zieger, *CIO*, 39–40; Kennedy, *Freedom from Fear*, 285; and Barone, *Our Country*, 106.

44 Leuchtenburg, *Roosevelt and the New Deal*, 175–96; Kennedy, *Freedom from Fear*, 280–87; and Barone, *Our Country*, 102–4.

45 Leuchtenburg, *Roosevelt and the New Deal*, 231–39; Kennedy, *Freedom from Fear*, 324–37; and William E. Leuchtenburg, *The Supreme Court Reborn: The Constitutional Revolution in the Age of Roosevelt* (New York: Oxford University Press, 1995), especially at 163–236.

46 Leuchtenburg, *Roosevelt and the New Deal*, 232–51; Kennedy, *Freedom from Fear*, 350–62; and Bruce Bartlett, "Are We About to Repeat the Mistakes of 1937?," *New York Times Economix* blog, July 12, 2011.

47 Leuchtenburg, *Roosevelt and the New Deal*, 232–51; Kennedy, *Freedom from Fear*, 350–62; James W. Cortada, *Before the Computer: IBM, NCR, Burroughs, and Remington Rand and the Industry They Created, 1865–1956* (Princeton: Princeton University Press, 1993), 146–47; David L. Stebenne, "Why the Social Security Rollout Worked Better," History News Network, December 9, 2013; and Bartlett, "Are We About to Repeat?"

48 Leuchtenburg, *Roosevelt and the New Deal*, 252–70; Kennedy, *Freedom from Fear*, 337–50; and Katznelson, *Fear Itself*, 151–82.

49 Leuchtenburg, *Roosevelt and the New Deal*, 261–63; and Kennedy, *Freedom from Fear*, 344–46.

50 Kennedy, *Freedom from Fear*, 345–46; and Katznelson, *Fear Itself*, 267–72.

51 Leuchtenburg, *Roosevelt and the New Deal*, 244, 256.

52 Leuchtenburg, 243–74; Kennedy, *Freedom from Fear*, 354–61, 374–75; and Katznelson, *Fear Itself*, 272–75.

53 Zieger, *CIO*, 66–102; and Gary Gerstle, *Working-Class Americanism: The Politics of Labor in a Textile City, 1914–1960* (New York: Cambridge University Press, 1989), 219–47.

54 Leuchtenburg, *Roosevelt and the New Deal*, 220–21, 226, 265–66, 273–86; Kennedy, *Freedom from Fear*, 396–97, 401–20; and Hamby, *For the Survival of Democracy*, 327–405.

4. The Good War

1 Kennedy, *Freedom from Fear*, 381–858; Leuchtenburg, *Roosevelt and the New Deal*, 275–325; Hamby, *For the Survival of Democracy*, 371–429; and Barone, *Our Country*, 125–81.

2 Kennedy, *Freedom from Fear*, 381–858; Leuchtenburg, *Roosevelt and the New Deal*, 275–325; Hamby, *For the Survival of Democracy*, 371–429; and Barone, *Our Country*, 125–81.

3 Allan R. Millett and Peter Maslowski, *For the Common Defense: A Military History of the United States of America* (New York: Free Press, 1994), 380–412.

4 Kennedy, *Freedom from Fear*, 409, 418–20; Leuchtenburg, *Roosevelt and the New Deal*, 285–86; and Hamby, *For the Survival of Democracy*, 400–407.

5 Barone, *Our Country*, 129; Kennedy, *Freedom from Fear*, 420–23; Leuchtenburg, *Roosevelt and the New Deal*, 287–92; and Hamby, *For the Survival of Democracy*, 405–8.

6 Kennedy, *Freedom from Fear*, 381–91, 393–96, 400–401, 420–25; Leuchtenburg, *Roosevelt and the New Deal*, 224–25, 288–89, 291–93; and Hamby, *For the Survival of Democracy*, 408–13.

7 Kennedy, *Freedom from Fear*, 425–38; and Leuchtenburg, *Roosevelt and the New Deal*, 293–95.

8 James L. Stokesbury, *A Short History of World War II* (New York: William Morrow, 1980), 89–102; and Leuchtenburg, *Roosevelt and the New Deal*, 297–98.

9 Kennedy, *Freedom from Fear*, 427–31; Lynne Olson, *Those Angry Days: Roosevelt, Lindbergh, and America's Fight Over World War II, 1939–1941* (New York: Random House, 2014), 12–114; and Leuchtenburg, *Roosevelt and the New Deal*, 278–97.

10 Kennedy, *Freedom from Fear*, 420–51; Olson, *Those Angry Days*, 12–114; and Leuchtenburg, *Roosevelt and the New Deal*, 275–97.

11 Kennedy, *Freedom from Fear*, 438–52; Leuchtenburg, *Roosevelt and the New Deal*, 29–301; and Olson, *Those Angry Days*, 97–138.

12 John Morton Blum, *V Was for Victory: Politics and American Culture During World War II* (New York: Harcourt, Brace, Jovanovich, 1976), 264; Olson, *Those Angry Days*, 170–71; Leuchtenburg, *Roosevelt and the New Deal*, 310–14; Kennedy, *Freedom from Fear*, 455–56; and Barone, *Our Country*, 135–36.

13 Recording of NBC's broadcast of Willkie's address to the Republican National Convention, June 28, 1940, Paley Archive, New York. See, too, the Wikipedia entry for Willkie; Olson, *Those Angry Days*, 171–82; and Leuchtenburg, *Roosevelt and the New Deal*, 312–14.

14 Leuchtenburg, *Roosevelt and the New Deal*, 314–17; Kennedy, *Freedom from Fear*, 456–57; Barone, *Our Country*, 137–40; and Olson, *Those Angry Days*, 184–90.

NOTES

15 Leuchtenburg, *Roosevelt and the New Deal*, 314–17; Kennedy, *Freedom from Fear*, 456–57; Barone, *Our Country*, 137–40; and Olson, *Those Angry Days*, 184–90.

16 Kennedy, *Freedom from Fear*, 452–64; Barone, *Our Country*, 135–44; Olson, *Those Angry Days*, 170–263; Leuchtenburg, *Roosevelt and the New Deal*, 301–23; and Gareth Davies, "The New Deal in 1940: Embattled or Entrenched?," in *America at the Ballot Box: Elections and Political History*, ed. Gareth Davies and Julian E. Zelizer (Philadelphia: University of Pennsylvania Press, 2015), 153–66.

17 Kennedy, *Freedom from Fear*, 149, 316, 431–32, 446; Powers, *Secrecy and Power*, 228–39; Leuchtenburg, *Roosevelt and the New Deal*, 280–81; Bradley F. Smith, *The Shadow Warriors: O.S.S. and the Origins of the C.I.A.* (New York: Basic Books, 1983), 20–36; Barone, *Our Country*, 137; and Gary Gerstle, *Liberty and Coercion: The Paradox of American Government from the Founding to the Present* (Princeton: Princeton University Press, 2015), 251–58.

18 Powers, *Secrecy and Power*, 218, 228–39; Gerstle, *Liberty and Coercion*, 251–58; Wadman and Allison, *To Protect and to Serve*, 101–4; and Smith, *Shadow Warriors*, 26–30.

19 Kennedy, *Freedom from Fear*, 459; Barone, *Our Country*, 141; Olson, *Those Angry Days*, 196–218; Leuchtenburg, *Roosevelt and the New Deal*, 306–8; and Cortada, *Before the Computer*, 201.

20 Kennedy, *Freedom from Fear*, 451, 459, 632–35; Olson, *Those Angry Days*, 196–219; Leuchtenburg, *Roosevelt and the New Deal*, 307–8; and Michael C. C. Adams, *The Best War Ever: America and World War II* (Baltimore: Johns Hopkins University Press, 1994), 76–79.

21 Kennedy, *Freedom from Fear*, 451, 459, 632–35; Olson, *Those Angry Days*, 196–219; Leuchtenburg, *Roosevelt and the New Deal*, 307–8; Lizzie Collingham, *The Taste of War: World War II and the Battle for Food* (New York: Penguin, 2011), 416–17; and Adams, *Best War Ever*, 76–79.

22 Michael S. Neiberg, *Making Citizen Soldiers: ROTC and the Ideology of American Military Service* (Cambridge: Harvard University Press, 2000), 12–34; Stephen Ambrose, *Eisenhower* (New York: Touchstone, 1983), 1:13–54; Kennedy, *Freedom from Fear*, 632–35; and Adams, *Best War Ever*, 76–79.

23 Barone, *Our Country*, 148–49; Leuchtenburg, *Roosevelt and the New Deal*, 301–8; and Kennedy, *Freedom from Fear*, 446–54, 460–62, 488–515.

24 Joseph P. Lash, *Roosevelt and Churchill, 1939–1941: The Partnership That Saved the West* (New York: Norton, 1976), 248–50; Kennedy, *Freedom from Fear*, 465–75; and Olson, *Those Angry Days*, 264–87.

25 Kennedy, *Freedom from Fear*, 482–85; and Millett and Maslowski, *For the Common Defense*, 418–19.

26 Kennedy, *Freedom from Fear*, 476–523; Olson, *Those Angry Days*, 341–461; and Doris Kearns Goodwin, *No Ordinary Time: Franklin and Eleanor Roosevelt: The Home Front in World War II* (New York: Simon & Schuster, 1994), 282–97.

27 Kennedy, *Freedom from Fear*, 524–858; James T. Sparrow, *Warfare State:*

NOTES

World War II Americans and the Age of Big Government (New York: Oxford University Press, 2011); and Mark R. Wilson, *Destructive Creation: American Business and the Winning of World War II* (Philadelphia: University of Pennsylvania Press, 2016).

28 Kennedy, *Freedom from Fear*, 615–23, 626–68, 709; Wilson, *Destructive Creation*, 48–189; Blum, *V Was for Victory*, 90–116; and Robert Gordon, *The Rise and Fall of American Growth: The U.S. Standard of Living since the Civil War* (Princeton: Princeton University Press, 2016), 535–65.

29 Sparrow, *Warfare State*, 122–24; Kennedy, *Freedom from Fear*, 624–26; and Blum, *V Was for Victory*, 228–30, 241–44.

30 Sparrow, *Warfare State*, 122–26; Kennedy, *Freedom from Fear*, 624–25; and Blum, *V Was for Victory*, 228–30.

31 Kennedy, *Freedom from Fear*, 619–30, 640–41, 644–47; Sparrow, *Warfare State*, 122–59; and Blum, *V Was for Victory*, 90–146.

32 Kennedy, *Freedom from Fear*, 619–30, 640–41, 644–47; Collingham, *Taste of War*, 418–19; Sparrow, *Warfare State*, 122–59; and Blum, *V Was for Victory*, 90–146.

33 Kennedy, *Freedom from Fear*, 619–30, 640–41, 644–47; Adams, *Best War Ever*, 131; Sparrow, *Warfare State*, 122–59; and Blum, *V Was for Victory*, 90–146.

34 Kennedy, *Freedom from Fear*, 644–46; and Collingham, *Taste of War*, 415–43.

35 Kennedy, *Freedom from Fear*, 256–57, 783; Musher, *Democratic Art*, 187–210; and Wikipedia entries for "God Bless America" and "This Is the Army"; Blum, *V Was for Victory*, 53; and Sparrow, *Warfare State*, 119–21, 150–52.

36 Blum, *V Was for Victory*, 53–89; Sparrow, *Warfare State*, 199–21, 150–52; and Dan DeLuca, "What's the Story behind Those Kate Smith Songs with Racist Lyrics," PhillyDailyNews.com, April 22, 2019.

37 Martin E. Marty, *Modern American Religion*, vol. 3, *Under God, Indivisible, 1941–1960* (Chicago: University of Chicago Press, 1996), 1–130; Mark Silk, "Notes on the Judeo-Christian Tradition in America," *American Quarterly* 36, no. 1 (1984): 65–85; Wikipedia entries for Irving Berlin and Kate Smith; and Leuchtenburg, *Roosevelt and the New Deal*, 184–85, 321–22.

38 Marty, *Under God, Indivisible*, 1–130; Kennedy, *Freedom from Fear*, 760–61; George H. Williams, "The Chaplaincy in the Armed Forces of the United States of America in Historical and Ecclesiastical Perspective," in *Military Chaplains: From a Religious Military to a Military Religion*, ed. Harvey Cox (New York: American Report Press, 1971), 11–58; and William Graebner, *The Age of Doubt: American Thought and Culture in the 1940s* (Prospect Heights, IL: Waveland Press, 1991), 61.

39 Marty, *Under God, Indivisible*, 1–130; Kennedy, *Freedom from Fear*, 760–61; and Williams, "Chaplaincy," 11–58.

40 Meinig, *Global America*, 116–21; Kennedy, *Freedom from Fear*, 637; Blum, *V Was for Victory*, 53–105; Graebner, *Age of Doubt*, 1–8; John Patrick Diggins, *The Proud Decades: America in War and Peace, 1941–1960* (New York: Norton, 1988), 22–25; and Wikipedia entries for "Don't Sit Under the Apple Tree (With Anyone Else but Me)" and "I'll Be Home for Christmas."

NOTES

41   Kennedy, *Freedom from Fear*, 644–46; Blum, *V Was for Victory*, 90–105; Graebner, *Age of Doubt*, 1–8; and Wikipedia entry for "Over the Rainbow."

42   Diggins, *Proud Decades*, 22–52; Graebner, *Age of Doubt*, 4; and Sparrow, *Warfare State*, 48–77.

43   Kennedy, *Freedom from Fear*, 748–60; Blum, *V Was for Victory*, 155–67; Roger Daniels, *Prisoners without Trial: Japanese Americans in World War II* (New York: Hill & Wang, 2004); and Wikipedia entries for *Ex parte Endo* and *Korematsu v. U.S.*

44   Kennedy, *Freedom from Fear*, 634, 711–12, 760–76; and Blum, *V Was for Victory*, 182–220.

45   Kennedy, *Freedom from Fear*, 760–76; and Blum, *V Was for Victory*, 182–220.

46   Kennedy, *Freedom from Fear*, 210, 342–44; Katznelson, *Fear Itself*, 90, 149, 160, 166–68, 176, 179–82; and Wikipedia entry for *Young Mr. Lincoln*.

47   Kennedy, *Freedom from Fear*, 776–82; Adams, *Best War Ever*, 132–35; and Susan M. Hartmann, *The Home Front and Beyond: American Women in the 1940s* (Boston: Twayne, 1984).

48   On that last point, see Hartmann, *Home Front and Beyond*.

49   Kennedy, *Freedom from Fear*, 710, 716, 808–58; Collingham, *Taste of War*, 415–63; recording of NBC's special V-E Day broadcast, Paley Archive; Blum, *V Was for Victory*, 90–116; Sparrow, *Warfare State*, 242–43; Graebner, *Age of Doubt*, 7–8; Diggins, *Proud Decades*, 14–34; and Adams, *Best War Ever*, 114–35.

50   Kennedy, *Freedom from Fear*, 710, 716, 809–58; Collingham, *Taste of War*, 415–63; Blum, *V Was for Victory*, 90–116; Sparrow, *Warfare State*, 242–43; Graebner, *Age of Doubt*, 7–8; Diggins, *Proud Decades*, 14–34; and Adams, *Best War Ever*, 114–35.

5. Postwar Fog

1   Leuchtenburg, *Perils of Prosperity*, 85, 100; James Patterson, *Grand Expectations: The United States, 1945–1974* (New York: Oxford University Press, 1996), 3–9, 13–15; Barone, *Our Country*, 185; William Manchester, *The Glory and the Dream: A Narrative History of America, 1932–1972* (Boston: Little, Brown, 1973), 1:485–86, 497–502; and Graebner, *Age of Doubt*, 9–18.

2   Kennedy, *Freedom from Fear*, 786–87; Patterson, *Grand Expectations*, 3–9, 185; Ira Katznelson, *When Affirmative Action Was White: An Untold History of Racial Inequality in Twentieth-Century America* (New York: Norton, 2005), 113–41; and Glen C. Altschuler, *The GI Bill: A New Deal for Veterans* (New York: Oxford, 2009).

3   Blum, *V Was for Victory*, 279–300; Barone, *Our Country*, 182–88; Kennedy, *Freedom from Fear*, 788–93; Patterson, *Grand Expectations*, 41–50; Diggins, *Proud Decades*, 95–102; Brogan, *History of the USA*, 582–92; and Manchester, *Glory and the Dream*, 445–55, 480–81, 487–96.

4   Blum, *V Was for Victory*, 90–105; Kennedy, *Freedom from Fear*, 644–47; Sparrow, *Warfare State*, 242–44; Patterson, *Grand Expectations*, 8–12,

61–76; Diggins, *Proud Decades*, 178–87; Gordon, *Rise and Fall*, 535–65; and Manchester, *Glory and the Dream*, 524–29.

5　Blum, *V Was for Victory*, 90–105; Kennedy, *Freedom from Fear*, 644–47; Sparrow, *Warfare State*, 242–56; Patterson, *Grand Expectations*, 8–12, 61–76; Diggins, *Proud Decades*, 178–87; Manchester, *Glory and the Dream*, 524–29; and Meinig, *Global America*, 123–34.

6　Blum, *V Was for Victory*, 90–105; Kennedy, *Freedom from Fear*, 644–47; Sparrow, *Warfare State*, 242–56; Patterson, *Grand Expectations*, 8–12, 61–76; Diggins, *Proud Decades*, 178–87; Gordon, *Rise and Fall*, 535–65; Manchester, *Glory and the Dream*, 524–29; and Meinig, *Global America*, 123–34.

7　Blum, *V Was for Victory*, 90–146; Kennedy, *Freedom from Fear*, 619–22; Wilson, *Destructive Creation*, 77–235; Howell John Harris, *The Right to Manage: Industrial Relations Policies of American Business in the 1940s* (Madison: University of Wisconsin Press, 1982), 3–104; and Stebenne, "Thomas J. Watson," 61, 64.

8　Blum, *V Was for Victory*, 90–146; Kennedy, *Freedom from Fear*, 619–22; Wilson, *Destructive Creation*, 77–235; Harris, *Right to Manage*, 3–104; and Stebenne, "Thomas J. Watson," 61, 64.

9　Alonzo Hamby, *Beyond the New Deal: Harry S. Truman and American Liberalism* (New York: Columbia University Press, 1973), 3–51; Nelson Lichtenstein, *Labor's War at Home: The CIO in World War II* (New York: Cambridge University Press, 1982), 203–32; and David Stebenne, *Arthur J. Goldberg: New Deal Liberal* (New York: Oxford University Press, 1996), 42–44.

10　Michael J. Hogan, *A Cross of Iron: Harry S. Truman and the Origins of the National Security State, 1945–54* (New York: Cambridge University Press, 1998), 1–40; Ambrose, *Eisenhower*, 1:409–32; Blum, *V Was for Victory*, 316–23; Melvyn P. Leffler, "National Security and U.S. Foreign Policy," in *Origins of the Cold War: An International History*, 2nd ed., ed. Melvyn P. Leffler and David S. Painter (New York: Routledge, 2005), 15–25; Smith, *Shadow Warriors*, 390–408; and Powers, *Secrecy and Power*, 275–92.

11　Robert Mason, *The Republican Party and American Politics* (New York: Cambridge University Press, 2012), 112–13; Michael Bowen, *The Roots of Modern Conservatism: Dewey, Taft, and the Battle for the Soul of the Republican Party* (Chapel Hill: University of North Carolina Press, 2011), 15–34; Hamby, *Beyond the New Deal*, 53–69; Alan Brinkley, *The End of Reform: New Deal Liberalism in Recession and War* (New York: Alfred Knopf, 1995), 265–69; and Patterson, *Grand Expectations*, 137–42.

12　Mason, *Republican Party*, 112–13; Bowen, *Roots of Modern Conservatism*, 15–34; Patterson, *Grand Expectations*, 127; and Blum, *V Was for Victory*, 265–79, 302–16.

13　Hamby, *Beyond the New Deal*, 53–69; Brinkley, *End of Reform*, 265–69; Patterson, *Grand Expectations*, 137–42; and Katznelson, *Fear Itself*, 362–90.

14　Patterson, *Grand Expectations*, 105–225; Melvyn P. Leffler, *The Specter of Communism: The United States and the Origins of the Cold War, 1917–1953* (New York: Hill & Wang, 1994); Hogan, *Cross of Iron*, 23–335; Graebner,

Age of Doubt, 9–148; Diggins, *Proud Decades*, 54–117; and Manchester, *Glory and the Dream*, 1:80–671.

15 John Lewis Gaddis, *The United States and the Origins of the Cold War, 1941–1947* (New York: Columbia University Press, 1972), 133–243; Leffler, *Specter of Communism*, 33–63; and Patterson, *Grand Expectations*, 105–26.

16 Gaddis, *United States*, 91, 246, 264, 289, 317, 336–37, 348–52; Leffler, *Specter of Communism*, 55–78; and Patterson, *Grand Expectations*, 128–33.

17 Hogan, *Cross of Iron*, 119–58; Leffler, *Specter of Communism*, 82–83; Kennedy, *Freedom from Fear*, 631–37, 710–11, 771–72; and Patterson, *Grand Expectations*, 134.

18 Leffler, *Specter of Communism*, 38, 41–45, 50–52, 54, 55, 59, 61, 64–65, 67, 71–80, 82–85, 89–90; Hogan, *Cross of Iron*, 3, 164–65, 182, 285, 479–80; Patterson, *Grand Expectations*, 85, 89, 98, 107, 111, 130–31, 134, 160, 167, 170, 183, 286; and Wikipedia entries for the North Atlantic Treaty Organization and the Berlin Blockade.

19 Patterson, *Grand Expectations*, 155–57; Diggins, *Proud Decades*, 103–6; and Barone, *Our Country*, 212–21.

20 Patterson, *Grand Expectations*, 157–63; Diggins, *Proud Decades*, 106–9; and Barone, *Our Country*, 221–23.

21 Leffler, *Specter of Communism*, 85–92; Patterson, *Grand Expectations*, 169–72; Michael H. Hunt and Steven I. Levine, "Revolutionary Movements in Asia and the Cold War," in *Origins of the Cold War*, ed. Leffler and Painter, 251–64; and Stebenne, "Thomas J. Watson," 64–65.

22 Leffler, *Specter of Communism*, 93–96; Hogan, *Cross of Iron*, 209–304; and Patterson, *Grand Expectations*, 172–78.

23 Leffler, *Specter of Communism*, 93–96; Hogan, *Cross of Iron*, 209–304; Patterson, *Grand Expectations*, 172–78; and Julian Zelizer, *Taxing America: Wilbur D. Mills, Congress and the State, 1945–1975* (Cambridge: Cambridge University Press, 1998), 1–54.

24 Leffler, *Specter of Communism*, 97–122; Hogan, *Cross of Iron*, 304–65; Patterson, *Grand Expectations*, 178; and Kathryn Weathersby, "Stalin and the Korean War," and Chen Jian, "Mao and Sino-American Relations," in *Origins of the Cold War*, ed. Leffler and Painter, 265–98.

25 Leffler, *Specter of Communism*, 97–122; Hogan, *Cross of Iron*, 304–65; and Patterson, *Grand Expectations*, 178.

26 Patterson, *Grand Expectations*, 13–15, 28, 31–38, 61–70, 76–81; Manchester, *Glory and the Dream*, 521–526; Barone, *Our Country*, 197–99; and Godfrey Hodgson, *America in Our Time* (Garden City, NY: Doubleday, 1976), 50–52.

27 Patterson, *Grand Expectations*, 13–15, 28, 31–38, 61–70, 76–81; Manchester, *Glory and the Dream*, 521–26; Barone, *Our Country*, 197–99; and Hodgson, *America in Our Time*, 50–52.

28 Patterson, *Grand Expectations*, 71–72; Diggins, *Proud Decades*, 181–83; and Jackson, *Crabgrass Frontier*, 231–38.

29 Patterson, *Grand Expectations*, 72–73; Jackson, *Crabgrass Frontier*, 234–38; Barbara M. Kelly, *Expanding the American Dream: Building and Rebuilding Levittown* (Albany: State University Press of New York, 1993); Herbert J.

NOTES

Gans, *The Levittowners: Ways of Life and Politics in a New Suburban Community* (New York: Columbia University Press, 1967); and Wikipedia entry for Levittown, NY.

30 Patterson, *Grand Expectations*, 73–76; Jackson, *Crabgrass Frontier*, 235–43; Kelly, *Expanding the American Dream*, 35–161; and Gans, *Levittowners*, 3–20.

31 Kelly, *Expanding the American Dream*, 21–154; Jackson, *Crabgrass Frontier*, 234–43; and Patterson, *Grand Expectations*, 73–74.

32 Kelly, *Expanding the American Dream*, 21–154; Jackson, *Crabgrass Frontier*, 234–43; and Patterson, *Grand Expectations*, 73–74.

33 Kelly, *Expanding the American Dream*, 21–154; Jackson, *Crabgrass Frontier*, 45–137, 231–43; Gans, *Levittowners*, especially at 22–43; Herbert J. Gans, *The Urban Villagers: Group and Class in the Life of Italian-Americans* (New York: Free Press, 1962), 3–278; Patterson, *Grand Expectations*, 10–38, 73–74; and Alan Ehrenhalt, *The Lost City: Discovering the Forgotten Virtues of Community* (New York: Basic Books, 1995), 194–249.

34 Kelly, *Expanding the American Dream*, 21–154; Jackson, *Crabgrass Frontier*, 45–137, 231–43; Gans, *Levittowners*, especially at 22–43; Patterson, *Grand Expectations*, 10–38, 73–74; and Ehrenhalt, *Lost City*, 194–249.

35 Patterson, *Grand Expectations*, 74–75; and Jackson, *Crabgrass Frontier*, 241.

36 Jackson, *Crabgrass Frontier*, 231–45; Michael Johns, *Moment of Grace: The American City in the 1950s* (Berkeley: University of California Press, 2003), 91–118; and Patterson, *Grand Expectations*, 76–81.

37 Ehrenhalt, *Lost City*, 139–89; Patterson, *Grand Expectations*, 15–16, 19–31; and Diggins, *Proud Decades*, 193–94.

38 Ehrenhalt, *Lost City*, 89–189; Johns, *Moment of Grace*, 1–6, 47–90; and Patterson, *Grand Expectations*, 15–16, 19–31.

39 Jackson, *Crabgrass Frontier*, 231–45; Johns, *Moment of Grace*, 91–118; and Patterson, *Grand Expectations*, 76–81.

40 Patterson, *Grand Expectations*, 14–15; Graebner, *Age of Doubt*, 14–15, 40–42, 101, 111; and Wikipedia entry for *The Best Years of Our Lives*.

41 Patterson, *Grand Expectations*, 14–15; Graebner, *Age of Doubt*, 14–15, 40–42, 101, 111; and Wikipedia entry for *Best Years of Our Lives*.

42 Wikipedia entry for *Adam's Rib*.

43 *Adam's Rib*.

44 *Adam's Rib*; Patterson, *Grand Expectations*, 36–38; and Cynthia Harrison, *On Account of Sex: The Politics of Women's Issues, 1945–1968* (Berkeley: University of California Press, 1988), 15–23.

45 Graebner, *Age of Doubt*, 10, 14, 17, 25–26, 32–33, 58, 112, 146–47.

46 Graebner, 40–120; and James L. Baughman, *Same Time, Same Station: Creating American Television, 1948–1961* (Baltimore: Johns Hopkins University Press, 207), 1–55.

47 Graebner, *Age of Doubt*, 60–61, 65–66, 75, 121, 135–37, 146; Diggins, *Proud Decades*, 231–47; and Jed Perl, ed., *Art in America, 1945–1960* (New York: Random House, 2014), 1–190.

48 Graebner, *Age of Doubt*, 137–40; and Diggins, *Proud Decades*, 231–47.

NOTES

49 Blum, *V Was for Victory*, 79–89; Graebner, *Age of Doubt*, 84–85; and Diggins, *Proud Decades*, 231–47.

50 Graebner, *Age of Doubt*, 137–40; and Diggins, *Proud Decades*, 231–47.

51 Patterson, *Grand Expectations*, 10–242; Branko Milanovic, *Global Inequality: A New Approach for the Age of Globalization* (Cambridge: Harvard University Press, 2016), 118–30; and Marty Jezer, *The Dark Ages: Life in the United States, 1945–1960* (Boston: South End Press, 1982), 13–105.

52 Patterson, *Grand Expectations*, 10–242; and Jezer, *Dark Ages*, 13–105.

53 Patterson, *Grand Expectations*, 10–242; and Jezer, *Dark Ages*, 13–105.

54 Patterson, *Grand Expectations*, 165–205; Jezer, *Dark Ages*, 77–105; Diggins, *Proud Decades*, 110–17; Allen, *Forgotten Men*, 203–9; and Margot Cannady, *The Straight State: Sexuality and Citizenship in Twentieth-Century America* (Princeton: Princeton University Press, 2009), 137–213.

55 Patterson, *Grand Expectations*, 165–205; Jezer, *Dark Ages*, 77–105; Diggins, *Proud Decades*, 110–17; Lillian Ross, "Onward and Upward with the Arts," *New Yorker*, February 21, 1948, 42–46; and Baughman, *Same Time*, 205–9.

56 Jezer, *Dark Ages*, 258–74; and John D'Emilio, *Sexual Politics: Sexual Communities*, 2nd ed. (Chicago: University of Chicago Press, 1998).

6. The Middle-Class Model

1 Hoff Wilson, *Herbert Hoover*, 209–68; Glen Jeansonne, *Herbert Hoover: A Life* (Berkeley: New American Library, 2016), 292–314; and George H. Nash, ed., *The Crusade Years, 1935–1955: Herbert Hoover's Lost Memoir of the New Deal Era and Its Aftermath* (Palo Alto, CA: Hoover Institution Press, 2013), xiii–xxii, 11, 53–97.

2 Jeansonne, *Herbert Hoover*, 315–44; James T. Patterson, *Mr. Republican: A Biography of Robert A. Taft* (Boston: Houghton Mifflin, 1972), 70, 81, 86–87, 146–79, 210, 216–31; and Nash, *Crusade Years*, xxiii, 198–231.

3 Jeansonne, *Herbert Hoover*, 344–78; and Nash, *Crusade Years*, xxiv, 11–12, 26–30, 232–90.

4 Roger Morris, *Richard Milhous Nixon: The Rise of an American Politician* (New York: Henry Holt, 1990), 258–337, 515–621; and Wikipedia entry for Lewis Strauss.

5 Jeansonne, *Herbert Hoover*, 344–78; Nash, *Crusade Years*, xxiv, 11–12, 26–30, 232–90; and Wikipedia entry for the Bohemian Grove.

6 Jeansonne, *Herbert Hoover*, 357–78; and Nash, *Crusade Years*, 253–90.

7 Patterson, *Grand Expectations*, 178–242; Barone, *Our Country*, 239–46; Mason, *Republican Party*, 130–42; Jeansonne, *Herbert Hoover*, 379–82; Patterson, *Mr. Republican*, 456–516; and Nash, *Crusade Years*, 295–327.

8 Patterson, *Grand Expectations*, 178–242; and Barone, *Our Country*, 239–46.

9 Patterson, *Grand Expectations*, 178–242; Barone, *Our Country*, 239–46; Mason, *Republican Party*, 130–42; Jeansonne, *Herbert Hoover*, 379–82; Patterson, *Mr. Republican*, 456–516; and Nash, *Crusade Years*, 295–327.

10 Ambrose, *Eisenhower*, 1:13–42; and Patterson, *Grand Expectations*, 245–47.

NOTES

11 Ambrose, *Eisenhower*, 1:13–437; and Patterson, *Grand Expectations*, 245–47.

12 Stebenne, "Thomas J. Watson," 65–67; Ambrose, *Eisenhower*, 1:437–517; and "Eisenhower," *American Experience* video, section entitled "Statesman."

13 "Ike's First Move," *New York Times Magazine*, November 14, 1993, 57; Ambrose, *Eisenhower*, 1:516–24; "Eisenhower—Statesman"; and William B. Pickett, *Eisenhower Decides to Run: Presidential Politics & Cold War Strategy* (Chicago: Ivan R. Dee, 2000), 118–80.

14 Leuchtenburg, *Roosevelt and the New Deal*, 312; Ambrose, *Eisenhower*, 1:516–41; and Bowen, *Roots of Modern Conservatism*, 56–148.

15 Ambrose, *Eisenhower*, 1:516–41; Bowen, *Roots of Modern Conservatism*, 56–148; Gerald F. Seib, "An Ike Analogy That Hits Home in a General Way," *Wall Street Journal*, September 27, 1995, A18; and "Eisenhower—Statesman."

16 Patterson, *Grand Expectations*, 251–60; Bowen, *Roots of Modern Conservatism*, 148–65; Mason, *Republican Party*, 144–47; "Eisenhower—Statesman"; and Kevin M. Kruse, "'Why Don't You Just Get an Actor?': The Advent of Television in the 1952 Campaign," in *America at the Ballot Box*, ed. Davies and Zelizer, 167–83.

17 Kruse, "'Why Don't You Just?,'" 167–83.

18 Patterson, *Grand Expectations*, 251–60; Bowen, *Roots of Modern Conservatism*, 148–65; Mason, *Republican Party*, 144–47; and "Eisenhower—Statesman."

19 Patterson, *Grand Expectations*, 251–60; Bowen, *Roots of Modern Conservatism*, 148–65; Mason, *Republican Party*, 144–47; "Eisenhower—Statesman"; and Kruse, "'Why Don't You Just?,'" 167–83.

20 Stephen Ambrose, *Eisenhower*, vol. 2: *The President* (New York: Simon & Schuster, 1984), 17–26; Chester J. Pach Jr. and Elmo Richardson, *The Presidency of Dwight D. Eisenhower*, rev. ed. (Lawrence: University Press of Kansas, 1991), 29–73; and Diggins, *Proud Decades*, 150–56.

21 Ambrose, *Eisenhower*, 2:17–26; Pach and Richardson, *Presidency*, 29–73; Nelson Lichtenstein, *The Most Dangerous Man in Detroit: Walter Reuther and the Fate of American Labor* (New York: Basic Books, 1995), 20, 139–40, 179, 229, 244, 277–80; and Diggins, *Proud Decades*, 150–56.

22 Arthur Larson, *A Republican Looks at His Party* (New York: Harper & Row, 1956); Stebenne, *Modern Republican*, 118–75; Mason, *Republican Party*, 148–77; Bowen, *Roots of Modern Conservatism*, 153–95; and Patterson, *Grand Expectations*, 243–75.

23 Stebenne, *Modern Republican*, 110–11, 154, 161–63, 168, 171.

24 Stebenne, 124–26, 159–60, 161, 163, 171, 187–88; and Ambrose, *Eisenhower*, 2:86–88.

25 Stebenne, *Modern Republican*, 114, 160, 167–68, 172–74, 178–96; "Eisenhower—Statesman"; Mason, *Republican Party*, 143–44, 147, 150, 154, 176–80; and Bowen, *Roots of Modern Conservatism*, 131, 149–50, 159–60, 164, 165, 174–75, 177–78, 183, 189, 191–92, 204.

26 Stebenne, *Modern Republican*, 120–21, 156, 172–74, 178–96; and "Eisenhower—Statesman."

27 Diggins, *Proud Decades*, 247–56; Hodgson, *America in Our Time*, 17–98;

NOTES

Wendy Wall, *Inventing the "American Way": The Politics of Consensus from the New Deal to the Civil Rights Movement* (New York: Oxford University Press, 2008), 163–240; and Robert Mason and Iwan Morgan, eds., *The Liberal Consensus Reconsidered: American Politics and Society in the Postwar Era* (Gainesville: University Press of Florida, 2017).

28 Pach and Richardson, *Presidency*, 75–87; A. E. Holmans, "The Eisenhower Administration and the Recession, 1953–5," *Oxford Economic Papers* (1958): 34–54; and Robert M. Collins, *The Business Response to Keynes, 1929–1964* (New York: Columbia University Press, 1982), 152–58.

29 Pach and Richardson, *Presidency*, 53–58; Stebenne, *Modern Republican*, 121–24, 128–37; and Ambrose, *Eisenhower*, 2:80, 158.

30 Pach and Richardson, *Presidency*, 106, 123–24; Patterson, *Grand Expectations*, 274, 316; Ambrose, *Eisenhower*, 2:250–51; and Meinig, *Global America*, 22, 61–69, 73–74, 108, 147, 256.

31 Pach and Richardson, *Presidency*, 106, 123–24; Patterson, *Grand Expectations*, 274, 316; and Meinig, *Global America*, 22, 61–69, 73–74, 108, 147, 256.

32 Wikipedia entries for Warren, Harlan, and Brennan; Ambrose, *Eisenhower*, 2:128–29; and Patterson, *Grand Expectations*, 388–90, 392, 416–17.

33 Pach and Richardson, *Presidency*, 140–43, 146, 149; and Patterson, *Grand Expectations*, 375–406.

34 Patterson, *Grand Expectations*, 375–406, 637–709.

35 Juan Williams, *Eyes on the Prize: America's Civil Rights Years, 1954–1965* (New York: Penguin, 1987, reprint 2013), 59–89; and Taylor Branch, *Parting the Waters: America in the King Years, 1954–1963* (New York: Touchstone, 1988), 105–205.

36 Pach and Richardson, *Presidency*, 75–104, 131–32; Patterson, *Grand Expectations*, 276–310; and "Eisenhower—Statesman."

37 Pach and Richardson, *Presidency*, 88–93, 108–12, 122, 136, 188, 193, 223; Patterson, *Grand Expectations*, 423–27; and "Eisenhower—Statesman."

38 Pach and Richardson, *Presidency*, 93–98, 198, 235, 238; Ambrose, *Eisenhower*, 2:174–76, 179, 182, 184–85, 204–10; and "Eisenhower—Statesman."

39 Pach and Richardson, *Presidency*, 17–18, 25, 62–63, 66–72; Patterson, *Grand Expectations*, 196–205, 250, 255–56, 264–69, 280; and "Eisenhower—Statesman."

40 Pach and Richardson, *Presidency*, 105, 124–26, 135–36; and Barone, *Our Country*, 277–94.

41 Hodgson, *America in Our Time*, 130; Diggins, *Proud Decades*, 251–52; Christopher Howard, *The Welfare State Nobody Knows: Debunking Myths About U.S. Social Policy* (Princeton: Princeton University Press, 2007), 25; and David Stebenne, "Social Welfare in the United States, 1945–1960," in *Liberal Consensus*, ed. Mason and Morgan, 108–26.

42 James A. Jacobs, *Detached America: Building Houses in Postwar Suburbia* (Charlottesville: University of Virginia Press, 2015); Nancy H. Kwak, *A World of Homeowners: American Power and the Politics of Housing Aid* (Chicago: University of Chicago Press, 2015); Stebenne, "Social Welfare," 116–17; Pach and Richardson, *Presidency*, 106, 123–24; Patterson, *Grand Expectations*, 274, 316; and Ambrose, *Eisenhower*, 2:250–51.

NOTES

43   Stebenne, "Social Welfare," 108, 111, 116–17.

44   Stebenne, 112–13.

45   Stebenne, 109–113, 116–18, 120–22.

46   Baughman, *Same Time*, 1–218; Patterson, *Grand Expectations*, 348–55; and Diggins, *Proud Decades*, 186–92.

47   Baughman, *Same Time*, 1–218; Patterson, *Grand Expectations*, 348–55; and Diggins, *Proud Decades*, 186–92.

48   Baughman, *Same Time*, 1–218; Patterson, *Grand Expectations*, 348–55; and Diggins, *Proud Decades*, 186–92.

49   Baughman, *Same Time*, 128–33, 207; Warren G. Harris, *Lucy and Desi: The Legendary Love Story of Television's Most Famous Couple* (New York: Simon & Schuster, 1991), 11–259; Coyne N. Sanders and Tom Gilbert, *Desilu: The Story of Lucille Ball and Desi Arnaz* (New York: Morrow, 1993), 9–200; the PBS *American Masters* profile of Lucille Ball; and the Wikipedia entry for *I Love Lucy*.

50   Baughman, *Same Time*, 128–33, 207; Harris, *Lucy and Desi*, 11–259; Sanders and Gilbert, *Desilu*, 9–200; *American Masters* profile of Lucille Ball; and the Wikipedia entry for *I Love Lucy*.

51   Baughman, *Same Time*, 128–33, 207; Harris, *Lucy and Desi*, 11–259; Sanders and Gilbert, *Desilu*, 9–200; *American Masters* profile of Lucille Ball; and the Wikipedia entry for *I Love Lucy*.

52   Baughman, *Same Time*, 128–33, 207; Harris, *Lucy and Desi*, 11–259; Sanders and Gilbert, *Desilu*, 9–200; *American Masters* profile of Lucille Ball; and the Wikipedia entry for *I Love Lucy*.

53   Baughman, *Same Time*, 25–218; and Wall, *Inventing the "American Way,"* 163–65.

54   Baughman, *Same Time*, 25–218; Guideposts.org; and the Wikipedia entry for *Life Is Worth Living*.

55   Baughman, *Same Time*, 25–218.

56   Baughman, 162–65, 209–10; and Patterson, *Grand Expectations*, 31, 351.

57   Baughman, *Same Time*, 25–218; and Patterson, *Grand Expectations*, 364–65.

58   Baughman, *Same Time*, 153–91; and the Wikipedia entry for *Marty*.

59   Baughman, *Same Time*, 183–86; and the Wikipedia entry for *Marty*.

60   David Michaelis, *Schulz and Peanuts: A Biography* (New York: Harper Perennial, 2007), 234–35. See, too, at 3–233.

61   Michaelis, 190. See, too, at 159–89.

62   Michaelis, 190–270.

63   Lawrence Jackson, *Ralph Ellison: Emergence of Genius* (New York: John Wiley, 2002); Martin Bauml Duberman, *Paul Robeson* (New York, Alfred Knopf, 1988), 336–445; David Levering Lewis, *W. E. B. Du Bois: A Biography, 1868–1963* (New York: Holt, 2009); and the Wikipedia entries for Paul Robeson and W. E. B. Du Bois.

64   Teachout, *Pops*, 312–13; and the Wikipedia entry for *High Society*.

65   Diggins, *Proud Decades*, 194; Patterson, *Grand Expectations*, 371; David Kaufman, *Doris Day: The Untold Story of the Girl Next Door* (New York: Virgin Books, 2008), 91–252; and the Wikipedia entry "Broadway theatre."

66   Diggins, *Proud Decades*, 177–219; Patterson, *Grand Expectations*, 337–74;

NOTES

David Halberstam, *The Fifties* (New York: Random House, 1993), 267–71; and the Wikipedia entries for Marlon Brando, James Dean, and Elvis Presley.

67 Diggins, *Proud Decades*, 196–98, 217; Patterson, *Grand Expectations*, 262, 365, 370, 372, 672; Halberstam, *Fifties*, 269, 456, 462, 479–85; and the Wikipedia entry for James Dean.

68 Diggins, *Proud Decades*, 194–96, 217; Patterson, *Grand Expectations*, 372–74; Halberstam, *Fifties*, 472–74; and the Wikipedia entry for Elvis Presley.

69 Diggins, *Proud Decades*, 177–219; Patterson, *Grand Expectations*, 337–74; Halberstam, *Fifties*, 267–71; and the Wikipedia entries for Brando, Dean, and Presley.

70 Diggins, *Proud Decades*, 177–219; Patterson, *Grand Expectations*, 337–74; and Halberstam, *Fifties*, 267–71.

7. Cracks in the Foundation

1 Patterson, *Grand Expectations*, 407–57; Barone, *Our Country*, 294–335; Diggins, *Proud Decades*, 312–44; and Jezer, *Dark Ages*, 251–309.

2 Patterson, *Grand Expectations*, 407–57; Barone, *Our Country*, 294–335; Diggins, *Proud Decades*, 312–44; and Jezer, *Dark Ages*, 251–309.

3 Patterson, *Grand Expectations*, 418–22; Diggins, *Proud Decades*, 307–18; and "Eisenhower—Statesman."

4 Patterson, *Grand Expectations*, 347, 408; Diggins, *Proud Decades*, 527–28; and Wikipedia entry for *On the Beach*.

5 Patterson, *Grand Expectations*, 418–20; Diggins, *Proud Decades*, 312–16; John Lewis Gaddis, *Strategies of Containment: A Critical Appraisal of Postwar American National Security Policy* (New York: Oxford University Press, 1982), 182–83; and "Eisenhower—Statesman."

6 Patterson, *Grand Expectations*, 418–22; Diggins, *Proud Decades*, 312–18; Gaddis, *Strategies*, 183–88; and "Eisenhower—Statesman."

7 Diggins, *Proud Decades*, 327–31; Patterson, *Grand Expectations*, 423–25; Gaddis, *Strategies of Containment*, 182–88, 195–97; and "Eisenhower—Statesman."

8 Diggins, *Proud Decades*, 336–38; Patterson, *Grand Expectations*, 425–27; and "Eisenhower—Statesman."

9 Patterson, *Grand Expectations*, 424–25; and Aleksandr Fursenko and Timothy Naftali, *Khrushchev's Cold War: The Inside Story of an American Adversary* (New York: Norton, 2006), 190, 196, 199–200, 201–10, 223–24, 281, 340.

10 Patterson, *Grand Expectations*, 427; Diggins, *Proud Decades*, 331–35; and Fursenko and Naftali, *Khrushchev's Cold War*, 295–97, 301–4.

11 Patterson, *Grand Expectations*, 427–29; Diggins, *Proud Decades*, 310; Fredrik Logevall, *The Origins of the Vietnam War* (New York: Routledge, 2001), 25–37; and Fursenko and Naftali, *Khrushchev's Cold War*, 323–29.

12 Patterson, *Grand Expectations*, 429–30; Logevall, *Origins*, 37–38; and Fursenko and Naftali, *Khrushchev's Cold War*, 329–35.

13 Patterson, *Grand Expectations*, 299–300; and Diggins, *Proud Decades*, 310.

14 Patterson, *Grand Expectations*, 306–8, 423; and Diggins, *Proud Decades*, 299–301, 308–9.

NOTES

15 Ambrose, *Eisenhower*, 2:378, 538, 581, 586–90; Diggins, *Proud Decades*, 307–9; and Fursenko and Naftali, *Khrushchev's Cold War*, 90, 111, 258, 294, 297–301, 307–13, 315–19.

16 Diggins, *Proud Decades*, 81–86, 311–12; Gaddis, *Strategies of Containment*, 25–53; and Steel, *Walter Lippmann*, 404–49, 502–11.

17 Stebenne, *Arthur J. Goldberg*, 154–232.

18 Stebenne, 154–232; and the Wikipedia entry for *Desk Set*.

19 Stebenne, *Arthur J. Goldberg*, 154–79.

20 Stebenne, 179–215.

21 Stebenne, 156–232, 299.

22 Stebenne, 25–232.

23 Stebenne, 25–232.

24 Iwan Morgan, "The Keynesian Consensus and Its Limits," in *Liberal Consensus*, ed. Mason and Morgan, 86, 93–94.

25 Stebenne, *Arthur J. Goldberg*, 45–187.

26 Stebenne, 188–215.

27 Patterson, *Grand Expectations*, 321–28; Barone, *Our Country*, 301–2; and Robert Lekachman, *The Age of Keynes* (New York: McGraw-Hill, 1966), 191–202.

28 Patterson, *Grand Expectations*, 321–28; Barone, *Our Country*, 301–2; Elaine Tyler May, *Homeward Bound: American Families in the Cold War Era* (New York: Basic Books, 1999), 163–85; and Lekachman, *Age of Keynes*, 191–202.

29 Elizabeth Tandy Shermer, "Sunbelt Patriarchs: Lyndon B. Johnson, Barry Goldwater and the New Deal Dissensus," in *Liberal Consensus*, ed. Mason and Morgan, 167–85; Rick Perlstein, *Before the Storm: Barry Goldwater and the Unmaking of the American Consensus* (New York: Hill & Wang, 2001), 3–68; and Jefferson Cowie, *Capital Moves: RCA's Seventy-Year Quest for Cheap Labor* (Ithaca, NY: Cornell University Press, 1999), 1–67.

30 Shermer, "Sunbelt Patriarchs," 167–85; Perlstein, *Before the Storm*, 3–68; and Cowie, *Capital Moves*, 1–67.

31 Shermer, "Sunbelt Patriarchs," 167–85; Perlstein, *Before the Storm*, 3–68; and Cowie, *Capital Moves*, 1–67.

32 Jeff Crane, *The Environment in American History* (New York: Routledge, 2015), 317–36; Diggins, *Proud Decades*, 325–30; and Jezer, *Dark Ages*, 154–75.

33 Crane, *Environment*, 317–36; Diggins, *Proud Decades*, 325–30; and Jezer, *Dark Ages*, 154–75.

34 "Rachel Carson's Silent Spring," *American Experience*, PBS video.

35 Patterson, *Grand Expectations*, 315–20; Diggins, *Proud Decades*, 178–87; Jezer, *Dark Ages*, 171–72; and Thomas Hine, *Populuxe* (New York: Knopf, 1990), 27–30.

36 Patterson, *Grand Expectations*, 315–20; Diggins, *Proud Decades*, 178–87; Jezer, *Dark Ages*, 171–72; and Hine, *Populuxe*, 27–30.

37 Patterson, *Grand Expectations*, 333–37; and Johns, *Moment of Grace*.

38 Patterson, *Grand Expectations*, 333–37; and Johns, *Moment of Grace*.

39 Patterson, *Grand Expectations*, 274, 336; Diggins, *Proud Decades*, 322–23; and Jezer, *Dark Ages*, 154–66.

NOTES

40 Patterson, *Grand Expectations*, 23, 64, 325; Jonathan Bell, "We Have Run out of Poor People," in *Liberal Consensus*, ed. Mason and Morgan, 208–26; Baughman, *Same Time*, 219–98; and Karal Ann Marling, *As Seen on TV: The Visual Culture of Everyday Life in the 1950s* (Cambridge: Harvard University Press, 1994).

41 "The 'Invisible' Unemployed," *Fortune*, July 1958, 105–11, 198, 200, 202, 204; and Michael Harrington, *The Other America: Poverty in the United States* (New York: Scribner, 1997).

42 "'Invisible' Unemployed," 105–11, 198, 200, 202, 204; and Harrington, *Other America*.

43 Patterson, *Grand Expectations*, 375–406; and Williams, *Eyes on the Prize*, 1–89.

44 Patterson, *Grand Expectations*, 395–96; Williams, *Eyes on the Prize*, 37–57, and the PBS video of the same name.

45 Patterson, *Grand Expectations*, 375–406; and Williams, *Eyes on the Prize*, 1–89, 121–42.

46 Patterson, *Grand Expectations*, 413–16; Williams, *Eyes on the Prize*, 91–119; and Teachout, *Pops*, 330–35.

47 Patterson, *Grand Expectations*, 411–16; Ambrose, *Eisenhower*, 2:414–26, 436–40; and Stebenne, *Modern Republican*, 208–10.

48 Ehrenhalt, *Lost City*, 188–89; and the Wikipedia entry for *A Raisin in the Sun*.

49 Ehrenhalt, *Lost City*, 188–89; Joel Dinnerstein, *The Origins of Cool in Postwar America* (Chicago: University of Chicago Press, 2017), 417–23; and the Wikipedia entry for *A Raisin in the Sun*.

50 Patterson, *Grand Expectations*, 361–69; Diggins, *Proud Decades*, 211–19; Jezer, *Dark Ages*, 219–34; and Harrison, *On Account of Sex*, 24–65.

51 Harrison, *On Account of Sex*, 25, 48, 110, 113; Patterson, *Grand Expectations*, 367–69; and Susan M. Hartmann, *From Margin to Mainstream: American Women and Politics Since 1960* (New York: Knopf, 1989), 1–22, 48–50.

52 Patterson, *Grand Expectations*, 328–33; Diggins, *Proud Decades*, 209–10, 257–63; Marty, *Modern American Religion*, 3:277–476; and Richard Fox, *Reinhold Niebuhr: A Biography* (New York: Harper & Row, 1985), 224–74.

53 Patterson, *Grand Expectations*, 358–59; and Diggins, *Proud Decades*, 204–7, 216, 257–63.

54 Patterson, *Grand Expectations*, 358–59, 371–74, 408–10; Diggins, *Proud Decades*, 204–7, 216–19, 257–71; the Wikipedia entry "Rat Pack"; and Dennis McNally, *Desolate Angel: Jack Kerouac, the Beat Generation, and America* (Cambridge, MA: Da Capo, 2003), 199–239.

55 *Grand Expectations*, 371–74, 408–10; and Diggins, *Proud Decades*, 216–19, 267–71.

56 Patterson, *Grand Expectations*, 329–33, 343, 355–58, 371, 407–8; Diggins, *Proud Decades*, 209–10, 349; and Darren Dochuk, *From Bible Belt to Sunbelt: Plain-Folk Religion, Grassroots Politics, and the Rise of Evangelical Conservatism* (New York: Norton, 2011), 3–222.

57 Patterson, *Grand Expectations*, 181, 374, 408–10; Michael Bronski, *A Queer History of the United States* (Boston: Beacon Press, 2011), 176–203; the Wiki-

NOTES

pedia entry for Frank Kameny; Joyce Johnson, *Minor Characters: A Beat Memoir* (New York: Houghton Mifflin, 1983); and Jezer, *Dark Ages*, 253–57.

58 Stebenne, *Modern Republican*, 142–43; Jezer, *Dark Ages*, 83–106, 293–96, 305–7; and Wikipedia entry for *The Man in the Gray Flannel Suit*.

59 Patterson, *Grand Expectations*, 433–35; Diggins, *Proud Decades*, 338–39; and Barone, *Our Country*, 314–19.

8. Trying to Cope

1 Hugh Brogan, *Kennedy* (London: Longman, 1996), 1–45; Barone, *Our Country*, 308–9; Ambrose, *Eisenhower*, 2:378; Theodore C. Sorensen, *Kennedy* (New York: Harper & Row, 1965), 11–108; and Allan Nevins, ed., *The Strategy of Peace* (New York: Harper & Brothers, 1960).

2 Brogan, *Kennedy*, 1–45; Barone, *Our Country*, 308–9; and Sorensen, *Kennedy*, 11–108.

3 Barone, *Our Country*, 278, 292, 310–11.

4 Barone, 307–14, 319–25, 329; Edmund F. Kallina Jr., *Kennedy v. Nixon: The Presidential Election of 1960* (Gainesville: University Press of Florida, 2010), 49–80; and Stebenne, *Arthur J. Goldberg*, 222–24.

5 Morris, *Richard Milhous Nixon*, 257–866; Stephen E. Ambrose, *Nixon* (New York: Touchstone, 1987), 1:117–555; Barone, *Our Country*, 331–32; "Richard Nixon Acceptance Address 1960," C-SPAN Video Library; Kallina, *Kennedy v. Nixon*, 117–23; and Theodore White, *The Making of the President 1960* (New York: Atheneum, 1961), 306–18.

6 Barone, *Our Country*, 332; Kallina, *Kennedy v. Nixon*, 123–25; and White, *Making of the President 1960*, 318–24.

7 Kallina, *Kennedy v. Nixon*, 135–49.

8 Kallina, 149–55; and Branch, *Parting the Waters*, 351–68.

9 Kallina, *Kennedy v. Nixon*, 154–57; Branch, *Parting the Waters*, 368–78; and Patterson, *Grand Expectations*, 440.

10 Kallina, *Kennedy v. Nixon*, 166–68; and Barone, *Our Country*, 333–34.

11 Kallina, *Kennedy v. Nixon*, 177–200; Barone, *Our Country*, 333–35; and Edward B. Foley, *Ballot Battles: The History of Disputed Elections in the United States* (New York: Oxford University Press, 2016), 217–28.

12 Patterson, *Grand Expectations*, 433–41; Diggins, *Proud Decades*, 338–44; and Brogan, *Kennedy*, 6–56.

13 Fursenko and Naftali, *Khrushchev's Cold War*, 338–42; and Patterson, *Grand Expectations*, 458–59, 486–88.

14 Patterson, *Grand Expectations*, 488, 492–96; and Fursenko and Naftali, *Khrushchev's Cold War*, 342–43, 346–49, 367, 395–96, 426–29.

15 Patterson, *Grand Expectations*, 497; Brogan, *Kennedy*, 757–58; and Fursenko and Naftali, *Khrushchev's Cold War*, 360–72.

16 Patterson, *Grand Expectations*, 497; and Fursenko and Naftali, *Khrushchev's Cold War*, 373–87, 410–12.

17 Fursenko and Naftali, *Khrushchev's Cold War*, 385, 390, 423–24; and Patterson, *Grand Expectations*, 498.

NOTES

18 Fursenko and Naftali, *Khrushchev's Cold War*, 426–29, 424–45, 451–56, 461–64; and Patterson, *Grand Expectations*, 498–99.

19 Aleksandr Fursenko and Timothy Naftali, *"One Hell of a Gamble": Khrushchev, Castro and Kennedy, 1958–1964* (New York: Norton, 1997), 204–34; Fursenko and Naftali, *Khrushchev's Cold War*, 465–68; and Patterson, *Grand Expectations*, 498–501.

20 Fursenko and Naftali, *"One Hell of a Gamble,"* 234–69; Fursenko and Naftali, *Khrushchev's Cold War*, 468–89; and Patterson, *Grand Expectations*, 501–4.

21 Fursenko and Naftali, *"One Hell of a Gamble,"* 257–89; Fursenko and Naftali, *Khrushchev's Cold War*, 468–92; and Patterson, *Grand Expectations*, 500–508.

22 Gaddis, *Strategies of Containment*, 267–69.

23 Barone, *Our Country*, 346–49.

24 Barone, 349; Stebenne, *Arthur J. Goldberg*, 279–315; and Gaddis, *Strategies of Containment*, 267–69.

25 Stebenne, *Arthur J. Goldberg*, 279–315; Stebenne, "Thomas J. Watson," 61–65; and Sparrow, *Warfare State*, 242–60.

26 Sparrow, *Warfare State*, 251–60; and Katznelson, *When Affirmative Action Was White*, 113–41.

27 Sparrow, *Warfare State*, 251–60; and Katznelson, *When Affirmative Action Was White*, 113–41.

28 Patterson, *Grand Expectations*, 508; Fursenko and Naftali, *"One Hell of a Gamble,"* 319–36; and Fursenko and Naftali, *Khrushchev's Cold War*, 483–523.

29 Patterson, *Grand Expectations*, 508–9; Fursenko and Naftali, *"One Hell of a Gamble,"* 336–38; Fursenko and Naftali, *Khrushchev's Cold War*, 523–26; and Stebenne, *Modern Republican*, 241–42.

30 Patterson, *Grand Expectations*, 508–9; Fursenko and Naftali, *Khrushchev's Cold War*, 526–28; Stebenne, *Modern Republican*, 241–43; and Brogan, *Kennedy*, 147–48.

31 Sparrow, *Warfare State*, 262.

32 Logevall, *Origins*, 40–41; Gaddis, *Strategies of Containment*, 212; Ambrose, *Eisenhower*, 2:614–15; and Brogan, *Kennedy*, 61–63.

33 Logevall, *Origins*, 41–42; Fredrik Logevall, *Choosing War: The Lost Chance for Peace and the Escalation of the War in Vietnam* (Berkeley: University of California Press, 1999), 23–27, 28–42; Gaddis, *Strategies of Containment*, 228–29, 237–46; and Patterson, *Grand Expectations*, 510–15.

34 Patterson, *Grand Expectations*, 509–11; Logevall, *Choosing War*, 26–42; *Strategies of Containment*, 237–46; and Logevall, *Origins*, 43–49.

35 Logevall, *Choosing War*, 26–42.

36 Patterson, *Grand Expectations*, 513–16; and Logevall, *Origins*, 49–57.

37 Blum, *V Was for Victory*, 333–40; and Woloch, *Women and the American Experience*, 439–508.

38 Baughman, *Same Time*, 149–50, 299–300; Wikipedia entry for *Gunsmoke*; Newton Minow, "How Vast the Wasteland Now?" (New York: Freedom Forum, 1993); and Patterson, *Grand Expectations*, 352–53.

39 Patterson, *Grand Expectations*, 321–28; Barone, *Our Country*, 301–2, 336–

NOTES

41; Lekachman, *Age of Keynes*, 191–202; and Stebenne, *Arthur J. Goldberg*, 233–315.

40 James N. Giglio, *The Presidency of John F. Kennedy*, 2nd ed. (Lawrence: University Press of Kansas, 2006), 20–21, 37, 128–29, 136–40; and Stebenne, *Arthur J. Goldberg*, 233–315.

41 Giglio, *Presidency*, 20–21, 128–29, 136–39; and Morgan, "Keynesian Consensus," 92–96.

42 Stebenne, *Arthur J. Goldberg*, 184–87, 233–78.

43 Stebenne, 312–13.

44 Stebenne, 313; Giglio, *Presidency*, 128–29, 136–40; Morgan, "Keynesian Consensus," 97–100; and Barone, *Our Country*, 341, 342–46.

45 Barone, *Our Country*, 342–43; Robert O. Paxton, *Europe in the 20th Century*, 2nd ed. (New York: Harcourt, Brace, Jovanovich, 1985), 589–97; J. A. S. Grenville, *A History of the World in the 20th Century* (Cambridge: Harvard University Press, 2000), 667–82; and Dillon's Wikipedia entry.

46 Giglio, *Presidency*, 136–41; and Morgan, "Keynesian Consensus," 97–100.

47 Giglio, *Presidency*, 137–40.

48 Barone, *Our Country*, 261–380; and Patterson, *Grand Expectations*, 243–523.

49 Barone, *Our Country*, 350–63; Patterson, *Grand Expectations*, 442–57; and Stebenne, *Arthur J. Goldberg*, 303–15.

50 Morgan, "Keynesian Consensus," 96–103; Patterson, *Grand Expectations*, 466–85, 524–42; and Stebenne, *Arthur J. Goldberg*, 310–15.

51 Robert MacNeil, ed., *The Way We Were: 1963—the Year Kennedy Was Shot* (New York: Carroll & Graf, 1988).

52 Perlstein, *Before the Storm*, 17–78; Phillips-Fein, *Invisible Hands*, 3–132; Donald M. Critchlow, *The Conservative Ascendancy: How the GOP Right Made History* (Cambridge: Harvard University Press, 2007), 6–52; and Jeansonne, *Herbert Hoover*, 394.

53 Hoff Wilson, *Herbert Hoover*, 230; Critchlow, *Conservative Ascendancy*, 53; and Barry M. Goldwater, *The Conscience of a Conservative* (Princeton: Princeton University Press, 2007), 81–120.

54 Goldwater, *Conscience*, 107–11, 116.

55 Perlstein, *Before the Storm*, 13, 49, 53–68, 70–75; Critchlow, *Conservative Ascendancy*, 7–8, 21–22, 25–26, 47, 56–59; and Phillips-Fein, *Invisible Hands*, 40–41, 50, 69, 77–81, 85–86, 101, 126–27.

56 Phillips-Fein, *Invisible Hands*, 44, 46, 51, 69, 135–37; Perlstein, *Before the Storm*, 418, 420–23; Critchlow, *Conservative Ascendancy*, 8, 13–16; and Milton Friedman, *Capitalism and Freedom* (Chicago: University of Chicago Press, 2002).

57 Stebenne, *Modern Republican*, 225–28, 244–46; and Theodore H. White, *The Making of the President 1964* (New York: Signet, 1965), 111–20.

58 Geoffrey Kabaservice, *Rule and Ruin: The Downfall of Moderation and the Destruction of the Republican Party from Eisenhower to the Tea Party* (New York: Oxford University Press, 2012), 1–71; Critchlow, *Conservative Ascendancy*, 52–60; and Perlstein, *Before the Storm*, 58–94.

59 Patterson, *Grand Expectations*, 444; Eric Foner, *The Story of American Freedom* (New York: Norton, 1998), 288–89; and Stebenne, *Arthur J. Goldberg*, 315.

60 Foner, *Story*, 287–90; and Wikipedia entry for *The Port Huron Statement*.

61 Foner, *Story*, 288–89; Dwight Macdonald, "Our Invisible Poor," *New Yorker*, January 19, 1963; Brogan, *Kennedy*, 93; and Patterson, *Grand Expectations*, 533–34.

62 Foner, *Story*, 288–89; Macdonald, "Our Invisible Poor"; and Patterson, *Grand Expectations*, 533–34.

63 Foner, *Story*, 288–89; Macdonald, "Our Invisible Poor"; and Patterson, *Grand Expectations*, 533–34.

64 Crane, *Environment*, 331–38; "Rachel Carson's Silent Spring"; and Wikipedia entries for *Silent Spring* and Rachel Carson.

65 Crane, *Environment*, 331–38; "Rachel Carson's Silent Spring"; and Wikipedia entries for *Silent Spring* and Rachel Carson.

66 Betty Friedan, *The Feminine Mystique* (New York: Norton, 1997), 43–53; Susan Oliver, *Betty Friedan: The Personal Is Political* (New York: Pearson, 2008), 1–76; Ehrenhalt, *Lost City*, 82; Hartmann, *From Margin*, 56; and Wikipedia entries for Friedan and *The Feminine Mystique*.

67 Hartmann, *From Margin*, 56; and Oliver, *Betty Friedan*, 53–78.

68 Hartmann, *From Margin*, 56; Oliver, *Betty Friedan*, 53–78; and Nelson Lichtenstein, *The Retail Revolution: How Walmart Created a Brave New World of Business* (New York: Picador, 2010), 13–52.

69 Hartmann, *From Margin*, 56; Oliver, *Betty Friedan*, 53–78; and Lichtenstein, *Retail Revolution*, 13–52.

70 Perlstein, *Before the Storm*, 3–68; and White, *Making of the President 1964*, 111–22.

71 Harrison, *On Account of Sex*, 69–126; and Hartmann, *From Margin*, 48–54.

72 Harrison, *On Account of Sex*, 89–105, 116–24; Hartmann, *From Margin*, 48–66; and Patterson, *Grand Expectations*, 462–63.

73 Williams, *Eyes on the Prize*, 121–81; and Branch, *Parting the Waters*, 225–672.

74 William H. Harris, *The Harder We Run: Black Workers since the Civil War* (New York: Oxford University Press, 1982), 123–57.

75 Williams, *Eyes on the Prize*, 121–83; Branch, *Parting the Waters*, 272–672; Douglas Field, *All Those Strangers: The Art and Lives of James Baldwin* (New York: Oxford University Press, 2015), 53; and Wikipedia entries for James Baldwin and *The Fire Next Time*.

76 Patterson, *Grand Expectations*, 468–82.

77 Patterson, 481; Branch, *Parting the Waters*, 822–24, 827–28; and Arthur M. Schlesinger Jr., *Robert F. Kennedy and His Times* (New York: Ballantine Books, 1978), 372–76.

78 Branch, *Parting the Waters*, 824–25; Schlesinger, *Robert F. Kennedy*, 652–53; and Giglio, *Presidency*, 191–202.

79 Branch, *Parting the Waters*, 821–22, 827–34; and Joseph Crespino, *Strom Thurmond's America* (New York: Hill & Wang, 2012), 127–42, 174–75.

80 Branch, *Parting the Waters*, 846–87; Williams, *Eyes on the Prize*, 197–205; Schlesinger, *Robert F. Kennedy*, 376–78.

81 Ed Ward, *The History of Rock and Roll: Volume One, 1920–1963* (New York: Flatiron Books, 2016), 253–303; and David Hajdu, *Positively 4th Street: The Lives and Times of Joan Baez, Bob Dylan, Mimi Baez Farina and Richard Farina* (New York: North Point Press, 2002), 3–193.

NOTES

82 Hajdu, *Positively 4th Street*, 157–93; and Wikipedia entry for "Blowin' in the Wind."

83 Ward, *History of Rock and Roll*, 1:59–303; Nelson George, *Where Did Our Love Go? The Rise and Fall of the Motown Sound* (Champaign: University of Illinois Press, 1986), 1–147; and Wikipedia entry "Diana Ross and the Supremes."

84 Teachout, *Pops*, 304–41.

85 Wikipedia entry for *The Andy Griffith Show*; and Williams, *Eyes on the Prize*, 147–95.

86 Norman Mailer, *Oswald's Tale: An American Mystery* (New York: Ballantine Books, 1995), 41–239, 354–423, 497–683; Barone, *Our Country*, 361–63; Patterson, *Grand Expectations*, 517–20; and Wikipedia entry for Lee Harvey Oswald.

9. Things Fall Apart

1 For overviews of the Johnson presidency, see the discussion in Patterson, *Grand Expectations*, 524–47, 709; Barone, *Our Country*, 364–457; and Allen J. Matusow, *The Unraveling of America: A History of Liberalism in the 1960s* (New York: Harper & Row, 1984), 93–439.

2 Robert Caro, *The Passage of Power: The Years of Lyndon Johnson* (New York: Vintage, 2013); Patterson, *Grand Expectations*, 525–30; Matusow, *Unraveling*, 131–33; and Barone, *Our Country*, 296–98.

3 Patterson, *Grand Expectations*, 524–63; and Barone, *Our Country*, 364–96.

4 Patterson, *Grand Expectations*, 562–677; Barone, *Our Country*, 396–430; Matusow, *Unraveling*, 153–79; and Stebenne, *Arthur J. Goldberg*, 337–46.

5 Patterson, *Grand Expectations*, 562–677; Barone, *Our Country*, 396–430; Matusow, *Unraveling*, 153–79; and Harrington, *Other America*, 72–81. Half of all black people living in urban areas during the 1960s were in high-poverty neighborhoods, where unemployment was greater than it had been for the overall population at any time since the Great Depression. On that point, see Harris, *Harder We Run*, 153.

6 Patterson, *Grand Expectations*, 593–636; and Barone, *Our Country*, 398–401, 405–7.

7 Patterson, *Grand Expectations*, 593–636; and Barone, *Our Country*, 398–401, 405–7.

8 Barone, *Our Country*, 420–26; Matusow, *Unraveling*, 153–79, 376–90; and Patterson, *Grand Expectations*, 593–677.

9 Patterson, 559–61, 650, 668–70; Barone, *Our Country*, 373–80; Perlstein, *Before the Storm*; and Mathew Dallek, *The Right Moment: Ronald Reagan's First Victory and the Decisive Turning Point in American Politics* (New York: Oxford University Press, 2000).

10 "Reagan," pt. 1, *American Experience*, PBS video.

11 White, *Making of the President 1964*, 375–412; Perlstein, *Before the Storm*, 122–24, 128, 166, 185, 297, 336, 350, 352, 372, 422, 499–504, 509–10, 512; and Dallek, *Right Moment*, 62–69, 103–27.

288

NOTES

12 "Reagan," pt. 1; White, *Making of the President 1964*, 375–412; Perlstein, *Before the Storm*, 122–24, 128, 166, 185, 297, 336, 350, 352, 372, 422, 499–504, 509–10, 512; and Dallek, *Right Moment*, 62–69, 103–27.

13 Meinig, *Global America*, 225–33, 258–95; Perlstein, *Before the Storm*, 3–157, 333–55; Barone, *Our Country*, 411–16; Elizabeth Tandy Shermer, *Sunbelt Capitalism: Phoenix and the Transformation of American Politics* (Philadelphia: University of Pennsylvania Press, 2013); and Dochuk, *From Bible Belt to Sun Belt*, 139–292.

14 Patterson, *Grand Expectations*, 621–24; Matusow, *Unraveling*, 308–25; Barone, *Our Country*, 384–85; and Stebenne, *Arthur J. Goldberg*, 337–43.

15 Patterson, *Grand Expectations*, 621–24; Matusow, *Unraveling*, 308–25; and Barone, *Our Country*, 384–85.

16 Patterson, *Grand Expectations*, 443–57, 598–600, 667–68; Matusow, *Unraveling*, 319–320; and Barone, *Our Country*, 384–85.

17 Patterson, *Grand Expectations*, 669–70; Matusow, *Unraveling*, 295–302; Barone, *Our Country*, 384–85; and Hajdu, *Positively 4th Street*, 192–298.

18 Patterson, *Grand Expectations*, 588–92, 659–68; Michael W. Flamm, *In the Heat of the Summer: The New York Riots of 1964 and the War on Crime* (Philadelphia: University of Pennsylvania Press, 2017); and Matusow, *Unraveling*, 345–69.

19 Patterson, *Grand Expectations*, 590, 672–74.

20 Harris, *Harder We Run*, 127–37, 152–56; and Patterson, *Grand Expectations*, 672–74.

21 Patterson, *Grand Expectations*, 447, 532–42, 588–92, 659–68; Flamm, *In the Heat of the Summer*; Michael W. Flamm, *Law and Order: Street Crime, Civil Unrest, and the Crisis of Liberalism in the 1960s* (New York: Columbia University Press, 2005); and Matusow, *Unraveling*, 345–69.

22 Patterson, *Grand Expectations*, 617; and Matusow, *Unraveling*, 206–16.

23 Jonathan Rieder, "The Rise of the Silent Majority," in *The Rise and Fall of the New Deal Order, 1930–1980*, ed. Steven Fraser and Gary Gerstle (Princeton: Princeton University Press, 1989), 243–68; Dan T. Carter, *The Politics of Rage: The Origins of the New Conservatism, and the Transformation of American Politics*, 2nd ed. (Baton Rouge: Louisiana State University Press, 2000); Alan Brinkley, *Voices of Protest: Huey Long, Father Coughlin & the Great Depression* (New York: Vintage, 1983), ix–xii, 3–81; and Patterson, *Grand Expectations*, 547–48.

24 Rieder, "Rise of the Silent Majority"; Carter, *Politics of Rage*; and Patterson, *Grand Expectations*, 548, 550.

25 Patterson, *Grand Expectations*, 579–85; Williams, *Eyes on the Prize*, 252–87; Matusow, *Unraveling*, 180–91; and Barone, *Our Country*, 401–3.

26 Patterson, *Grand Expectations*, 565–68, 584–85; Matusow, *Unraveling*, 187–92; Barone, *Our Country*, 402–3, 545; and David Stebenne, "Re-Mapping American Politics: The Redistricting Revolution Fifty Years Later," *Origins* 5, no. 5 (February 2012): 1–7.

27 Barone, *Our Country*, 402–3, 434–36, 449–53, 545–46; Patterson, *Grand Expectations*, 565–68, 584–87, 650, 698–707; and Matusow, *Unraveling*, 422–39.

NOTES

28   Hartmann, *From Margin*, 48–59; and Patterson, *Grand Expectations*, 642–48.

29   Hartmann, *From Margin*, 60–65; Patterson, *Grand Expectations*, 644–48; Matusow, *Unraveling*, 194–98; Oliver, *Betty Friedan*, 98–110; and Dorothy Sue Cobble, *The Other Women's Movement: Workplace Justice and Social Rights in Modern America* (Princeton: Princeton University Press, 2004), 145–90.

30   Hartmann, *From Margin*, 60–65; Patterson, *Grand Expectations*, 644–48; Matusow, *Unraveling*, 194–98; Oliver, *Betty Friedan*, 98–110; and Cobble, *Other Women's Movement*, 145–90.

31   Crane, *Environment*, 316–52; Patterson, *Grand Expectations*, 725–26; and Wikipedia entries for the Wilderness Act, the Clean Air Act, the Clean Water Act, and the Endangered Species Act.

32   Dochuk, *From Bible Belt to Sun Belt*, xi–xxiv, 1–332; and Wikipedia entry for Joseph Kraft.

33   Matusow, *Unraveling*, 275–305; Patterson, *Grand Expectations*, 445–47; Hodgson, *America in Our Time*, 402–3; and Manchester, *Glory and the Dream*, 1352, 1361–68, 1408.

34   MacNeil, *Way We Were*; Hajdu, *Positively 4th Street*, 192–298; and Patterson, *Grand Expectations*, 373, 446, 621–23, 669.

35   Patterson, *Grand Expectations*, 467, 672–74; and Lichtenstein, *Retail Revolution*, 23–45.

36   Lichtenstein, 23–45.

37   Patterson, *Grand Expectations*, 40–46, 63–65, 373, 446, 449, 467–68, 565–68, 574–77, 637–38, 665, 672–74; Eric Rhode, *A History of the Cinema* (New York: Da Capo, 1976), 587–632; Wikipedia entry for *Bonnie and Clyde*; Matusow, *Unraveling*, 293–304; Barone, *Our Country*, 420–21; and Manchester, *Glory and the Dream*, 1347–50. In the mid-1960s, roughly half of the US population was under the age of twenty-seven. On that point, see Manchester, *Glory and the Dream*, 1348.

38   Patterson, *Grand Expectations*, 446, 454; Hodgson, *America in Our Time*, 140; and Manchester, *Glory and the Dream*, 1223, 1227.

39   Wikipedia entry for *My Three Sons*.

40   Wikipedia entries for *The Big Valley* and *Gunsmoke*.

41   Wikipedia entry for *The Fugitive*.

42   Wikipedia entry for *Guess Who's Coming to Dinner*; and PBS's *American Masters* profile of Sydney Poitier.

43   Wikipedia entry for *I Spy*.

44   Wikipedia entry for *Star Trek*; and Stephen E. Whitfield, *The Making of Star Trek* (New York: Ballantine Books, 1968), 252–54.

45   Alex Prud'homme, *The French Chef in America* (New York: Knopf, 2016), 7–53, 202–6; and Wikipedia entry for *The French Chef*.

46   Patterson, *Grand Expectations*, 77–78, 671–72; and Barone, *Our Country*, 198–99, 301–2, 390–91.

47   Patterson, *Grand Expectations*, 577–79, 637–38, 671; Manchester, *Glory and the Dream*, 1343–54; Hodgson, *America in Our Time*, 310–52; and Barone, *Our Country*, 301–2, 385–86, 389–93, 420–22, 602–3.

48   Brinkley, *Publisher*, 419–59; and Robert Gottlieb, *Avid Reader: A Life* (New York: Farrar, Straus & Giroux, 2016), 36–193.

49 Matusow, *Unraveling*, 389–92; Patterson, *Grand Expectations*, 678–82; and Barone, *Our Country*, 426–32.

50 Patterson, *Grand Expectations*, 681–85; Matusow, *Unraveling*, 391–94; and Barone, *Our Country*, 432–34.

51 Patterson, *Grand Expectations*, 425–41; Matusow, *Unraveling*, 395–98, 404–11; and Barone, *Our Country*, 432–41.

52 Patterson, *Grand Expectations*, 449, 650, 685, 688–94, 708; Matusow, *Unraveling*, 395–96; and Barone, *Our Country*, 436–37.

53 James A. Colaiaco, *Martin Luther King, Jr.: Apostle of Militant Nonviolence* (New York: St. Martin's, 1993), 196–97. See, too, 5–195; and Branch, *Parting the Waters*, 27–142.

54 Patterson, *Grand Expectations*, 683–708; Matusow, *Unraveling*, 389–430; and Barone, *Our Country*, 436–451.

55 Patterson, *Grand Expectations*, 607–8; and Kenneth O'Reilly, *Racial Matters: The FBI's Secret File on Black America, 1960–1972* (New York: Free Press, 1989), 40–60.

56 Patterson, *Grand Expectations*, 681–84, 689, 696–702; Matusow, *Unraveling*, 397–405, 425–29; and Barone, *Our Country*, 441–49.

57 Nelson, *Jumping the Abyss*, 364–65.

58 Stebenne, *Arthur J. Goldberg*, 355–71.

59 Wikipedia entry for "What a Wonderful World"; and PBS's *American Masters* profile "This Is Bob Hope."

60 Stephen E. Ambrose, *Nixon: The Education of a Politician, 1913–1962* (New York: Simon & Schuster, 1987), 650–74; Patterson, *Grand Expectations*, 697–709; Matusow, *Unraveling*, 398–404, 422–39; and Barone, *Our Country*, 441–43, 447–53.

10. The Era in Retrospect

1 Steven Brill, *Tailspin: The People and Forces Behind America's Fifty-Year Fall—and Those Fighting to Reverse It* (New York: Knopf, 2018), 24–25; Patterson, *Grand Expectations*, 700–725; Matusow, *Unraveling*, 398–404, 426–39; and Barone, *Our Country*, 447–88.

2 Barone, *Our Country*, 441–53; Matusow, *Unraveling*, 398–404, 422–39; and Patterson, *Grand Expectations*, 607–709.

3 Morris, *Richard Milhous Nixon*, 21–254; Ambrose, *Nixon*, 1:21–674; and Perlstein, *Before the Storm*, 3–355.

4 Morris, *Richard Milhous Nixon*, 21–254; Perlstein, *Before the Storm*, 3–355; Shermer, *Sunbelt Capitalism*, 1–330; Allen J. Matusow, *Nixon's Economy: Booms, Busts, Dollars and Votes* (Lawrence: University Press of Kansas, 1998); and Brill, *Tailspin*, 24–168.

5 Mike Davis, *City of Quartz: Excavating the Future in Los Angeles* (London: Verso, 2006).

6 Davis; and Bruce J. Shulman, *The Seventies: The Great Shift in American Culture, Society and Politics* (New York: Da Capo Press, 2001).

Index

INDEX

New Deal and, 49–50, 51, 53–54
postwar challenges to middlebrow,
123–24
postwar years, 122–23
See also middlebrow culture
Asian Americans. *See* Japanese Americans
automation, 165, 207, 221
automobility, xvi–xvii, 10, 140, 144,
170–71, 234
average vs. majority, x

baby boom
Eisenhower years, 144, 151
Johnson years, 222, 226
Kennedy years, 199, 216
postwar years, 113, 118, 119
waning of, 241
Baldwin, James, 198, 205, 211
Ball, George, 246
Ball, Lucille, 147–48
Banking Act (1935), 66–67
bank policy. *See* monetary and bank
policy
Batista, Fulgencio, 161
Battle of Britain (1940), 81, 85–86
Bauch, Beatrice (case study). *See*
Sindt, Beatrice Bauch
Bay of Pigs invasion (1961), 189–90
Beatles, 235
beat movement, 181–82
Beiderbecke, Bix, 56
Bellow, Saul, 124
Berlin, Irving, 92
Berlin crises, 109–10, 160–61, 190
Berlin Wall, 190
The Best Years of Our Lives, 119–20
big-band music, 95
big government. *See* federal govern-
ment role
The Big Valley, 238
birth control, 241
Black Americans. *See* African Americans
Black Power movement, 229
"Blowin' in the Wind" (Dylan), 215
Bohemian Grove, 131
Bonnie and Clyde, 237
Book of the Month Club (BOMC),
55, 123

books. *See* arts and literature
Boone, Pat, 180
Bozell, L. Brent, 204
Brando, Marlon, 153–54
Breen, Joseph, 40, 42
Brennan, William, 141
Broadway, 152
Brooks, Gwendolyn, 124
*Brown v. the Board of Education of
Topeka, Kansas*, 141, 176
Brugler, Frank, 167
Buckley, William F., Jr., 204, 230
Business Advisory Council (BAC), 30–31
business sector
causes of Great Depression and, 5
Eisenhower moderate conservatism
and, 137
environmentalism and, 207–8
Kennedy years, 199
late 1950s, 170
New Deal and, 69
opposition to New Deal, 27, 32, 43,
46, 49, 60–61, 65, 69, 130, 134
postwar years, 104, 112
support for New Deal, 30–32
union relationships with, 166–67
Vietnam War and, 245–46
Byrnes, James, 102

Capitalism and Freedom (Friedman),
202–3, 204–5
Capote, Truman, 124
Carson, Rachel, 171, 205, 207–8
Carter, Jimmy, 232
Castro, Fidel, 161, 190
Castro, Raúl, 161
Catholic Americans
civil rights movement and, 212
immigrants, xii, xiii
motion-picture industry and, 12,
39, 40
1928 presidential election and, xv
1960 presidential election and, 186,
187
World War II and, 93
Central Intelligence Agency (CIA),
109, 142, 191
charitable giving, 201
Chayefsky, Paddy, 150

INDEX

301

INDEX

About the Author

David Stebenne is a specialist in modern American political and legal history. He has published political commentary in the *Conversation*, the *Huffington Post*, the *New Republic*, the *Observer*, and *Salon* and has appeared on National Public Radio's *All Things Considered* to discuss politics, the economy, and labor issues. A native of Rhode Island and Maryland, he teaches history and law at Ohio State University.